JOHN GREENLEAF WHITTIER

Books by EDWARD WAGENKNECHT
Published by Oxford University Press

NATHANIEL HAWTHORNE: Man and Writer (1961)
WASHINGTON IRVING: Moderation Displayed (1962)
EDGAR ALLAN POE: The Man Behind the Legend (1963)
HARRIET BEECHER STOWE: The Known and the Unknown (1965)
HENRY WADSWORTH LONGFELLOW:
Portrait of an American Humanist (1966)
JOHN GREENLEAF WHITTIER: A Portrait in Paradox (1967)

CHAUCER: Modern Essays in Criticism (1959)
Edited by Edward Wagenknecht

John G. Whittier

JOHN GREENLEAF WHITTIER

A Portrait in Paradox

EDWARD WAGENKNECHT

Who comes with his hat-brim resembling the wing
  Of the bird which old Sinbad the mariner saw?
Such hats must be surely admirable things,
  The wearer to shield from the elements' war.

WHITTIER, "THE QUAKER," 1827

NEW YORK OXFORD UNIVERSITY PRESS 1967

Frontispiece: John Greenleaf Whittier in 1836
Etched by S. A. Schoff after a painting by Bass Otis

LIBRARY OF CONGRESS CATALOGUE CARD NUMBER: 67-20407

PRINTED IN THE UNITED STATES OF AMERICA

For ELEANOR AND ALFRED AMES
Good Quakers and Good Friends

The truth is, the "small craft" of poetry in which we have indulged ourselves is not fitted for the voyage of Immortality. We shall perish, and verily *our works will follow us.* The hearts which know us and love us will also soon cease to beat, and with them our very memories will die. The utilitarian of the twentieth century will not heed whether, in treading on our graves, he shakes the dust of prose or poetry from his feet. And after all what matters it? Who cares for the opinions of the twentieth century? Not I, for one.

WHITTIER to LUCY HOOPER, 1837

It has been his chief glory, not that he could speak inspired words, but that he spoke them for the despised, the helpless and the dumb; for those too ignorant to honor, too poor to reward him. Grace was given him to know his Lord in the lowest disguise, even in that of the poor hunted slave, and to follow him in heart into prison and unto death.

HARRIET BEECHER STOWE, 1877

Oh, you're witty, but the author of *Snow-Bound* was Whittier.

American schoolboy lore of the 1940's

PREFACE

The aims and methods of this study of Whittier are the same as those of my other books in this series.

In writing it I have met with almost unparalleled kindness. Professor John B. Pickard of the University of Florida, great-grandson of Matthew Franklin Whittier, the poet's brother, and grandson of the authorized biographer, Samuel T. Pickard, is the literary editor of the Whittier Estate. When Professor Pickard learned that I was contemplating a study of Whittier, he at once gave me permission to quote anything I should need from unpublished materials, but his kindness did not stop there. He is himself engaged in collecting and editing Whittier's letters, and he turned over his files to me, thus saving me the enormous labor of trying to collect the letters for myself. I know of no way adequately to reward such generosity, but if report be true, it is rewarded in heaven.

My manuscript has been read by both Professor Pickard and by Mr. Roland H. Woodwell, of Amesbury, Massachusetts, who, I suspect, knows more about Whittier than Whittier ever knew about himself. When he publishes his own biography of the poet, which I hope will be soon, I am sure it will at once take its place as standard. Mr. Woodwell has gladly shared his knowledge with me, and I am very grateful for his guidance and advice. It must be understood, however, that neither he nor Professor Pickard is to be held responsible for any of my interpretations.

I have quoted from letters owned by the following, to all of whom I express my gratitude for their courteous co-operation: Columbia University, Essex Institute, Harvard University (Houghton Library), Haverford College, The Huntington Library, Massachusetts Historical Society, Northwestern University, Swarthmore College, the University of Michigan, Mr. Roland H. Woodwell, Yale University. I also wish to thank Mrs. Cecil B. Williams for permission to quote from her late husband's University of Chicago doctoral dissertation on Whittier.

Naturally I have also drawn freely from materials in print. My heaviest indebtedness here is to Samuel T. Pickard's *Life and Letters of John Greenleaf Whittier*, a far more scholarly work than most authorized nineteenth-century biographies, and to John A. Pollard's fine modern book, *John Greenleaf Whittier, Friend of Man.*

Like many nineteenth-century writers, Whittier had a habit of using the ampersand; in quoting from unpublished materials I have consistently replaced this with "and." He also often used double punctuation (for example, a comma coupled with a dash), and I have generally removed one mark or the other. Very occasionally I have changed some other obviously incorrect mark of punctuation but only when I feared it might trouble the reader. I have not tried to standardize, but in a book in which many letters had to be quoted from printed texts which had already been standardized by others, it seemed fanatical to try to reproduce documents with complete fidelity. For uniformity's sake I have used italics for book titles and quotation marks for short poems and articles, even in quoting from writers who used a different system.

EDWARD WAGENKNECHT

West Newton, Mass.
October 15, 1966

CONTENTS

JOHN GREENLEAF WHITTIER

BIOGRAPHY

John Greenleaf Whittier was born December 17, 1807,[1] on a farm near Haverhill, Massachusetts, the elder son and second child of John Whittier and his wife Abigail Hussey. The house, now open to the public and visited by many each year as the scene of *Snow-Bound,* had been built about 1688 and inhabited ever since by Whittiers.

Though an "Abram Whityeare" is mentioned in the Essex County court records for 1637, Thomas Whittier is regarded as the founder of the Whittier family in this country. Born in England in 1620, he came to America in 1638, where he received a grant of land including what is now known as Whittier Hill in the township of Amesbury. Later he moved to Job's Hill, near Haverhill. Thomas Whittier was a huge man, who, even in his youth, weighed more than 300 pounds, and who fathered ten children. Though he was not a Quaker, he risked his standing in the community and incurred legal disability when he defended Quakers in disfavor. He also treated the Indians as Penn and other Quakers were to treat them—and got similar results. When his neighbors insisted upon having a garrison house, he helped them build it, but he would never use it. In times of trouble, Indians on the warpath are said to have presented their paint-daubed faces at his windows, but the family was never endangered.

Though the poet believed the Whittiers to have been of Huguenot origin, this now seems more than doubtful. Thomas Whittier's ancestors have been traced in Hampshire and Wiltshire almost to the beginning of the sixteenth century.[2] The name, which occurs in many different forms, is probably a trade name, from "white tawyer," a whitener of leather. Recent research has also made it necessary to give up another of Whittier's own beliefs—that his mother was descended from the Reverend Stephen Bachiler, which would have made the poet a relative of Daniel Webster, whom he blasted in "Ichabod." [3] There *was* a French strain, but this did not enter the family until the poet's grandfather, the second Joseph, married Sarah Greenleaf, whose name was a translation of the French Feuillevert.[4] Since the seventeenth century the Whittier line of descent had been almost entirely through younger sons: Whittier's father, John, born in 1760, but not married until 1804, was the tenth child of Joseph II, born in 1716, who was the ninth child of Joseph I, born in 1669, and in his turn the youngest son of the American progenitor, Thomas Whittier, born in 1620. The Whittiers became Quakers when, in 1694, Joseph I married Sarah Peasley, granddaughter of the man in whose defense Thomas Whittier had jeopardized his standing in the community, and the Husseys, the maternal ancestors, had joined the Society even earlier.

John and Abigail Whittier had four children—Mary, born in 1806; John Greenleaf; Matthew Franklin, born in 1812; and the poet's favorite, Elizabeth Hussey, born in 1815. During Whittier's childhood, as all readers of *Snow-Bound* know, the family group also included Uncle Moses Whittier and Aunt Mercy Hussey.

Whittier always felt closer to his mother than he did to his father, the "prompt, decisive man" of *Snow-Bound*, who wasted no breath, and whose two best-known sayings are "That's enough for stand now, John," when his son halted his farm work to dream or meditate, and "Sir, poetry will not get him bread," when William Lloyd Garrison urged him to send the boy to school and give him a chance to cultivate his literary gifts. Nevertheless, John Whittier was an honorable man and a devout Quaker and democrat; though he had nothing of the artist or scholar in him, he would have shared most of John Greenleaf's beliefs in later years. He was not opposed to learning as such; neither did he fail to recognize his son's gifts; he simply knew that human beings could not live without some means of livelihood, and he did not propose that, through his very brilliance, the boy should leave himself unprovided for.

The district school was in session only twelve to fourteen weeks each winter, and Whittier said he could recall only two teachers who had been very good. (Since his teachers were paid only twelve dollars a month, he would still seem to have been lucky.) Joshua Coffin, who was much at the Whittier home, became a lifelong friend; what he did to introduce his pupil to the work of Robert Burns would alone have made him Whittier's best teacher, even if he had never done anything else.

In 1827 an "academy" was established in Haverhill, and between then and 1829 Whittier spent two twenty-six-week terms there, earning the fees (eight dollars per term, plus four dollars extra for French) for the first term by making slippers, and for the second by teaching school in the Birch Meadow district of West Amesbury and posting the ledgers of a Haverhill merchant. Partly because he had by this time published many poems in local papers, he was regarded as a prodigy at the academy; he had even composed, upon request, a dedicatory ode for the opening exercises, which must surely be a unique distinction for a student entering a newly established school.

Whittier had indeed been scribbling poems since his childhood. In 1826, without his knowledge, his sister Mary sent "The Exile's Departure" to the Newburyport *Free Press*, whose editor, William Lloyd Garrison, published it on June 8. By 1827 the young man had some eighty published poems to his credit, of most of which he was later heartily ashamed.

From January to August 1829 he held his first editorship, that of the pro-Clay *American Manufacturer* in Boston. From January to July 1830 he edited the Haverhill *Gazette*, and from then until January 1832 he was in Hartford, editing the *New England Weekly Review*. He edited the *Gazette* again between May and December of 1836, and from June to August 1837 he was acting editor of *The Emancipator and Anti-Slavery Record* in New York. He was editor of the *Pennsylvania Freeman* from 1838 to 1840. From July 1844 to March 1846 he edited the *Middlesex Standard* in Lowell, Massachusetts, and during these same years also served as acting editor of the *Essex Transcript*, Amesbury and Salisbury. He was a contributing editor to Dr. Gamaliel Bailey's *National Era*, Washington (the paper in which *Uncle Tom's Cabin* was serialized) from 1847 to 1860.

Whittier was an extremely able and aggressive editor, but his health was too delicate long to endure the strain of editorial work and his labors were often interrupted by physical breakdowns. This circumstance aborted his editorial career and in later years reduced it to functions which he could perform at home. By 1836 he had sold the farm and moved to Amesbury.

He was an avowed abolitionist from 1833 when he published his anti-slavery manifesto, *Justice and Expediency*. He afterwards said, "I set a higher value on my name as appended to the Anti-Slavery Declaration of 1833, than on the title-page of any book." More than once he was in danger of mob action.

He served in the Massachusetts state legislature in 1835, but most of his political work was done behind the scenes. He was a skillful lobbyist and a power in the careers of both Caleb Cushing and Charles Sumner. Early in life he left the Whig Party, and, in 1839, became one of the founders of the Liberty Party. Later he worked through the Free-Soil Party, and after 1856, always through the Republican Party. He was a presidential elector in 1860 and 1864, voting for Lincoln both times. It pleased him that he was the only man who had had a chance to vote for Lincoln for President four times—twice as an elector and twice at the polls.

Whittier's first book, *Legends of New England*, which includes both verse and prose, was published in 1831. With *The Super-*

naturalism of New England (1847), it gives him an honorable place among the pioneer workers in New England legendry. The first authorized collection of poems appeared at Philadelphia in 1838. *Lays of My Home* (1843) was the first book on which Whittier had the valuable advice of James T. Fields and the first to be published, like all its successors, by the great New England house which, after many realignments of ownership, and changes of name, finally came to be known as Houghton Mifflin Company. In 1857 the establishment of *The Atlantic Monthly*, which did not belong to this firm at the beginning but was soon acquired by it, gave Whittier a distinguished magazine outlet and contributed importantly to both his purse and his fame.

Lays of My Home was followed by, among other titles, *Voices of Freedom* (1846); *Songs of Labor* (1850); *Home Ballads* (1860); *In War Time* (1863); *Snow-Bound* (1866); *The Tent on the Beach* (1867); *Among the Hills* (1869); *The Pennsylvania Pilgrim* (1872); *The Vision of Echard* (1878); *The King's Missive* (1881); and *At Sundown* (1890). In 1857 the "Blue and Gold" edition of his poems was issued, followed in 1874 by the "Household Edition." In 1888-89 Horace E. Scudder did a magnificent job editing the seven-volume "Riverside Edition" of Whittier's writings.[5] *Snow-Bound* marked the turning of the tide financially, quite unexpectedly so far as Whittier was concerned. Samuel T. Pickard says he earned $10,000 from the "first issue." The next year *The Tent on the Beach* also became a best-seller.

Whittier's mature prose works include *The Stranger in Lowell* (1845); *Old Portraits and Modern Sketches* (1850); *Literary Recreations and Miscellanies* (1854); and, above all, his one prose work of the first rank, the radiant *Leaves from Margaret Smith's Journal* (1849), a kind of novel in the form of a journal kept by an English girl of great heart and liberal temper, during a visit to Massachusetts in 1678-79. This book, one of the inexplicably neglected classics of American literature, is, next to *Snow-Bound*, Whittier's unquestionable masterpiece. Into it he poured all his Quaker "concerns," his vast knowledge of old New England, and all the imaginative power that he possessed. With the assistance of his protégée, Lucy Larcom, he also published three anthologies: *Child Life* (1871); *Child Life in Prose* (1874); and *Songs of Three Centuries* (1876).

During his later years Whittier's fame and popularity were very great. His birthday was almost as widely celebrated as Longfellow's, and the celebrations became quite as great a burden. This "graduate of a district school" received many academic honors. Both Haverford and Harvard gave him an M.A. in 1860, and Harvard followed this in 1886 with an LL.D. He was an overseer of Harvard College from 1858 to 1871 and a trustee of Brown University from 1869 to 1892. The Massachusetts Historical Society, the American Academy of Arts and Sciences, the New England Historic Genealogical Society, the American Philosophical Society, and the Western Reserve Historical Society were among those who sought him as a member. Whittier College in Iowa was named for him, and the town of Whittier in California. How much these honors meant to him we do not know; the duties involved cannot have been onerous since we are told that during his entire term of service at Brown he managed to attend only one meeting of the board.

His mother died in 1857, leaving his sister Elizabeth in charge of Whittier's house. Elizabeth's death in 1864, just in time to miss his prosperity, was one of the great disappointments of his life. She was succeeded by another "Lizzie," his brother Matthew's daughter, who in 1876 married Samuel T. Pickard, the Portland journalist, later Whittier's authorized biographer. If the consciousness of being "wanted" can mitigate the loneliness of an old man's last years, Whittier had it in abundant measure. Though he always maintained his legal residence in Amesbury, he spent much of his time from 1876 on with his cousins—Mrs. Abby J. Woodman and the Misses Johnson, and Mrs. Woodman's adopted daughter Phebe—at the luxurious sixty-acre farm and estate in Danvers, which he named "Oak Knoll." The Newburyport home of his Cartland cousins was always open to him also, and he often summered with them in the White Mountains or at Centre Harbor on Lake Winnepesaukee and elsewhere. He was a welcome guest at the Boston homes of Governor and Mrs. Claflin and Mr. and Mrs. Fields; at Celia Thaxter's house in the Isles of Shoals; and at "Elmfield," the home of a family friend, Sarah Abbie Gove, in Hampton Falls, New Hampshire. It was here that he died on September 7, 1892.

CHAPTER ONE

A SIDE TO FACE THE WORLD WITH

I

Painters often indulge in self-portraits; creative writers autobiographically inclined generally prefer to present themselves somewhat more indirectly. But Whittier's self-portrait in *The Tent on the Beach* strikes so many of the essential notes that it may be well to have it before us at the outset.

And one there was, a dreamer born,
  Who, with a mission to fulfil,
Had left the Muses' haunts to turn
  The crank of an opinion-mill,
Making his rustic reed of song
A weapon in the war with wrong,
Yoking his fancy to the breaking-plough
That beam-deep turned the soil for truth to spring and grow.

Too quiet seemed the man to ride
  The wingëd Hippogriff Reform;
Was his a voice from side to side
  To pierce the tumult of the storm?
A silent, shy, peace-loving man,
He seemed no fiery partisan
To hold his way against the public frown,
The ban of Church and State, the fierce mob's hounding down.

For while he wrought with strenuous will
The work his hands had found to do,
He heard the fitful music still
Of winds that out of dream-land blew.
The din about him could not drown
What the strange voices whispered down;
Along his task-field weird processions swept,
The visionary pomp of stately phantoms stepped.

The common air was thick with dreams,—
He told them to the toiling crowd;
Such music as the woods and streams
Sang in his ear he sang aloud;
In still, shut bays, on windy capes,
He heard the call of beckoning shapes,
And, as the gray old shadows prompted him,
To homely moulds of rhyme he shaped their legends grim.

In another poem, "My Namesake," written for Francis Greenleaf Allinson, who had been named after him, Whittier describes himself somewhat more elaborately. These passages are too long to be quoted in their entirety, but their interest for the present writer is considerably increased by the evidence they afford of Whittier's lack of sympathy for the kind of enterprise essayed in this volume.

Let Love's and Friendship's tender debt
Be paid by those I love in life.
Why should the unborn critic whet
For me his scalping-knife?

Why should the stranger peer and pry
One's vacant house of life about,
And drag for curious ear and eye
His faults and follies out?—

Why stuff, for fools to gaze upon,
With chaff of words, the garb he wore,
As corn-husks when the ear is gone
Are rustled all the more?

Let kindly Silence close again,
  The picture vanish from the eye,
And on the dim and misty main
  Let the small ripple die.

It seems clear, then, that Whittier saw himself as a creature of mingled good and evil, but this was not the only paradox of which he was conscious.

In him the grave and playful mixed,
  And wisdom held with folly truce,
And Nature compromised betwixt
  Good fellow and recluse.

Moreover,

His eye was beauty's powerless slave,
  And his the ear which discord pains;
Few guessed beneath his aspect grave
  What passions strove in chains.

Loving goodness and wisdom, he yet owned his kinship to all

Who met him on the common ground
  Of suffering and of sin.

He shared his neighbors' griefs also, and

For all the ills he could not cure
  He held himself to blame.

"The patient peace of Nature" was an unfailing solace to him, and he remained faithful to the ways of his Quaker forebears, but he never claimed to have pierced the heart of the human mystery.

The arrows of his straining sight
  Fell quenched in darkness....

Hence he sympathized with all religious aspiration, whether Christian or pagan.

He dared not mock the Dervish whirl,
  The Brahmin's rite, the Lama's spell;
God knew the heart; Devotion's pearl
  Might sanctify the shell.

These, to borrow the language of the pulpit, might be called the "texts" of this study, and it will take the rest of the volume to expound them.

Whittier is often thought of as having devoted his early life to reform activities and his later years to literature. As we have already seen—and as we shall see more elaborately—this is a gross oversimplification. Though he grew up in a house with few books in it, he was a slave to print from the moment he could read; his formal education was limited but he became a well-read man. He was conscious of the conflicts between various aspects of his temperament; in "The Two Voices" (1854), he describes his temptation to turn away from efforts for social amelioration. But when, in 1833, he published his anti-slavery manifesto, *Justice and Expediency*, he took his place with the outcasts, and he knew exactly what he was doing. Once he had fully awakened, he never ceased his anti-slavery work until freedom had been won, but the years during which agitation was his primary business were not many, and even then he did not lay poetry aside. Few of his anti-slavery poems can be placed among his finest achievements, yet it may reasonably be argued that through them he found his way.

Nor are these the only paradoxes to be found in him. He lived celibate, but he was always strongly attracted to women and, in his turn, powerfully attracted them. It seems unquestionable that he was a much more passionate man than Longfellow, who married twice and fathered six children. Another interesting contrast between the two poets emerges in connection with their attitudes toward war. Whittier was the most convinced pacifist among all the major American poets, but he was also very "patriotic," and if, as Oliver Wendell Holmes and many others have believed, the abolitionists had their share in bringing on armed conflict between the North and the South, then Whittier.

whose poems and fiery editorials chronicled almost every ebb and flow in the anti-slavery struggle, must be said to share, in some measure, in whatever blame may be thought to have accrued. Though he hated war, Longfellow was not, in the ideational sense, a pacifist, and once the hour had struck, he seems to have had no doubts about the Northern cause; but there was none of Whittier's militancy about him, and taken as a whole, his poetry was, more than Whittier's, an influence toward conciliation.[1]

II

Whittier was five feet, ten and one half inches tall, with a lean, spare figure. His complexion was olive, his hair black. The bushy eyebrows never turned; in his old age, when the rest of his hair was white, they formed a startling black bar over the brilliant eyes. The head was long, the forehead exceptionally high. Thomas Wentworth Higginson was not the only one who thought him Jewish-looking; this was also said of his sister Elizabeth.

To the end, he carried himself erectly, giving an impression of quick nervous energy. Elizabeth Stuart Phelps says he seemed so eager to see his friends that his heart outran his feet, and Edmund Gosse, who met him as an old man, was particularly impressed by the absence of "the immobility so frequent with very aged persons." Helen Burt found "the lines of Puritanic firmness in his face . . . illumined by his kindly, sympathetic smile and by the humorous twinkle of his fine brown eyes, which on occasion, nevertheless, could dart a shrewd flashing look as piercing as an eagle's." Julia Ward Howe says his eyes "glowed like black diamonds," and one can well believe the story that they once "looked down" some "roughs" who stood in his path as he emerged from an anti-slavery meeting. In ordinary conversation he was rather slow and deliberate, but everybody who heard him read poetry aloud was startled by the fullness and depth of his voice. "He scanned his lines with a majestic movement and the effect was heightened by a peculiar hoarseness to which he was subject, at least in the last part of his life." It is interesting to see the dramatic temperament emerging here; it shows again, I think, in his handwriting, which is hardly that of a self-effacing man. His most marked mannerism was a habit of slapping his knee when he was amused or impressed; "his hands might have been called almost another feature, such emphasis did they give to his expression."

Many have made the point that Whittier's portraits do not do him justice. "In them," says W. H. Rideing, "he is represented as a severe and ascetic man, cold in eye, and unsympathetic in manner." Whittier himself objected that the ambrotype process gave him "a blanched look," and in 1878 he did not think that his picture in *Snow-Bound* looked like "anybody's face! If I remember rightly it is a trifle harsh and severe—something of 'the Sword of the Lord and Gideon' in it." [2]

Whittier's friends, at least, thought him handsome. Unfortunately some of these were impressible ladies like Gail Hamilton, and one cannot take their impressions at face value. But Lyman Abbott was a bird of another feather. Abbott rejects the word "handsome," and he obviously did not know much about photography, but his report, written in old age, is all the more interesting because it comes from so unsentimental a writer:

> No one would call his face handsome; it was better, it was beautiful. The features were homely, though the forehead was high and the eyes were luminous. The photograph but poorly represents him. For his face was a transparency; the spirit within it lighted it up; and photographs rarely, the older photographs never, interpret the spirit. His illuminated face has made quite real to me the picture given in Exodus, of Moses when he descended from the mount where he had talked with God and "his face shone." Whittier's was a shining face.[3]

Whittier dressed well. "His coat was a perfect fit," says Mary Claflin, "and his outside garment, with its fine fur collar, was very becoming, which fact his friends sometimes suspected he understood as well as they." He was very observant of clothes, particularly in women, though fond of rallying them. In later years his cousins used to tell him that "a man who has to go to Philadelphia to get his coat cut should not criticize women's bonnets." But he sent to Philadelphia only because he clung to the Quaker cut, though discarding the traditional broad-brimmed hat and adopting the fashionable stovepipe instead, and he does not seem to have given much time or thought to his clothes. Since his figure varied but slightly through the years, he ordered by mail, according to the measurements, "which I suppose thee still has in thy books," though he might add, "the one last year was a good fit" or "it might be well to have this a trifle looser—only a trifle, however."

Whittier's great handicap was his wretched health. Sometimes this is indicated in general terms—"half sick—half mad"—or "I am a bundle of nerves for pain to experiment upon," or "I remember Lindley Murray's Grammar defined a verb as 'a word signifying to be, to do, or to suffer,' which is just my predicament, leaving out the 'to do.'" Often, however, he is more specific, as when he writes Elizabeth Lloyd in 1860 that a

> complicated nervous affection, combined with the old trouble in my head and stomach, has rendered me so much of an invalid that the slightest change of weather, any extra physical or mental exertion, or responsibility is sufficient to entirely prostrate me. I am compelled to avoid, as far as possible, all excitement and mental labor as the only condition of preserving anything like quiet and self control, and of obtaining relief from pain.

And twelve years later he is writing William J. Allinson of "weakness and pain in my left side often accompanied with difficulty of breathing and great prostration of strength, dizziness, and pain in the head."

He complains of rheumatism and "palpitation of the heart," and he dreaded the New England winter more and more as he grew older, though even in his early days he thought that if he ever committed suicide it would be during a northeaster. As early as Civil War times, we hear of failing sight, and he was certainly partly deaf during his last years, a condition which he was not above slyly taking advantage of to help him escape from the bores by which his fame had caused him to be plagued.[4] After the death of his sister Elizabeth he was so afflicted with boils that he compared himself to Job. He would also seem to have had rather more than his share of accidents. When he was an infant, his sister Mary tried the experiment of rolling him downstairs in a blanket, from which he escaped without injury, but he was nearly asphyxiated when his parents bundled him up too heavily for a ride on a cold winter's day. In 1847 he received a bullet wound in the cheek from a boy who was engaged in target practice not far from his garden,[5] and in 1872 he was thrown to the floor and knocked insensible when the Amesbury house was struck by lightning. But his real afflictions were headaches and insomnia: one of his earliest recollections was "pain in the head." He "worked between headaches," often only half an hour at a time. In those days, when there were no barbiturates, insomniacs had to choose between narcotics and just staying awake. Whittier has at least one reference to the use of laudanum for sleeplessness, but since he once went without sleep for 120 hours, he certainly did not make a habit of using it.

Various diagnoses of Whittier's ill health have been attempted. Dr. H. I. Bowditch, who examined him, thought the trouble was with his heart, and Dr. George M. Gould, who did not, was equally confident that the difficulty was eyestrain, never accurately diagnosed or corrected with proper glasses.[6] There has been no lack of those who have even found what are now called "psychosomatic" factors, and Whittier may well have had his neurotic aspects. He himself writes:

> Soon or late to all our dwellings come the spectres of the mind,
> Doubts and fears and dread forebodings, in the darkness undefined;
> Round us throng the grim projections of the heart and of the brain,
> And our pride of strength is weakness, and the cunning hand is vain.[7]

He has one perfect Mrs. Gummidge passage (it seems odd that so devoted a Dickensian could have written it without thinking of her): "The miserable wet weather—hard for everybody—is particularly so to me." And it almost goes without saying that his piety often expressed itself in the miserable nineteenth-century fashion of expecting one's end at any moment, whether there was any reason for anxiety or not, and of welcoming it should it be God's will, as when, in 1840, he writes Gerrit Smith that he intends to vote for Birney and Earle in November "if my life is spared." (This might, he adds, be the last vote he will ever have a chance to cast for a Presidential candidate.) But there is less of this kind of thing in Whittier than might be expected. He was not incapable of finding humor even in woe, as when, upon giving himself a black eye through striking his head in 1889, he told Mrs. Fields that he did not wish to be seen in the likeness of "a Modoc Indian in his war-paint." Though he took no stock in faith healing, never having seen any reason to believe that the good were less subject to the ills of the flesh than the bad, he still admits that "it seems to me wrong to be sick, and I dare say it is somehow, for it seems so necessary to be well." [8] He found it humiliating to be reminded of human limitations by the weakness of the body and wanted nobody to think that, as country people would put it, he "enjoyed poor health." He certainly seems normal enough when he writes Mrs. Fields that he would not mind suffering if it did not put a stop to his work, and again, "I can't pity anybody who can work and sleep." In his later days, he did not regard his inability to read newspapers as a great deprivation, "but to put books aside, and not to be able to write to my friends, is another matter." [9]

In addition to his physical ailments, Whittier had one peculiarity. His mother discovered it when she sent him out as a boy to gather wild strawberries. Even when the woods were blazing with autumn colors, he could not tell the difference between the red and the green. He made up for this in a measure by his unusual appreciation of yellow and, not unnaturally, championed the goldenrod as the national flower. He once said that rainbows were very beautiful to him—and all yellow. Desmond Powell argues that because of his disability, Whittier does not paint scenes but etches them, and that "*Snow-Bound* is memorable largely because it gave full play to his powers as an artist in black and white." [10]

But even Powell admits that "crimson-blooded maples" in "The Ranger" is good, and J. Warren Thyng says that Whittier often called his attention to "the most delicate tints in a landscape" and quotes from "Sunset on the Bearcamp":

> The gold against the amethyst,
> The green against the rose.

I am not sure that we should be aware of Whittier's color-blindness from his writings alone. "I wish thee could have seen our maple woods and our scarlet oaks and purple ash trees, in the golden tints of autumn," he once wrote Mrs. Alexander. And Charlotte Forten Grimké quotes him as saying that Celia Thaxter had sent him flowers "whose hues he thought were more brilliant in her little garden among the rocks of the Isles of Shoals than he had seen elsewhere."

III

Though Whittier did not like farm work, the countryman's ways and outlook clung to him all his life. His strongest oath seems to have been "Hang me!" but one can hardly imagine any of his peers writing as he did in 1840: "Only think of it. H. V. Stanton it is rumored, will get married and go out with his woman to Europe!" In some ways he shows the countryman's freedom from softness also. We have his own word for it, in a letter written in the 'thirties, that he had never shed a tear since being birched at the village school. "I have sometimes wished I *could* shed tears —especially when angry with myself or with the world. There is an iron fixedness about my heart on such occasions when I would gladly melt away."

He was not so foolish, however, as to count this unto himself for righteousness, nor yet to imagine that he had achieved a calm religious detachment from the passions of life. His blood boiled over slavery outrages, and it is clear that many of his anti-slavery pieces were written in a rage; had he been able to avoid this, he might have been spared some of his breakdowns too. When he first read *Evangeline* he was disappointed at the calmness with which Longfellow had described the fate of the exiles, though later he came to feel that the Cambridge poet had managed the matter quite rightly. "Looking at the materials before him with the eye of an artist simply, he has arranged them to suit his idea of the beautiful and pathetic, leaving to some future historian the duty of sitting in judgment upon the actors in the atrocious outrage which furnished them." But he also knew that he himself could never have done it that way. He writes of the "wrecks of passion and desire" and less metaphorically in prose, of "my temperament, ardent, impetuous, imaginative, powerfully acted upon from without, keenly susceptible to all influences from the intellectual world, as well as to those of nature."

Despite his Quaker training, Whittier knew himself "ill adapted to that quiet, submissive, introverted state of passive and patient waiting for direction and support" which he regarded as the ideal. He cried "Hallelujah" when he heard that the Douglass family had escaped the slavecatchers, and he is said to have thrown his presentation copy of *Leaves of Grass* into the fire.[11] If he feared mobs, it was because he resented an assault upon his dignity; he never trembled for his life. He once considered a lawsuit, and he may himself at times have been in danger of breaking the libel laws. Nor did his Quaker principles ever prevent him from defending himself when he was attacked. "He will yet have to learn," he wrote of a brother-editor, "that although far from being pugnacious in our general temperament, we can for his special benefit divest ourselves of Quakerism in our paper at least." When in his later years sentimental admirers called him a saint, he would have none of it.

"Jordan is a hard road to travel." . . . Only a day or two ago I lost my temper because somebody who was not a saint, but only an average church-member, was perverse and ill-dispositioned; and I disputed the bill of an Irishman who thought it right to make spoil of a Protestant Egyptian, and I dare say he went away with no satisfactory evidence of my saintship.

There can be no question that Whittier was naturally nervous and impatient. Even in the 'seventies Elizabeth Hume found him "certainly a very nervous man to travel with, constantly walking back and forth from end to end of the car, putting down and taking up his bag and changing his seat." The same thing shows in his unwillingness to listen to a prolonged discourse. He would always much rather read sermons than hear them delivered, and it may not have been ill health alone which kept him from attending Lyceum lectures at Amesbury, even when the lecturer was staying at his house. He was quite capable of interrupting a conversation which bored him by getting up to tend the fire or perform other chores, and once at least he got a volume of Emerson off the shelf and asked a member of the circle to read aloud. "Heaven knows how hard I have all my life striven to control this nervous excitability," he writes in one letter, and Edna Dean Proctor would seem to have been quite right when she wrote, "I have always been impressed by the mingled volcano and iceberg of your character."

The only really bitter vituperation in which Whittier ever engaged was in connection with slavery, and this he seems to have justified to himself, in part at least, by the example of Milton, whose controversial works he admired "for their stern dignity and terrible invective, the bitter scorn, the annihilating retort, the solemn eloquence and devout appeals." The classical example is, of course, "Ichabod"—the great 1850 attack on Daniel Webster for his support of the Compromise and the Fugitive Slave Law—one of Whittier's finest achievements and a world classic in the literature of public invective. The Biblical grandeur of the assault made the impact more deadly, and the victim was not named only because he needed no identification. Whittier had had serious doubts about Webster for some time. The next year he attacked him again in "Kossuth," his poem about the Hungarian patriot then visiting America—

Who shall be Freedom's mouthpiece? Who shall give
Her welcoming cheer to the great fugitive?
Not he who, all her sacred trusts betraying,
  Is scourging back to slavery's hell of pain
  The swarthy Kossuths of our land again!—

and when Webster had the bad judgment to declare that most Friends agreed with his position, Whittier contradicted him directly and authoritatively.[12]

If Webster alone inspired Whittier to powerful castigation in verse, he was far from being the only public figure to feel the lash of his tongue in prose. Nor was the poet's bitterness altogether limited to the advocates of slavery. As a book reviewer he was not gentle. His reviews of *Atlantic Souvenir* and of *The Token* for 1831 [13] are dull and pernickety and as irritatingly self-confident as Poe at his worst. When Bryant, as editor of the New York *Evening Post*, assaulted William L. Stone of the *Commercial Advertiser* on Broadway, Whittier headed his very sarcastic commentary on the fracas in the *New England Weekly Review* with the poet's own lines—

> And leave the vain low strife
> That makes men mad.

Oh for the pen of a Diedrich Knickerbocker, the same which sketched the terrific picture of the war-like Peter Stuyvesant! The chivalry of the Dutch Dynasty has returned to New York. We marvel why something of a belligerent nature cannot be got up in Hartford [where the *Review* was published]. We are far behind our neighbors in matters of pugnacity.

The next year, trying to sting Bryant, James Lawson, and William Leggett into taking an anti-slavery stand, Whittier published anonymously in the Haverhill *Iris* a poem "To a Poetical Trio in the City of Gotham," [14] in which, among other things, they found themselves described as "lost miscreants" and "hirelings of traitors." And when Whittier himself was pilloried among others in a pamphlet called *Truth: A New Year's Gift for Scribblers*, his reply was masterly: "This is the title of a pamphlet, in imitation of *English Bards and Scotch Reviewers*, recently published in Boston. It possesses all the marks which distinguish its copy, except genius, spirit, satire, and poetry."

It is only fair to add, however, that compared to what others were writing and saying at the time, even Whittier's worst invective was temperate. Edmund Quincy, for example, compared Daniel Webster with Professor John Webster, the Boston killer of Dr. Parkman, "the other criminal of the same name who is now on trial by God and his country." Whittier publicly apologized to James K. Polk, having become aware that he had inadvertently brought a false accusation against him, though, in a way, the apology was itself an insult: he thought that "as a slaveholder," Polk had "already sins enough to answer for, without charging him falsely." Though he was displeased with Bancroft's conduct as minister to England and disappointed over his own failure to win him to abolitionism, he ridiculed a reviewer who ignored Bancroft's achievement as an historian, and when Edward Everett died, he astonished everybody by publishing a laudatory notice of him in spite of all their disagreements. Perhaps the testimonial which a group of Southerners presented to the old poet on his eightieth birthday is more a witness to their moderation than to his, but it must still be significant that it was to him rather than to another of their old opponents that they chose to send it. Whittier aimed to smite evil wherever he encountered it, but having smitten, he was always sincerely mindful of the unworthiness of the smiter.

> The longer I live, I see the evil in myself in a clearer light, and more that is good in others; and if I do not grow better, I am constrained to be more charitable. I shudder sometimes at my fierce rebuke of evil-doers, when I consider my own weakness and sins of omission as well as commission.

He had his disagreements with allies as well as with opponents —with the curious cynicism about human nature that ran alongside his idealism, he once remarked that he had "long ceased to expect that because men are reformers, they will therefore be better than other people" [15]—but he was right and Garrison was wrong in the differences that developed between them, and he treated Garrison with great forbearance while Garrison treated him outrageously, even accusing him of a desire to obtain "peace at the expense of consistency, if not of principle," and expressing the fear that he might eventually truckle to the slave states.[16]

IV

I must not leave the impression that Whittier associated with his fellows only in connection with their campaigning for "causes." But his abstention from both alcohol and tobacco applied a brake to his social life to the extent of causing him to incline to shun social gatherings where drinking and smoking might be done. This is presumably what Longfellow meant when he wished that Whittier had some vices "so he could come and see me." Temperance was always one of his "causes." Whittier lived in a hard-drinking age, and he saw all around him the ravages of alcohol in the lives of many persons who were otherwise useful and amiable. Nor was there ever any doubt in his mind that the organized liquor traffic was the enemy of everything that makes for social progress and the ally of all the vices that drag men down. In a letter to the New York *Sun*, January 17, 1888, he called Frances Willard, founder of the Women's Christian Temperance Union, "the noblest woman of her age." He showed that he had some understanding of the social causes of drinking when, as early as 1858, he advocated the cultivation of social and popular amusements as counter attractions to the saloon, though I think it must be admitted that the particular amusements he favored were somewhat too exalted in tone to reach many of John Barleycorn's victims. Yet here as elsewhere he carefully avoids extremism. "I am a Prohibitionist," he writes in 1884, but he proposes to vote the Republican, not the Prohibition, ticket. "I question whether the Temperance cause at present should be transferred into a *national political party*, but there is abundant reason for urging Prohibition in the *states*." Whittier would have been quite incapable of such an act as Thoreau committed when he advised an intemperate man who came to see him under the influence of liquor to go home and cut his throat and do it quickly. As early as 1836 he condemned the aristocrats who "with the wine-glass at their lips . . . grow eloquent over the vices and drunkenness of 'the rabble.' " He could read Holmes's lines "On Lending a Punch Bowl" without shuddering over the contents of the vessel, and he tells us specifically that the Whittiers did not refuse hard cider to the "Yankee Gypsies." [17] Pollard has called attention to the amazing facts that the *New England Weekly Review* carried liquor advertisements and that Whittier himself contributed an article to *The American Manufacturer* on "Cultivation of the Vine." [18]

Whittier did not care much for the pleasures of the table either. "I am far from indifferent to the good things of life," he wrote Elizabeth Lloyd, July 14, 1859, "but I could live, if necessary, on the black broth of Sparta, or the oatmeal porritch of the Scotchman. . . . With the Scriptural injunction I 'eat what is set before me, asking no questions.' " Such preferences as he had seem to have been more negative than positive, but he had a fondness for squash pie, and it may be significant that when he writes Phebe Woodman about the cuisine at Asquam House, Holderness, New Hampshire, in 1884, though he mentions "meat nice and well cooked," the stress of the letter falls on such things as "fritters and buckwheats in the morning, Indian and Graham cakes, and pies of all kinds." He considered the traditional New England boiled dinner a "detestable" messy dish and feared that New Englanders had weakened their native fibre by eating too much pork and potatoes. He loathed both cabbage and cucumbers, declaring that after cabbage had been cooked in a house, you had to burn it down to get rid of the smell.

Sports and games were not important in Whittier's America; it is not surprising that for such a man as he was they should hardly have existed. He had some share in the country pleasures of his youth; he also told Elizabeth Hume that he had played High Low Jack as a boy, "but of course the folks did not know." His Uncle Moses was a great hunter and fisherman, and Whittier sometimes went with him on his fishing expeditions at least. Judging by the piece he afterwards wrote for children, "The Fish

I Didn't Catch," he was not, at the outset at least, what would be called successful, and I do not imagine such excursions were numerous, even in childhood. Many country boys enjoyed swimming in the lakes and pools about Haverhill, but Whittier never took to the water; neither did he become a good sailor. When he stayed at Bearcamp House, at White Osipee, New Hampshire, in his old age, he came into close association with bear hunters, enjoyed hearing them tell of their experiences, and even helped them eat their kill, but that was as far as he went. Indeed, the only reference I have found to Whittier's personal participation, during his mature life, in any sport or game is Moncure D. Conway's account of having once found him playing croquet against himself.[19] When Swarthmore College named its "field of Recreation and Exercise" after him, he professed to be honored, but his letter of acknowledgement was about as stiff as they come:

> As the graduate only of a district school I know little of the needs of a college, but I have no doubt that the "Field" will be found an important adjunct to Swarthmore. The old Greeks—whose example in many things is worthy of imitation—were wise in combining physical with mental culture. Recreation is doubtless as necessary in a Friends' school as in any other, though in this as in everything else, it is well to let our moderation be known to all. Life is a very earnest thing: and the time allotted us too precious to be wasted in idle sports....

He did not do much more with travel. Alone among the famous American poets of his time, he never crossed the ocean. "One vast world-page remains unread." Nor did he travel widely in his own country, for though he was continentally minded more than any of the others—being thrilled, for example, at the prospect of building a railroad from Chicago to the mouth of the Columbia River —he was never north of the White Mountains, west of Chambersburg, Pennsylvania, or south of Washington, D.C. Mrs. Stowe could not lure him to Florida nor the founders of Whittier, California entice him west by naming the town after him and giving him a parcel of land on the central square. In 1840 he nearly went to London to an anti-slavery meeting, or at least he toyed with the idea. "It would be pleasant—nay it would be glorious to visit the wild scenery of Scotland—to glide along the Rhine by moonlight—by vineyard, and forest—old German castles—ghost-tenanted perhaps—grey towers built by the Roman conquerors of the blue-eyed barbarians of Germany—to drop in upon Paris," but health considerations and his fear of his inability to stand up under the excitement involved, caused him to give up the idea in the absence of a clear mandate of duty. Later he made something of a principle of his abstention:

He who wanders widest, lifts
No more of beauty's jealous veil
Than he who from his doorway sees
The miracle of flowers and trees.

"Munich, the Louvre, and the Vatican are doubtless well worth seeing," he wrote Emerson, "but I fancy I see all and much more in my own painted woodlands." And when he was asked whether he did not wish to visit Quebec, he replied, "Oh no. I know it all by books and pictures just as well as if I had seen it." At the end, he even applied this principle when asked to go for a drive in the country around Oak Knoll: "I know just how everything looks, we should see nothing more beautiful than what we have at home."

In a way, all this was in line with the Transcendentalist attitude toward travel. But Whittier was much less theoretical about it. The Transcendentalists downgraded travel because they believed that all the essential elements of human experience might be encountered in one's native environment. If Whittier had actually believed this, he would probably not have pored over books of travel with such avidity. The truth of the matter seems to have been that he preferred to do his traveling by proxy (this was not the only area in which he demonstrated a gift for vicarious experience). Once, welcoming Bayard Taylor home from one of his endless jaunts, he wrote, "I have followed thee all over the world without any share of the expenses, trouble or fatigue." He took up much the same attitude toward Edna Dean Proctor when she enchanted him with stories of her journeys in Russia and Asia.

But it was not merely economy and love of ease that kept Whittier from travel—nor health considerations either. He was enough of an artist to care nothing for experience until it had been intellectually apprehended and aesthetically recreated. If he had traveled, he would probably have enjoyed his travels much more in retrospect than in actuality. That was the way he enjoyed the places he did see, and he writes Celia Thaxter concerning her letters from the Isles of Shoals:

> They are wonderfully hospitable letters—they give me the freedom of the Island: I sit by the parlor fire in the stormy nights. I see the tossing boats in the little harbor—the islands ringed round with foam and I feel the spray as it tosses up through cleft and gorge; and I hear thee telling stories to the young folks, and half fancy myself a boy among them, nestling close to thee with "not unpleasing horror" as the tragedy deepens.

Sometimes it must even have seemed to him that he *had* traveled: "The weather is delightful—the air is soft and warm as any air of Italy or South Spain." And, indeed, in his own way, he had, for his Italian pieces have reminded both Pollard and Bliss Perry of Browning. It is hard to believe that the man who thus described Strasbourg Cathedral not only never saw it but never set eyes upon any other cathedral either:

> he saw, far down the street,
> A mighty shadow break the light of noon,
> Which tracing backward till the airy lines
> Hardened to stony plinths, he raised his eyes
> O'er broad facade and lofty pediment,
> O'er architrave and frieze and sainted niche,
> Up the stone lace-work chiseled by the wise
> Erwin of Stenbach, dizzily up to where
> In the noon brightness the great Minster's tower,
> Jewelled with sunbeams of its mural crown,
> Rose like a visible prayer.[20]

V

The arts are not, like sports and games, *essentially* social enjoyments, though they are probably at their best when shared with others. From the most social of them all, the theater, Whittier was barred by his Quaker prejudices: he seems to have read Shakespeare with a clear conscience, but there is no record that he ever saw a play. Mrs. Fields says that he promised to go with her and James T. Fields to see Ristori in 1886, but he backed out at the last minute. His closest approach was when he attended Dickens's last reading in Boston in 1867, and the rapture which that experience brought him gives us some idea of how much he missed.[21] He mentions David Garrick in "The Quaker Alumnus" and Barnum in *The Tent on the Beach*.[22] He once received a social invitation from Edwin Forrest but he did not accept it. Yet whenever his path crossed that of a famous actor, he seems to have been aware of it: in 1837 he was on shipboard with "the celebrated Miss Ellen Tree of theatrical notoriety."

In 1860 he met Charlotte Cushman, "a great woman, with a large heart, and a reformer of the better stamp," as he tells Elizabeth Lloyd. But to Elizabeth's sister, Mrs. Neall, he writes more condescendingly: "I spent a pleasant day with Emerson this fall, in company with Charlotte Cushman, who, apart from her actress vocation, is one of the noblest of women, a warm abolitionist, and friend of all good causes." (When what he respects and admires is coupled with what he mistrusts, what is a poor man to do?) Three years later he wrote Mrs. Fields of "the coal-touched lips of Charlotte Cushman." Had she read for him, I wonder, or was he indulging his not unfamiliar habit of describing what he had only experienced in his imagination? "Coal-touched" is from Isaiah 6:5-8, which describes the call of a prophet of Yahweh; it seems a lofty figure for Whittier to apply to a stage artist. All in all, he would seem to have found himself quite of a mind with the Mount Auburn grave-digger who remarked of Charlotte, as Gamaliel Bradford delightedly reports, that "she was considerable of a woman for a play-actress." [23]

There is an interesting but puzzling passage, too, in a letter to Mrs. Fields, in which Whittier reports of Boston that

> The shop-windows are a delight to me, and everything and everybody is novel and interesting. I don't need to go to the theatre. I have more theatre than I can take in every time I walk out.

But how can you think of life in terms of theater when you have never seen a play?

The thing which delights me most in this connection, however, is an incident which occurred during Whittier's first visit to Boston, as a country boy very proud of his "boughten buttons." He met on this occasion a very charming lady, who evidently took an interest in the simple country lad and went out of her way to make his visit agreeable. But alas, he could not take advantage of the crowning kindness she offered him, which was a pass to the theater where she was playing, for she was an actress! The shock was evidently a great one, for at that time an actress must have been almost as fabulous a creature to young Whittier as a griffin or a Gorgon.

Whittier is sometimes inclined to minimize the beauty of art as opposed to that of nature, as when he writes Mrs. Alexander: "No doubt your picture galleries at Florence are beautiful with art, but nothing like the pictures of God hung over all our hills." But he was certainly not indifferent to painting, and sometimes he even looks at nature herself from an artist's point of view. "We have just returned from the banks of the Saco, where it is joined by the Swift River—a very fine bit for a painter." His most famous artistic figure is certainly the reference to his recollections of the farm life at Haverhill as "these Flemish pictures of old days."

Among the painters he mentions, some of them repeatedly, are Raphael, Fra Angelico, Leonardo da Vinci, Tintoretto, Ary Scheffer, Claude Lorraine, and Poussin. He seems to have associated Hogarth with gaiety and Salvator Rosa with Gothic gloom; I should have thought there would have been much more to horrify the moralist in Hogarth's subject matter. He wrote poems inspired by pictures by Raphael, Tintoretto, Ary Scheffer, James

Barry, Edwin Austin Abbey, and George Fuller. In 1859 he went with Henry Ward Beecher to see one of the century's favorite pictures—"The Heart of the Andes" by Frederick Church: "It is a great picture, and I am glad to hang it up in my memory as a joy forever." In 1856 he thanked Lucy Larcom for the "welcome gift" of "a splendid picture of Dante and Beatrice," but three years later, when she invited him to go to see some pre-Raphaelite pictures at the Fieldses, he said he was "snow-bound" and sent some nonsense verses instead.[24] He liked pictures that had a moral meaning, but he was not narrow about it, nor aesthetically snobbish either, and he also liked pictures which told a story and appealed simply to human feeling. A picture of an "Arab at Prayer" appealed to him so much that he would have liked to own it: "It is not, I think, much of a work of art, but it is suggestive and appeals to the imagination." As early as 1830, when he was narrower about such things than he afterwards became, he quite fell in love with a picture representing

> one of the cowled brotherhood of merry England in her time of priests and monks and tournaments. There was something in the good monk's features so expressive of satisfaction and contented indolence, and so mild and benevolent withal, that we could not but envy the original, and wish ourself certain of being so happily disposed of.

And as late as Christmas 1866 he could rejoice at receiving "a chromo-lithograph copy of 'Old Mother Hubbard,' very queer and very finely done."

Possibly he was a little more wary of sculpture, or perhaps it only interested him less. Mary Claflin tells of a life-size figure of Ruth which turned on a pivot in the home of one of his friends and which he frequently admired in silence. When by accident it got turned about, he was disturbed and said to his hostess, "Thy graven image appears to be backing folks t'much. I think thee had better turn her round." Story's "Lybian Sybil," which he saw "at Mrs. Lodge's" in Beacon Street in 1869, is one of the few statues he mentions by name; he thought the figure "a grand and awful creature." There are few references to nude sculpture, but all are morally neutral, which is interesting in view of Hawthorne's difficulties with this matter and even Mrs. Longfellow's sense of chagrin that a Yankee girl could have stooped to pose for Palmer's "White Captive." An 1855 letter to Fields indicates that Whittier was himself invited to be sculptured but had refused. Eventually he succumbed however. "Does thee know that when I was in Boston," he wrote Gail Hamilton in 1873, "I was caught by Powers the younger and made a graven image of? Such is the melancholy fact. To such strange uses may even Quakerism come!" Two years later he even suggested that this "graven image" might be purchased by the Haverhill Library, "unless Mr. Powers sets too high a price on the blockhead."

When it comes to music, there are two questions to consider: What musical capacity, if any, did Whittier possess? And to what extent was his attitude toward music determined by the traditional Quaker prejudice against it?

The incapacity he himself affirms uncompromisingly to Mrs. Fields: "The gods have made me most unmusical." And he reaffirms it to Higginson as late as 1882: "I don't know anything of music, not one tune from another."

In the early days he seems rather proud of his shortcoming:

> In my opinion man was not endowed with those high faculties which distinguish him from the brute creation to devote them to the attainment of an art, in which few arrive to perfection, and which he is incapable of exercising to soothe his hours of illness, or to warm the frozen spirits of age; and considering it as a part of those religious exercises which Christians are called upon to perform, I presume every reflecting person will admit that it is only that music which proceeds from a heart under the immediate influence of the spirit of truth which can be acceptable to heaven.

Two years later, in *The American Manufacturer*, he was equally uncompromising:

> We have seen and heard a great deal about the power of music, the charms of music, &c. but for ourself we have no great predilection for this kind of amusement. Charms of music, forsooth!—the shocking

amalgamation of a choir of human voices—croaked hoarse and squalling—the harsh growl of the bass-viol contrasted with its sharp scream, which operates on the nerves like the whetting of a hand-saw; and the provoking squeak of the violin, imitating in the language of Burns "the dying agonies of a pig under the hands of the butcher"! And then to see a young lady, pushing up and down pieces of ivory, screwing her pretty mouth into all manner of shapes, but the right one—imposing silence on all, who are unfortunate to be within hearing—and pausing only in the painful monotony of her employment, to receive the plaudits of a company, who have all along been wishing her delectable instrument at the bottom of the Red Sea, why, it is enough to weary the genius of patience itself. We had rather hear the creaking of the cider-mill, or the music of a high pressure steam engine. Away with such unnatural efforts. Give us the melody of mind—the music and the eloquence of thought.

And when a rival editor, George D. Prentice, twitted him about this in the *New England Weekly Review*, he replied:

A Quaker! we glory in the name. Unworthy as we are of the appellation, we can feel a pride in its application to ourself. A Quaker! he can boast of no chivalric ancestors, no war-like heroes in the simple annals of his family. But he *can* boast of their moral power—of their triumph over self—of their heroic firmness in the dark days of New-England persecution. No blood has flowed to the demon of intolerance on the peaceful altars of his sect. In the hour of bigotry and persecution, when the scaffold of death was erected on the grave of liberty, the Quakers alone stood forth—not in arms—not in worldly power, but in calm and unbending opposition to tyranny. And they died in their firmness—perished on the ignominious scaffold—the pioneers in the cause of religious liberty.

This is about as close to sectarian bigotry as Whittier ever came, nor did he often display such skill in drawing red herrings over the trail.

Many years later, when the Friends School at Providence considered the possibility of introducing musical instruction, he was much less bigoted, though he still could not qualify as a musical enthusiast. Opposing the proposition, he was careful to stipulate that he was not opposed to music as such, and that he saw no more reason why Quakers should mistrust music than any other art. What he did fear was

> that the teaching of music in the school might be found in many instances the preparation of our young folks to practice it in our meetings. They might come back to us, to sing Moody and Sankey songs about "Holding the Fort." I like the old reverent waiting better than the "Howlish Dervish" style of "carrying on" a meeting.

He closed with the suggestion that if the non-Quakers in the school desired musical instruction, "an 'outside barbarian,' a city music teacher [might] come and attend to it."

In sharp contrast to the comparatively large number of painters mentioned by Whittier, I have noted references to only two great composers—Beethoven and Haydn. Yet his favorite sister Elizabeth loved music and was, we are told, abnormally sensitive to sound, so that "voices took shapes to her; they were round, and square, and of different shapes," and there are indications that Whittier's own capacity was greater than he sometimes wished to believe. In 1868 he was interested in the famous Norwegian violinist Ole Bull, partly perhaps because he had heard that a woman had been reminded by him of "such a music-ignoring Quaker as I am." It may possibly have been only politeness which, twelve years later, caused him to write very kindly to E. P. Whipple about another famous violinist who had expressed a desire to meet him and play for him.[25] But there are a number of late references to his having listened with pleasure to the singing of Scottish and other songs, though once, at Bear Camp, a lady sang a setting of his "Barbara Frietchie" to harp accompaniment, and he failed to recognize it and therefore let her go unthanked! After visiting Harriet McEwen Kimball, on the other hand, he remembered her sister's singing gratefully; once he even went so far as to tell a singer that he wished he could write a song for her. Naturally, the Negro Spirituals appealed to him profoundly, both for their religious value and their association with the race he had helped to free, and when the Fisk Jubilee Singers visited him at Amesbury in 1879 and sang for him, he was overcome for once and wept for joy, and wrote the poem "The Jubilee Singers" afterwards.

Actually, Whittier not only *wished* he *could* write songs: he *did* write them. "Lexington, 1775" was written for the centenary celebration of the battle; the next year came the "Centennial Hymn" for the great exposition in Philadelphia. In his early days he wrote songs in imitation of Burns, and for Frémont's 1856 campaign he turned out a campaign song written to a tune from *I Puritani*. During the Civil War the Hutchinsons sang the "furnace-blast" song which he had composed to "Ein' Feste Burg ist unser Gott" with such effect that McClellan prohibited repetition, but Lincoln countermanded the order, saying that this was just the kind of song he wanted the soldiers to hear. "I am glad to know that there is any *sing* in my verses," wrote Whittier to John Hutchinson. "Of course I can have no objection to thy use of them. If thee can get any music out of them, I shall be pleased and gratified." But the oddest paradox concerns the use of Whittier's poems in hymnology. He once said that "a good hymn is the best use to which poetry can be devoted, but I do not claim that I have succeeded in composing one." It would have been difficult for him to do so, for he belonged to a body which made no use of Congregational singing. Yet a very large number of hymns have been drawn from his poems in the hymnals of nearly all leading Protestant denominations, and two of these—"We may not climb the heavenly steeps" from "Our Master" and "Dear Lord and Father of mankind" from "The Brewing of Soma"—rank with the most beloved hymns of the English-speaking world.

VI

Fortunately, sociability can exist quite apart from any of the organized interests of mankind.

> My friends, like Charles Lamb's [wrote Whittier to Elizabeth Lloyd], are to me a glorious possession—a rich mine of wealth—calling forth from my heart, silent thanksgivings when I look them over in memory

as a miser does his gold—one by one passing in their veiled beauty and goodness before me. Is it nothing that I have felt the kindly smile of the pure-spirited Follen, "sliding into my soul"—that I have enjoyed the rare and beautiful companionship of Lucy Hooper, and of others who dead to the world are to me living realities? Who shall set a value in the world's coin upon the worth of the intellectual communion I have enjoyed and still enjoy with the Channings, the Pierponts, the Longfellows and Bryants, with Weld and Birney and Goodell and others engaged in the cause of humanity?

No doubt he was entirely sincere when he wrote such things. But taken by itself such an utterance gives the impression of a much richer social life than he actually enjoyed. Because he grew up on a farm without near neighbors, he had few close friends in childhood, and the habits formed at that time were never entirely cast off. At Haverhill Academy his relations with his fellow students were cordial but not intimate. If he was really sociable at any period, it would seem to have been during his Hartford and Philadelphia days, though, looking back, he thought of himself in early life as "full of the wisdom of inexperience, diffident and trying to hide my shyness by brusqueness and affectation of indifference, with vague dreams and ambitions interweaving with my commonplace surroundings."

Theoretically he never wanted anybody to stand on ceremony with him. "A truce to your apologies when writing a letter to me," he wrote Edwin Harriman in 1829. "Write on unconcernedly and never trouble yourself whether you are right or wrong. . . . What is the use to disguise human nature?" But probably he himself achieved this goal more successfully in letters than in conversation, for the very same year he writes Mary Nesmith to excuse himself for his "stupid behavior" in company.

The truth was I was suffering from the effects of the toothache—I felt moreover out of humor with the whole world. I scarce know how it is, or why it is, but there are some times when I can feel no enjoyment in society; and when I can neither converse myself, nor pay any attention to what is going on around me.

Thirty years later he is still explaining his dislike of big dinners on the ground that "at such times when I break through my natural reserve I am liable to say more than I mean—to be extravagant and overstrong in my assertions." He was a member of the Saturday Club, but he attended so seldom that Emerson seems not to have been aware that he belonged.[26] He had no small talk, and he found it hard work to be idle, though he seems to have felt fairly comfortable with the members of the Radical Club of Chestnut Street and with his publishers and their friends. Yet when the famous Seventieth Birthday Dinner was planned to honor him, he complained because he would have to buy a new pair of pants, and it was touch-and-go up to the last minute whether he would attend or not.

One form of communication he completely abjured—public speaking; Pollard found only "perhaps three public addresses" in his whole life. Though he was a skillful lobbyist—a "buttonhole man"—he would not speak for a cause ("I am, heart and soul, an Abolitionist, but by no means, a *speaking* one") nor for his friends (since he turned down Mrs. Fields's urgent request that he participate in a poetry reading for charity); nor, apparently, even for the Holy Spirit (since there seems to be no record of his having spoken in Quaker meeting). "My voice is of a timorous nature and rarely to be heard above a breath." He did go to the birthday dinner, but he got Longfellow, who was no lion in such matters himself, to read the response he had prepared to all the lovely things that were said about him. Yet Mrs. Fields thought him a gifted story-teller in private, and many seem to have relished his poetry readings when he could be persuaded to read to a small group.

How much at ease he was in small gatherings seems to have depended upon circumstances and conditions. In some moods he liked the combined sociability and privacy which a hotel affords, especially a small one. Apparently he talked about religion freely with Lyman Abbott, Elizabeth Stuart Phelps, and others, but he would have preferred chopping wood to talking about poetry with strangers. Though he did not believe in capital punishment, he was inclined to think it might be well to make interviewing "a state prison offence." When he first visited Julia Ward Howe, he was so persistent in moving his chair away from hers that she feared he might end by backing into the fireplace and up the chimney, and when Thomas Wentworth Higginson introduced him to Harriet Prescott (Spofford), it was, he said, "like bringing a girl and a gazelle together; each visibly wished to run away from the other."

What Whittier really seems to have wanted was to have his friends available when he needed them but to be left alone when he craved solitude; and during his later years with his cousins in Danvers, this is just what they provided for him. J. Warren Thyng, who knew him at Bearcamp, says:

> When he sat alone under his tree no one presumed to intrude upon him. Indeed, if one desired to retain his friendship, it was well to keep away when he chose to be by himself, and sometimes it was best to be a better listener than talker.

And Helen Burt adds that care was always taken to give him a quiet out-of-the-way room, with "few neighbors, or at least quiet ones." He always took his leave suddenly, often while his companions believed themselves to be in the midst of a conversation, and once when the Fieldses asked him why he could not stay longer, he replied bluntly that it was because he didn't want to.[27]

In a way, Whittier's loneliness increased during his later years, partly because he outlived so many of his contemporaries but also because he was obliged, now that he had become a celebrity, to spend so much energy trying to escape from the bores and intruders who swarmed over him. Perhaps his most trying experience along this line was with the lady who was so impressed by the honor of meeting him that she burst into tears, leaving him to stand there "dumb ... like a gentle martyr." "*Thee* could run away," he told the amused Nora Perry reproachfully afterwards, "but *I* had to stay." On the whole, however, he managed himself very well, and there are times when one sympathizes with Gail

Hamilton who concludes an invitation with "Don't say you have a cold—you always have a cold." According to Martha Hale Shackford, he once made a scene when he found a group of friends mulling over his latest photograph in his absence. "With a sudden swoop, without a word, the irate poet seized the offending photograph, flung it indignantly across the room, then stalked away in the midst of an awful silence."

Yet he was not a hermit, either by temperament or by conviction. "It is possible to be too quiet, and a change from solitary Nature to human contact and voices is sometimes desirable. There are always nice people to be found in any crowd. For my own part, I like folks generally. Very few come amiss to me." Yet it is clear that he preferred observing to being observed, and trains, resorts, and hotels afforded him a means of that not-too-intimate contact with humanity which he enjoyed as much as he relished reading autobiography. In an 1839 letter to Elizabeth Neall from Saratoga Springs he even sounds a little like Hawthorne. He wishes she were present to laugh with him

> at the ten thousand ridiculous things which are constantly occurring around us. As it is, I have laughed alone, and that is a hard business. It is an admirable place here to study human nature—to watch the manifestations of its pride, vanity, and jealousy—to note the early developments of love—the agony of disappointments—of baffled aims—of wasted affections—of unshared sympathies—Hope and Despair, Love and Hatred, Chastened Desire, and unbridled Passion—all crowded together . . . mingling in the same dance and promenade. For myself, I have been somewhat of a laughing Philosopher and have found amusement wherever I could.

This is hardly characteristic however. The Quaker belongs to a "Society," and his worship itself is communion with man as well as with God.

> The meal unshared is food unblest:
> Thou hoard'st in vain what love should spend;
> Self-ease is pain: thy only rest
> Is labor for a worthy end.[28]

Not even books can take the place of humanity, though it is necessary to have them.[29] Indeed God Himself cannot satisfy us alone,[30] and since Christ thought it no shame to wear human nature, it cannot be disrespectful toward Divinity to acknowledge this. In *Snow-Bound* the re-establishment of contact with the outside world after the isolation which had been imposed upon the Whittier family by the blizzard is very exhilarating:

> The chill embargo of the snow
> Was melted in the genial glow;
> Wide swung again our ice-locked door,
> And all the world was ours once more!

Poor as the Whittiers were by our standards during the early days, they had social standing in the community. At Quarterly Meeting time, they sometimes had forty people to dinner, and we are told that Whittier "enjoyed carving roast beef for the multitude." In 1840 he regretted that Elizabeth Lloyd had not mingled more with society during her stay in Philadelphia. "I am persuaded, thee would have found brothers and sisters, where thee looked for strangers, and sympathizing friends, where thee expected but coldness, and reserve, and suspicion." When he was in Brooklyn in 1870 Whittier paid an unsolicited call on the clergyman Theodore L. Cuyler and gladly agreed to attend a group meeting, where Cuyler found his talk "fresh, racy and humorous." On February 15, 1874 he attended a dinner in honor of Wilkie Collins at the St. James Hotel in Boston, and a copy of the menu, on silk, with a hand-painted border, and with Whittier's own name imprinted on the outside, was in his library when he died. In 1876 he seems to have met his royal admirer, Dom Pedro of Brazil, with ease and even to have evaded his embrace gracefully.

"Oftentimes," says Martha Hale Shackford, "there was a sly sarcasm in his comments on people, revealing a shrewdly humorous appreciation of human nature." He once looked over a portfolio of photographs of "various persons who had achieved a rapid but dubious notoriety . . . pointing out eccentricities of countenance and making this a text for a jesting criticism of the literary work of each." Miss Sparhawk says he lamented his ability to read character because it sometimes made him uncomfortable, and adds that he once told a young woman she was not fit to travel alone and that she would lose her trunk at Dover, which she did!

That Whittier had a capacity for hero-worship is evident in his attitude toward General Gordon and others, but generally speaking, he expected to be disappointed. "I expect to see faults and frailties, and to grieve over the mistakes of those I love and respect."

> No perfect whole can our nature make;
> Here or there the circle will break;
> The orb of life as it takes the light
> On one side leaves the other in night.

And so he asks of George Whitefield in "The Preacher":

> He erred: shall we count his gifts as naught?
> Was the work of God in him unwrought?
> The servant may through his deafness err,
> And blind may be God's messenger;
> But the errand is sure they go upon,—
> The word is spoken, the deed is done.

He quotes Richard Baxter approvingly—"The good are not so good as I once thought, nor the bad so evil, and in all there is more for grace to make advantage of, and more to testify for God and holiness, than I once believed"—and he even felt that Baxter's own unearthliness was a defect, not a virtue. He did not admire "a cold and passionless virtue," and he was not afraid to say that he preferred "folks" to angels. He admitted the faults of both Sumner and Samuel J. Tilden in the memorial poems he wrote for them, while as for James T. Fields, he was anxious that he should

> Keep the human heart of thee;
> Let the mortal only be
> Clothed in immortality.

For himself, he was too much attached to the good green earth to be eager to die, however much he might believe in immortality.

Whittier's own descent from the picturesque New England cleric of unsavory reputation, Stephen Bachiler, has now been disproved (and, for that matter, Bachiler himself may well have been considerably better than his legend), but the poet never doubted the connection; neither does he seem really to have been ashamed of Bachiler or any other shady ancestor, real or supposed. One gathers that the presence of an ancestral taint may even have comforted him at times in reflecting upon what he considered his own shortcomings: "we are weak," he would say, "on the Hussey side."[31] His human sympathies were not bounded by race or creed; like Emerson and Thoreau, but unlike most of his Yankee contemporaries, he was quite undisturbed by the invasion of New England by Irish immigrants. He admired John Randolph, not because he was a slave holder but because he desired to free his slaves; and he loved Burns for his great qualities and despite his obvious failings.

Florence Maybrick, accused of having poisoned her husband, was the heroine of one of the most controversial murder trials of the nineteenth century.[32] In all probability innocent, she was sentenced to death, then reprieved, and the sentence commuted to penal servitude for life; she served fifteen years before she was pardoned. One day Gail Hamilton showed Whittier two pictures of her.

> one before her trouble came—only a piquant young face with a toss of curly hair above it and a careless curve of round white arm and dimpled hand and falling flowers; the other after the blow had fallen, and all the piquancy was gone and only an infinite trouble and bewilderment looked out of the large eyes—the amazement and *uncomprehendingness* of a child. He looked long from the one picture to the other, with moans of pity and sympathy, and to her . . . he was moved to send a token of tenderness, a spray of his glossy birthday ivy, bidding her be, in his own words,
>
> Strong
> In the endurance that outwearies wrong.[33]

I know that a certain type of sentimentalist is almost fatally drawn toward a convicted or suspected murderess, but nothing could have been more alien than this to Whittier's character, and I submit that no moral snob could have sent such a message as he sent under the circumstances related.

He was the same with those he knew. Once a woman who felt that she had offended him went to him to confess her fault, beginning by saying that she feared he would be angry. "I shall not be angry long," he replied gently.

> The day I got thy letter [he wrote Elizabeth Lloyd in 1860], we were dreadfully shocked by the death (by his own hand) of a neighbor and dear friend, to whose kindness and love we owed much. A genial, generous, warm-hearted man, the derangement of his wife and other troubles broke him down and destroyed the balance of his mind. Elizabeth and I had been very anxious about him weeks before. He was greatly beloved; at his funeral the great congregation "lifted up their voices and wept." We have not got over the shock; it overpowered me for the time.

Better still is his attitude toward Henry Ward Beecher when he was publicly accused of adultery. Whittier was by no means sure that he was innocent. "I have been sorely pained by this miserable Scandal at Brooklyn," he wrote Lydia Maria Child. "I have loved Beecher so much! I *cannot* believe him guilty as is charged, and yet it looks very dark. God pity him in any case!" And to Elizabeth Stuart Phelps: "I love Beecher and believe in him. He has done good to thousands. If he has fallen into temptation I shall feel grieved, but would be ashamed of myself were I less his friend." When Beecher died, he added:

> I am saddened by the death of Beecher; he was so strong, so generous, so warm-hearted, and so brave and stalwart in so many good causes. It is a mighty loss. He had faults, like all of us, and needed forgiveness; and I think he could say, with David of old, that he would rather fall into the Lord's hands than into the hands of man.

All in all, Whittier would seem to have been quite in character when he ended his story of Skipper Ireson,

> Tarred and feathered and carried in a cart
> By the women of Marblehead!

with a sudden change of heart on the part of the women themselves, who, once they had wrought vengeance, found that there was little satisfaction in it after all.

> Then the wife of the skipper lost at sea
> Said, "God has touched him! why should we?"
> Said an old wife mourning her only son,
> "Cut the rogue's tether and let him run!"
> So with soft relentings and rude excuse,
> Half scorn, half pity, they cut him loose,
> And gave him a cloak to hide him in,
> And left him alone with his shame and sin.

Unlike many nineteenth-century men, Whittier was able to face even impurity on the part of women without hysteria. When he read Lamartine's *History of the Girondins*, he was fascinated by a French Revolutionary courtesan,

> the brown-locked and peerlessly beautiful Gheroigne de Mericourt—the impure Joan d'Arc of the Parisian populace—fearfully sinned against and sinning—selling her charms to aristocratic voluptuaries, and casting their purchase money, with rigid self-denial, into the treasury of the Republic.

In the early uncollected poem, "The Weird Gathering," his sympathy with the betrayed girl who turns to witchcraft in order to avenge her wrongs upon her betrayer is obvious, and when Elizabeth Stuart Phelps dared to make a woman who had "fallen" the heroine of a novel, *Hedged In,* which shocked the generally unprudish Harriet Beecher Stowe, Whittier urged Lucy Larcom, in a rhymed letter, to review for the *Atlantic* a book which, as he saw it,

> teaches and helps folk
> To deal with offenders
> In love which surrenders
> All pride unforgiving,
> The lost one receiving
> With trustful believing

That she like all others,
Our sisters and brothers,
Is only a sinner
Whom God's love within her
Can change to the whiteness
Of heaven's own brightness.

Mordell becomes an unconscious humorist when he suggests, on the basis of such passages,[34] that Whittier sympathized with sexual sin. He simply knew that there is such a thing as Christian charity. It is true that in popular speech a chaste woman is still a "good" woman, whatever other faults she may have, and that an unchaste woman is "bad," whatever other admirable qualities she may possess; but there has never been any sanction for such judgments in any responsible system of Christian ethics. Sins of passion have always been regarded by Christian moralists as less culpable than sins of permanent evil disposition, while the sins that are committed deliberately, in cold blood, to win selfish advantage over others or to betray those who have trusted us, are the worst of all. Whittier never glossed over the sins of the fornicator or the drunkard, but he never forgot that there are much worse transgressions, and that many of them are committed by the most successful and respectable people.[35]

Two special qualities were useful to Whittier socially—his optimism and his humor. He was no cheerful idiot by temperament. He did not desire to live his life over again, and he knew "those 'azure demons' vulgarly called the 'Blues,' " but he did not cherish nor cultivate them. If he was too much of a nineteenth-century pietist to escape "kissing the rod" altogether, it never became his favorite form of osculation. As late as 1857 he did not expect to see slavery abolished during his lifetime, but he never doubted that sooner or later it would pass, and toward the end he was so sure that progress was being made that he thought he would have liked to live a hundred years to see it. "Of course the world is growing better," he wrote in 1881; "the Lord reigns; our old planet is wheeling slowly into fuller light. I despair of nothing good. All will come in good time that is really needed.

All we have to do is work—and wait." He once said that he was still a boy at forty-six, and even when he was eighty-three it seemed to him it had been but a very little time since he had been a boy playing on the farm at Haverhill. "I suppose we all need to feel our weakness and dependence upon our Father, and that it is well for us to find ourselves walking the Valley of Humiliation; but I like the hills and the sunshine, after all." It is the last part of the sentence that is characteristic. "I have blessings beyond my deserts," he writes Lucy Larcom in 1856; "life, in spite of its care and pain, is beautiful; and my heart is often filled with gratitude toward the Merciful Providence whose bounty I enjoy." And twenty years later, despite all the ills of age, he is writing Celia Thaxter: "Life is still good."

Humor helped even when there was nothing to be immediately cheerful about. It is true that Elizabeth Cady Stanton thought the atmosphere of the Whittier home solemn.[36] Apparently the Whittiers did not feel at their ease with her. His close friends found Whittier a fountain of delight. His laughter was "visible instead of audible," but the convolutions it produced were delightful to see. When he became an overseer of Harvard College he playfully told Lowell that he would turn him out of his professorship unless he behaved as Whittier desired in his capacity as editor of the *Atlantic*.

He thought Gail Hamilton's writing "wise and witty, with just enough of unwisdom to make it spicy and enjoyable." He even relished the outrageousness of the old Quaker John Roberts, about whom he wrote a sketch.[37] His humor never stopped short at himself either, and he writes of one of his portraits that it was said to be "an excellent likeness, barring a slight grip of the mouth, giving it a twist by way of variety. Never mind that; twists are natural to men of one idea." He would face a mob when it needed to be faced, but if what he himself calls an "undignified trot" would help him to get away, he employed it. After having been mobbed with George Thompson at Concord, New Hampshire, in 1835, he wrote Harriot Minot to counteract any reports she might have received that he had "betrayed symptoms of fear."

> I was a hero—a moral Leonidas—a spiritual Epaminondas. I was John Knox before the Catholic Queen—Martin Luther before the Pope's council where "every tile upon the housetop was a devil." I was Geo. Fox before the mob of Castle Bosworth—Wm. Penn before the bench of Judges. Yea, verily of a Truth, I maintained the testimony and resisted not—I gave place unto wrath.

But when he and Thompson stopped in their flight at an inn, where the landlord asked them if they had heard about the Englishman Thompson and the Quaker Whittier, who had been stirring things up about the "niggers," he could not resist introducing Thompson as he jumped into the chaise, who, in turn, presented "the Quaker Whittier," whereupon both drove off as rapidly as possible, leaving the landlord "standing, mouth wide open, gazing after us in the greatest astonishment." When Pennsylvania Hall was burned in Philadelphia in 1838, and his office with it, Whittier did not enjoy the spectacle, but it is difficult not to believe that he did enjoy disguising himself and mingling with the mob in order to be able to get in and rescue some of his papers.

None of this means, however, that Whittier was in any sense a hail-fellow-well-met sort of man. Howells, indeed, thought him very difficult with strangers, and he thought he knew why also: "the Quaker calm was bound by the frosty Puritanic air, and he was doubly cold to the touch of a stranger, though he would thaw out to old friends, and sparkle in laugh and joke." [38] I think there is no doubt that, socially speaking, women were easier for him than men, and Elizabeth Stuart Phelps testifies that at their very first meeting, "we talked till our heads ached and our throats were sore; and when we have finished we began again." But even she carried in her heart an "almost painful" picture of his "patient and cheerful but heavy loneliness."

> Who can claim to have come nearest to him? In truth, I believe no one of us all.... His reserve, after all, was something unapproachable.... Faithful to the uttermost, he never fell short of the loyalty of friendship; but he did not go beyond that vague line where it is impossible to fulfil the just expectations of one whom we love. He kept his friendships where he could sustain them.[39]

CHAPTER TWO

POWER AND LOVE

I

The popular idea of Whittier's (in the Meredithian sense) "ordeal" is that there was a conflict between the comparatively selfish desire to win fame as a poet and the sense of moral obligation which impelled him to serve his day and generation as a reformer, primarily in the area of anti-slavery activity. Though the two interests did not ultimately prove irreconcilable, there was such a conflict, but to see the ordeal in these terms alone is to oversimplify it greatly. Politics was in the picture too, and so was journalism. Nor were the lines of demarcation between power and love always quite clearly drawn.

Just how early Whittier's self-consciousness awakened it would be hard to say; he professed to be able to remember nothing that happened before he was six. But he must have determined to make something of himself very early. We are told that as he drove home the cows at the age of seven, he pondered such questions as: Why am I different from these cows? What have I got to do in life? What *is* life? When he gave up the idea of going to college rather than be beholden to others for his education, he simply testified to his pride; there is no implication that ambition was lacking. He was quite in character when he wrote A. W.

Thayer that he might as easily expect to "catch a weasel asleep, or the Old Enemy of Mankind in a parsonage house" as to find him contented to be a good cobbler.

As editor of *The American Manufacturer*, Whittier did not find that what the sectarians call "worldly ambition" was censurable. On the contrary, he thought of it as "one of the best incentives to the exertion of moral power." Puritan though he was, he even sought to excuse Burns's transgressions by reference to "the strongest palliation which vice can offer—the blight of disappointment acting on the exquisite sensibility of genius." As to his own desires it is hard to see how he could have been franker during his early years:

> To George Prentice, 1829: I am haunted by an immediate ambition —perhaps a very foolish desire of distinction, of applause, of fame, of what the world calls immortality.
>
> To Mrs. L. C. Tuthill, 1831: I am naturally . . . an egotist. . . . I have placed the goal of my ambition high—but with the blessing of God, it shall be reached. . . . If my life is spared, the world shall know me in a loftier capacity than *as a writer of rhymes.*
>
> To Mrs. Lydia H. Sigourney, 1832: I would have fame visit me *now* —or not at all. I would not choose between a nettle or a rose to grow over my grave. If I am worthy of fame, I would ask it now—now in the spring-time of my years—when I might share its smile with the friends whom I love, and by whom I am loved in return. But who would ask a niche in that temple where the *dead* alone are crowned—where the green and living garland waves in ghastly contrast over the pale, cold brow and the visionless eye; and where the chant of praise and the voice of adulation fall only on the deafened ear of Death?

If this is not sufficiently "unquakerish," as Whittier might say, there is still the Indian-like "I can no more forget a kindness than an injury. I feel both deeply"—to Caleb Cushing in 1832—or the even more surprising letter to Jonathan Law, written that same year after recovering from an illness: "But I am in tolerable spirits. Life itself is a jest, and I will laugh at it." "Phrenologically," he told Harriot Minot, somewhat playfully, in 1837, "I have too much self-esteem to be troubled by the opinions of others—and

I love my old friends too well to deny them the gratification (if it be one) of abusing me to their hearts' content."

To be sure, there were also times when Whittier abjured fame, and when he thought he was not going to have it he could renounce it nobly on religious grounds, as in the 1848 poem, "The Wise of Today." In "My Soul and I," written at the same period, he probes his motives mercilessly, frankly recognizing that even pure public service may be inspired by selfish, and therefore tainted, motives. In "Ego" (1843), he had reached the extreme of self-abnegation, for here he seemed to be rejecting not only fame but poetry itself:

> ...garlands wreathed from Folly's bowers,
> Of idle aims and misspent hours.

On the other hand, there are two 1857 poems in which he shows his consciousness that fame was already his in some measure even before *Snow-Bound*. "The Last Walk in Autumn" was sent forth to

> Go, find a place at home and hearth
> Where'er thy singer's name is known;

while in "The First Flowers" he exclaims:

> Who knows but that my idle verses
> May leave some trace by Merrimac!

In "A Name," written in 1880, he compares himself to the French poet Marot, and in "An Autograph" (1882) he recognizes that oblivion may well claim him and declares that though he does not care to have an inventory made of his accomplishments,

> Yet, as when dies a sound
> Its spectre lingers round,
> Haply my spent life will
> Leave some faint echo still.

But by this time fame had been long since won, and the situation was changed.

The desire to be known to the world "in a loftier capacity than *as a writer of rhymes*" in the letter to Mrs. Tuthill is particularly interesting. In 1842 Whittier wrote to Ann Wendell that the political "ambitions and selfish hopes of other years" no longer disturbed him. The clear implication is that he once had been disturbed by them, and there can be no question that this is true. Though Whittier may always, in his heart, have wished to be a "friend to man"–

To all who dumbly suffered,
His tongue and pen he offered;
His life was not his own,
Nor lived for self alone– [1]

it is clear that there was a time when the Inner Light shone but dimly, and if there is such a thing as selflessness, Whittier certainly did not achieve it until after he had received a number of hard knocks and rejections, for he himself recalled the time

. . . when ambition's lip of flame and fear
Burned like the tempter's to my listening ear.[2]

Senator Hoar, who was in a good position to judge, described him as "one of the wisest and most discreet political advisers and leaders who ever dwelt in the Commonwealth" of Massachusetts.[3] He never had any illusions about politics or the persons engaged in it, but he tried to believe in politicians as long as he could, and when this was no longer possible, he continued to use them for the causes he believed in as far as they were willing to go.

Up to 1833 Henry Clay was the one he believed in most, partly because he, like Clay, was committed to the "American system" of internal improvements,[4] but he dropped him when it finally became clear that Clay would not join the anti-slavery forces. Jackson was his *bête noire*, partly, no doubt, because the political principles he had learned from Edmund Burke were antipathetic to Jacksonism, but, from Whittier's point of view, there were also other sound reasons for his opposition. Not only did Whittier detest Jackson's Indian policy; he regarded him as a "bloodthirsty old man," enmeshed in the spoils system and relentlessly driving on toward dictatorship, to whom the control of the army might no more safely be entrusted than to the devil himself. Perhaps Frémont was the political figure Whittier most seriously overestimated, though it should not be forgotten that he persuaded him not to oppose Lincoln in 1864, and in 1872 he refused to be nominated for Vice-President by the Independence Party, with Frémont as the nominee for President. And perhaps Andrew Johnson was the president toward whom he was most inclined to be unfair. In February 1866 he was "saddened" by the "folly and stupidity" of Johnson's veto of the bill extending the functions and term of the Freedmen's Bureau, though still willing to give him credit for unenlightened good intentions, but by August 24 he was ready to support impeachment proceedings.

Whittier's behind-the-scenes activities in politics were very important; as Bliss Perry conveniently summarizes, "it was he who devised the conditions which sent Cushing, the Whig, and Rantoul, the Democrat, to Congress, which made Boutwell governor of Massachusetts and sent Sumner to the United States Senate."[5] Before the war he nearly always belonged to a minority party and was largely indifferent to the party affiliations of the candidates he supported so long as he could pledge them to anti-slavery or even to the support of some particular measure which, in his view, militated against the slave system.

Whittier knew that the anti-slavery forces could not really count on Caleb Cushing, but, preferring half a loaf to no bread, he was still influential in getting him elected to Congress in 1834, 1836, and 1838, on his pledge to support the right of petition and the abolition of slavery in the District of Columbia. When in 1838 Cushing tried to abandon this stand, Whittier maneuvered him into a position where he was forced to sign a letter which Whittier wrote for him, renewing his promises to the abolitionists. Two years later, now feeling sure of re-election without abolitionist help, Cushing went his own way, but though he won the election, he paid a heavy price for it; for when President Tyler nominated him as Secretary of the Treasury, Whittier published the 1838 letter to demonstrate that "our distinguished and talented fellow-citizen of Essex North" was "no less an abolitionist than Edward Everett" (whom the pro-slavery Senate had previously rejected), whereupon they proceeded to reject Cushing also, though Tyler sent his name up three times. In 1842-43 Whittier quite as cleverly caused a stalemate in Essex County and prevented the election of a pro-slavery man to Congress by himself remaining a candidate of the Liberty Party, though he had no desire to be elected.

Sumner was a very different breed from Cushing; on the slavery issue and much besides, he and Whittier saw eye to eye. Whittier had the highest regard for Sumner and never found it necessary to play games with him. But it was he who engineered the "deal" that sent Sumner to Washington the first time: the Free-Soilers in Massachusetts agreed to support the Democratic candidate for governor, George S. Boutwell, in return for Democratic support for Sumner as senator. Whittier made sure that Sumner would accept, and the senator frequently sought his advice all through the 'fifties.[6]

All this activity was perfectly legitimate, but it was shrewd and cunning too; it does not suggest a man who was innocent of the realities of human nature or who feared power, and much the same must be said of Whittier's journalistic work. What could have been more "cocky" than his inaugural statement upon taking over the *New England Weekly Review* in 1830?

We have been called a clever fellow heretofore; and it shall go hard with Jacksonism and all the other plagues of the land, but that we will continue to deserve the appellation. We shall take the liberty of speaking our mind upon any subject that may thrust itself into our notice. We shall take occasion to speak of *Men*, too, as well as measures;—and whether hunting down the impudent office-seeker, or exposing the unprincipled Demagogue, we shall never spoil a joke to avoid a libel-suit, or soften a sentence under the apprehensions of a duel *a la Jackson* —that is to say, a flourish of rattans and the visitation of a mahogany stocked pistol. Why should we? Are we not *hors de combat*—a disciple of William Penn? ... Depend upon it, reader, we have too great a respect for our outward man to make a target of it for every scoundrel to shoot at. We never, in all our life, received but one challenge, and that, of course, came from a poor, miserable devil of a Jackson editor. Had no other motive save that of *pity* actuated us, we should certainly have declined the fellow's invitation. . . . Had we accepted the challenge, we should have been the death of the poor fellow. Pistols would never have reached him. Our courtesy would have finished him without the aid of gunpowder.

Another thing, dear reader of ours—we are a cold water man. Intemperance and Jacksonism go hand in hand—an unclear pair of lubberly giants, who rely upon each other for support.

But should they think it proper to make an experiment upon our good nature they may raise a spirit which not even the "Great Magician" himself can lay at his bidding. Let them begin the strife, and we stand ready to cast the scabbard of our war-knife in their faces—hoist the red flag and do battle for extermination.[7]

Whittier struck the same note when in 1831 he wrote Gideon Wells, an editor of the Hartford *Times*, after what he considered an attack upon his character as editor of the *New England Weekly Review:*

Sir, if you know anything against my character, a character dearer to me than life itself, in God's name publish it to the world, as becomes a man—but deal no longer in dark insinuations. I am a stranger here—with no wealth, save that of honorable reputation, for which I have struggled long and wearily; and believe me Sir, I will not tamely see the only abiding hope of my existence sported with by the wanton and malicious.

Wells replied that since he had never spoken of him disparagingly, he did not know what Whittier was talking about, and that, so far as he knew, nobody's character had been attacked, but he added, "you know me not, if you suppose I would in the least injure your reputation or tarnish your just fame—still less do you know me, if you suppose that threats could influence me." After which, both the turkey-cocks seem to have retreated from an altercation which had, after all, been much less dangerous and more civilized than many disputes between gentlemen were in those days.

One element of motivation which generally looms large with ambitious men seems to have been quite lacking in Whittier's case, and this is the desire for money. It never seemed to him that he had been reared in poverty. "We had no spare money," he says, "but with strict economy we lived comfortably and respectably." The circumstances look much like penury to us of another time, however. To support himself at the Academy he made slippers at twenty-five cents a pair, and he calculated his expenses so closely that he had just twenty-five cents left over at the end of the first term.[8] Five hundred dollars a year was about as much as he could expect from one of his anti-slavery editorships, and he did not always get that much. The first book from which he made any money was *Lays of My Home* (1843). "In regard to the matter of publication," he wrote Fields, "I know little or nothing about it. I shall leave it altogether to you, thinking that if the work meets with a ready sale, you will do me justice." In 1849 B. B. Mussey offered him five hundred dollars plus royalties on the first collected poems. But the watershed was not crossed until *Snow-Bound* came out in 1866, followed by *The Tent on the Beach* in 1867. From then on to the end of his life Whittier enjoyed what was for him great prosperity.

Think of bagging in this "tent" of ours an unsuspecting public at the rate of a thousand a day [so Whittier wrote Fields]! This will never do. The swindle is awful. Barnum is a saint to us. I am bowed with a sense of guilt, ashamed to look an honest man in the face. But Nemesis is on our track; somebody will puncture our "tent" yet, and it will collapse like a torn balloon. I know I shall have to catch it; my back tingles in anticipation. If a promise of never doing such a thing again would avail, I am more than ready to make it.

On January 11, 1890, the New York *Ledger* ran "The Captain's Well" with pictures by Howard Pyle and paid $1000 for it to a poet who had published most of his verses—including the great anti-slavery songs which had modified history—without any compensation whatever. When he died in 1892, he left $8500 in real estate and $125,229.39 of personalty.[9]

He seems to have been modest in his demands even after he had "arrived" financially, but he knew the value of money and did not pretend to despise it. As we shall see later in another connection, his publishers conducted their transactions with authors in a very irregular and informal way. On May 24, 1872, Whittier wrote James R. Osgood, "I have received nothing from any of my writings for nearly two years except the copyright on the new volume *Miriam*." And on June 10, again: "I am in need of money just now. Is there not something due me...?" And on November 8, 1873, when Osgood was apparently disturbed about Whittier's having given a piece to be published elsewhere, he declared:

> You have no idea what magnificent offers I have had from time to time and how peremptorily I have set them aside, to stand by my old publishers. As Jeanie Deans' Dumbiedikes would say even "siller" wouldn't "do it."

But he withdrew the piece from the other publisher, and at the same time told Osgood that he expected to be in Boston shortly, "and, as I am rather in need of funds just now, I hope you will be able to let me have an installment of what is due me, if you can do so without detriment."

It is the opinion of Mr. Roland H. Woodwell that Whittier's investments were made for him and that consequently he never really knew how much he had. This hypothesis would explain much. (In 1866 he speaks of "a little speculation" of $300 having given him $1200, a rate of increase which would surely have pleased even Hetty Green.) That Whittier continued to live as frugally after prosperity as before should surprise nobody. His tastes were simple and his wants few; he would not have known how to live otherwise. What may need explaining, however, is why he should have felt nearly as poor after *Snow-Bound* as he had felt before. In 1880 he sent Helen Colcord twenty dollars, wishing he could give more. "I have so much to do and so inadequate means to do it, that I cannot see how I can be of much service to thee." And in 1888 he was still talking about having "disposed of my limited means in a will." He had always been charitable, sharing with others even when he had nothing to share, and when he could not cover the need himself, he would canvass his friends.[10] He was on the alert, too, to help friends in other ways than with money; when the abolitionist Theodore Weld fell upon evil days, he tried to get him a Lowell lectureship.[11] The point is that when he was poor he made small donations, and when he became rich (for him), he still made small donations, though he did make many of them, and it should be remembered that donations of fifty or one hundred dollars went much farther in his time than they do now.

No doubt part of this was his inbred New England frugality. He did not lack human kindness, but nobody had ever spoiled him, and he could perceive no reason why he should spoil other people. Once a youngster appealed to him for funds for a college education. He sent five dollars, which was very likely more than the beggar deserved, and with it he sent some good advice: "But, as to education, use thy leisure in *educating thyself*. Read and study a little every day, and before thee art 20 years of age, thee will find that a school is not needed." He was still a poor man when he wrote this, but I wonder if he would have replied differently at a later date. Once, from a neighboring town, he received a request for $100. If it was not forthcoming, the writer said, he would blow his own brains out. Whittier did not believe the man had any brains to blow out, and he did not send the money. "I must confess, however, I looked rather anxiously at the newspapers for the next few days, but seeing no news of a suicide in the neighboring town, I was relieved." [12]

II

This consideration of Whittier's charities may perhaps afford a convenient point of transition from power to love, but here again we must be careful not to oversimplify. Of course he was moved by the inhuman aspects of slavery, but he did not oppose the "peculiar institution" primarily upon this ground. Opposition was a matter of principle to him, and of justice, going back ultimately to the basic religious conviction that every man was a child of God, that a human being was an end in himself and not a means toward an end, and that therefore it was unthinkable that man should hold property in man. There is little that is sentimental—or even highly emotional—in Whittier's attitude toward Negroes. I do not know whether he really "liked" them or not, or whether it ever occurred to him to put the question to himself. As a matter of fact, I do not believe that he thought very much about them as individuals, and he was quite right in regarding this as largely irrelevant to his attitude, for those who "like" Negroes (or any other minority group) are, in a sense, quite as condescending as those who "dislike" them. What all such persons have a right to ask is that they should be thought of as individual human beings, with the same rights and privileges (including the "right" to possess moral failings) that belong to other members of the race.[13] Whittier opposed every assumption of racial inferiority; he furiously attacked Carlyle's racism; and, pacifist though he was, he vindicated the record of "The Black Man in the Revolution and the War of 1812." But he had no sympathy whatever with miscegenation, or "amalgamation" as he calls it, and he points out quite justly that it was Southern planters, not Northern abolitionists, who were bringing this about. He has a very few references to Negroes which the twentieth century might consider disrespectful, though I am not sure that he meant them so.[14] But he certainly never excused a Negro for an offense which would have been condemned if perpetrated by a white man. When in 1831 a band of black men went through the streets of Hartford knocking down whites, he wrote Mrs. Tuthill: "Eight or ten were injured—and two it is feared will not recover. I hate these negroes, and would think favorably of John Randolph's proposition of shooting them without ceremony."

Unlike Garrison and Mrs. Chapman, he was never fanatical about abolition;[15] I think the one significant exception is the hysterical passage in the poem "To William Lloyd Garrison" where he almost urges martyrdom upon that leader:

Go on, the dagger's point may glare
  Amid thy pathway's gloom;
The fate which sternly threatens there
  Is glorious martydom!

His general tendency was to make fun of the abolitionists who regard themselves as martyrs; abolition, he thought, had done much more for him than he was ever able to do for abolition. In 1841 he wrote his cousin Moses Cartland that the anti-slavery cause "has been to me what the vision on the house-top of Cornelius was to Peter—it has destroyed all narrow sectarian prejudices, and made me willing to be a man among men." Hyatt H. Waggoner says finely: "If all the reformers of the age had had Whittier's humility and his faith and vision, Hawthorne might not have been moved to satirize reformism in *The Blithedale Romance* or James in *The Bostonians*."

Whittier always disclaimed any ill-will toward Southerners. "I was never an enemy to the South, or the holders of slaves. I inherited from my Quaker ancestors hatred of slavery, but not of slaveholders. To every call of suffering or distress in the South I have promptly responded to the extent of my ability." His best chances to prove this came after the war. Reasonable doubts may be entertained concerning the wisdom of his Reconstruction policies—which were, in general, Sumner's Reconstruction policies—but there was no malice in either man. When his poem about John Randolph came out, Judge Beverley Tucker's daughter wrote to him expressing her gratitude and surprise, and he replied:

> Permit me to express the hope that the time is close at hand when the different sections of our country shall do full justice to the great names and cherished memories and great traditions of each other; and when all old prejudices and feuds shall be lost in the common hope and mutual interest of a united people. . . . God knows that our people as a whole have no unkind feelings nor rankling resentments toward you: we love and honor all your illustrious names, we are proud of all you

are justly proud of, as a part of the priceless treasure of a common country.[16]

He would not write a poem for the fiftieth anniversary of the Anti-Slavery Society in 1883, because he did not wish to reopen old wounds, but he did write a letter in which he declared that

we are beginning to feel that we are one people, with no really clashing interests, and none more truly rejoice in the growing prosperity of the South than the old abolitionists, who hated slavery as a curse to the master as well as the slave.

And he added, generously:

If, in looking back, we feel that we sometimes erred through impatient zeal in our contest with a great wrong, we have the satisfaction of knowing that we were influenced by no merely selfish considerations. The low light of our setting sun shines over a free, united people, and our last prayer shall be for their peace, prosperity and happiness.[17]

Perhaps it was easy to say such things after the war, but Whittier had said something like them beforehand. When John Brown committed his mad act at Harpers Ferry, Emerson lost his head but Whittier did not.

It is time for all to pause and enquire with what feelings and motives they have acted in the great controversy between Freedom and Slavery. Who ever fans the flames on either side from mere selfishness and for party ends assumes a fearful responsibility.

He faced—and triumphantly passed—a more difficult test when Southern chivalry disappeared into Southern hoodlumism with Preston Brooks's attack upon Sumner in the Senate Chamber in 1856, and Whittier told the citizens of Amesbury:

It is worse than folly to talk of fighting slavery, when we have not yet agreed to vote against it. Our business is with poll boxes, not cartridge boxes; with ballots, not bullets. The path of duty is plain: God's providence calls us to walk in it.

The whole history of the anti-slavery battle could be written from the point of view of Whittier's observance of and participation in it.[18] At the beginning it was necessary to repudiate the

Colonization Society, which was supported by pro-slavery Southerners (because they wished to get free Negroes out of the country), by conservative business men, and sometimes, no doubt, by romantic Northerners as a kind of sop to their conscience, giving them an excuse to believe that they were somehow freeing themselves from the guilt of supporting slavery. By 1839 Whittier feared that the anti-slavery movement was moribund and sighed for "a new baptism of the old anti-slavery feeling—for the self-forgetfulness of our early consecration!" By 1842 he thought the cause had been renewed "not so much by anything which we abolitionists do—as by the inevitable current of events, which in the Providence of God, seems setting with constantly augmenting strength toward the South, and its doomed 'peculiar institution.'" In 1845 he was greatly heartened by Sumner's great anti-war, anti-slavery oration on "The True Grandeur of Nations." By 1849 it was as difficult to find a pro-slavery man in the North as it had been to find an abolitionist in 1833, but Whittier could hardly suppose that "this marvellous conversion is altogether genuine and heartfelt." In 1851 he congratulated Sumner "not so much on thy election, as upon the proof which it affords of the turning of the tide—the recoil of the popular feeling—the near and certain doom of the wicked Slave Law." He was displeased by the Compromise of 1850 and even more by the Kansas-Nebraska Act, four years later, which reopened a subject that was supposed to have been "settled," and which convinced him that the time was now ripe for the organization of a new political party which should take a firm and meaningful stand on slavery.

Whittier was not quite accurate when, in 1854, he sent a correspondent a list of his books "as near as I can now recollect," saying, "My attention has been devoted more to political reforms than to literature." Actually, it was only from 1833 to 1843 that he was "a whole-souled and single-minded abolitionist"; from 1843 on he was rather "a moderate reformer with literature again his greatest natural interest and the object of the major part of his devotion." [19] One might say that he consecrated literature to abolition (but the consecration was never complete); another way of putting it would be to say that he found in abolition fresh subject matter for literature. His approach to the problem was very different from Garrison's. Garrison, an ethical absolutist, opposed political action, under the Constitution, as a means of abolishing slavery, because in his view the fact that the Constitution recognized slavery made it "an agreement with death and a covenant with hell." Until slavery should "cease to pollute our soil," "REPEAL OF THE UNION between the North and the South" became the paramount duty of all who were not God's enemies. Garrison was prepared to tolerate "no union with slaveholders" in any area of activity. Theoretically he was a pacifist, but as the anti-slavery struggle intensified he became more and more militant. In 1843 he declared that "peace or war is *a secondary consideration*," and that "slavery must be conquered, 'peaceably if we can, forcibly if we must.'" When John Brown was hanged he told an audience in Tremont Temple that he could not but "wish success to all slave insurrections," on the curious ground that this was "one way to get up to the sublime principle of non-resistance; and... God's method of dealing retribution upon the head of the tyrant," which is much like the reasoning of a well-known American clergyman who, some years ago, advocated universal military training as a step toward disarmament because you cannot disarm until after you have armed, or of those madmen who have appeared from time to time during the history of the Christian Church, devoting themselves diligently to every kind of vice and crime, in order that where sin has abounded, grace may much more abound.

Yet it cannot be said that Whittier never flirted with the vampire named "Disunion." In *Justice and Expediency* he argued rightly that the danger to the Union came not from the abolitionists but from an aggressive slave power. In 1842 he cried, "*Disunion* before Texas!" By the fall of 1845 he was convinced that Texas could not be kept out of the Union, whereupon he bent all his efforts to prevent her coming in as a slave state, and when this too failed, he was, like all anti-slavery people, bitterly disappointed. What he really believed on the subject was well stated in a letter to Emerson, September 20, 1845:

> Some of my non-resistant friends say, "*Dissolve the Union.*" I am, for one, no blind worshipper of the Union. As an abolitionist, I am shut out from its benefits.[20] I prize liberty far above it. But I see nothing to be gained by an effort—necessarily limited, sectional and futile—to dissolve it. The moral and political power requisite for doing it could far more easily abolish every vestige of slavery.

Whittier, then, was not a disunionist, but clear down to Fort Sumter he often gives the impression that it would not be impossible for him to accept disunion. In 1836 he declared that he would obey no censorship law; in 1850 he wrote of the Fugitive Slave Law: "So far as that law is concerned, I am a nullifier." When Kossuth was in this country, Whittier urged Sumner to alert him to the danger of allowing himself to be used by the "Union Savers," which, being interpreted, meant those who were willing to compromise with slavery. "Naturally he [Kossuth] would deprecate a dissolution of the Union—but he ought to understand that it is not in the slightest jeopardy." About that, as the event proved, Whittier could hardly have been more wrong, though he was quite right in his attempt to discourage the possible giving of advice on a domestic issue by a visiting foreigner. But a score of utterances, in prose and in verse, show where he himself placed the emphasis: "At all events, with the Constitution, or without the Constitution, *Slavery must die*." Though he would not actually advocate disunion, he could be pretty scornful of those who seemed unduly alarmed by it.[21] "If I had any love for the Union remaining," he wrote when the fugitive Anthony Burns was captured in Boston and returned to slavery, "the events of the last few weeks have 'crushed it out.'" In 1856, in "The Panorama," he spoke scornfully of those

> who, with instinctive dread,
> Whenever Freedom lifts her drooping head,
> Make prophet-tripods of their office-stools,
> And scare the nurseries and the village schools
> With dire presage of ruin grim and great,
> A broken Union and a foundered State!

As late as November 21, 1860, he declared:

> With slavery in the States we have no right to interfere, and no desire to do so beyond the mild persuasion of the successful example of Freedom; but outside of State sovereignty, Slavery has no more legal right or constitutional guaranty than Polygamy out of Utah. Its home is only in the States; everywhere else it is an outlaw.

But at the same time he regarded

> the menace of disunion from the South as more likely to prove mischievous than really dangerous. It may do injury to the industrial and financial interests of the country, but the evil will work its own cure. Business men at the South will not long indulge in the childish folly of setting fire to the clothes on their backs, in the expectation that their neighbors' fingers will be scorched in putting it out.

Clear to the end he was willing to do anything except compromise principle to avoid either war or disunion, but he felt that "we must not be forced into a crime against humanity by threats of disunion, nor dishonor ourselves and sin against God by concessions of principle today, which will only invite new demands, backed by the same old threat tomorrow." If the slave states could live without the free, then "the free States can not only live but prosper without them; and it is neither expedient to buy them back by unmanly concessions nor to fight them back." And at the end of March he found himself writing, "The current of events seems to me to be setting toward the separation of the free and slave states. . . . Better this than the sin and dishonor of bowing yet lower to the evil spirit of slavery."

Albert Mordell and others have scolded Whittier for what they consider his turning away from reform activities after the Civil War. At times his own words during later years seemed to furnish a foundation for such charges. In 1868 he wrote Mrs. Howard that he was "not willing now to connect myself with *any* organization" and that with slavery gone, he felt himself "released from *all* societies, save the one I was born in." Ten years later he was telling Gail Hamilton:

For myself I do not feel called upon to enter into these present contests. The game seems to me hardly worth the candle. The issues seem small and poor. I suppose I am getting old, and am disposed to ask for peace in my day. I have had enough of fighting in the old days.

And to Elizabeth Stuart Phelps, who, like himself, had the reformer's zeal coupled with a sensitiveness of temperament that made public agitation much more difficult than it is for more coarse-grained people, he wrote:

I quite sympathize with what thee say of the "causes." Against my natural inclinations I have been fighting for them half my life. . . . I have suffered dreadfully from coarseness, self-seeking vanity, and asinine stupidity among associates, as well as the coldness, open hostility and worst the ridicule of the outside world.

Nevertheless, it is a great mistake to suppose either that Negro emancipation was the only "cause" in which Whittier was enlisted or that he was ever so foolish as to suppose that once the Emancipation Proclamation had been signed, the Negro problem was solved for good and all. The year before he died he wrote John Murray Forbes:

I am thankful that we have outlived chattel slavery, but the rights of the colored citizens are denied, and the entire vote of New England in Congress is neutralized by that of thirty or forty Southern suppressors of the colored vote. Will the time ever come when the Sermon on the Mount and the Declaration of Independence will practically influence our boasted civilization and Christianity? [22]

He was vitally concerned for the welfare of Negroes and of all human beings as long as he lived, and the causes he supported were many. In 1872 he wrote that "no consideration of private interest, nor my natural love of peace and retirement and the good will of others, have kept me silent when a word could fitly be spoken for human rights," and this was no idle boast.

About the only time he failed to speak out was when William Dean Howells asked him to plead for the Chicago anarchists who were facing execution after the so-called "Haymarket Riot" of

1886. Whittier missed his opportunity here and refused, as all the other American writers did also, leaving Howells standing alone, and all the more honor to him. But I think we should be able to understand why Whittier refused. The condemned men were not rioters, but they had incited riot. They were not murderers, but the whole trend of their thinking and agitating had moved in the direction of justifying killing in the name of social justice. Whittier simply could not bring himself to take his place beside those whose whole way of thought and life was so antithetical to his own. Howells had no more sympathy with violence than he had, but because he was younger, he understood the industrial age better, and he was more cosmopolitan; consequently he cut through irrelevant considerations to the basic issue, which was that men were being destroyed not for their deeds but for their opinions. Whether they were right or wrong, good or bad, was not important. If that could happen to one man, then no man was safe.

That Whittier would champion woman suffrage and freedom of speech and press, oppose capital punishment, and take a sympathetic interest in liberal movements abroad might almost have been taken for granted, his background and basic convictions being what they were. He knew the danger of a venal press, but he wished to guard against its abuses "not by direct proscription, not by fettering the press, the mouth-piece of Liberty and Equal rights, but by a just discrimination in the all-important disposal of their patronage" on the part of "the truly virtuous portion of the community." Evidently the only time he was even tempted to renege on this issue was in 1867 when the newspapers reported him engaged to be married!

Complete equality of the sexes has always prevailed in the Society of Friends, and Whittier supported women's rights as a simple demand of justice—"I have seen no good reason why mothers, wives, and daughters should not have the same right of person, property, and citizenship which fathers, husbands, and brothers have"—though he annoyed some suffragettes and suffragists by opposing Garrison when he complicated the slavery issue by advocating Negro emancipation and woman suffrage simultaneously. But here again he was realistic enough to warn those who looked to woman suffrage as a cure-all for political corruption and other social ills that they would certainly be disappointed, as they have been abundantly since his time.

Whittier was working for the abolition of capital punishment in Massachusetts as early as the thirties, and if he was less optimistic about Negro emancipation than he might have been, he was much more optimistic about capital punishment than the event was to justify, for in 1843 he expected to see "the overthrow of the Gallows in this State at the next session of the Legislature." He was always infuriated when clergymen defended what seemed to him social iniquities, and he wrote two poems inspired by such defenses of capital punishment—"The Gallows" and "The Human Sacrifice." "The Human Sacrifice" testifies not only to Whittier's humanity but also to his imagination, for he shows that the "murderer" is also a human being, cherishing happy memories of his earlier normal life and enjoying contacts with others. In "The Gallows" the poet thanks God

> that I have lived to see the time
> When the great truth begins at last to find
> An utterance from the deep heart of mankind,
> Earnest and clear, that all Revenge is Crime,
> That man is holier than a creed....

but does not, I think, really face any of the fundamental issues involved in the debate over capital punishment.[23]

In the year of Revolution, 1848, Whittier wrote Sumner: "What glorious changes in the Old World! I feel almost like going to France myself, and would if I could do anything more than gratify my feelings by so doing." From him who never went abroad for any other purpose, such a statement, even considered as rhetoric, serves as a reasonable yardstick to measure enthusiasm. He kept his eye on Italy, Poland, Hungary, and other countries also. Sometimes his enthusiasm for freedom tempted him to compromise his peace principles, but he reserved his special admiration for those like Daniel O'Connell in Ireland and the Emperor Dom Pedro in Brazil, who achieved reform by peaceful means. If he was unfair to any nation, it was England, partly because, like so many Americans in his time, he had not yet quite recovered from Revolutionary War patriotism, and partly because of his sympathy for the Irish. "There is a taint of blood in the landed estates of Ireland," he says. "Founded in robbery and violence, they have been held in succession by reckless, extravagant, absentee landlords."

Toward Indians, Whittier took up a more advanced position in life than his references to them in his published works (except *Margaret Smith's Journal*) might suggest. He criticized Cooper for his "stock" Indians, but in his early poems he himself did not do nearly as well as Cooper. Consider, in "Pentucket":

> No,–through the trees fierce eyeballs glowed,
> Dark human forms in moonshine showed,
> Wild from their native wilderness,
> With painted limbs and battle-dress!

And

> Then rang the rifle-shot, and then
> The shrill death-screams of stricken men,–
> Sank the red axe in woman's brain,
> And childhood's cry arose in vain.

In "The Bridal of Pennacook,"

> The Indian's heart is hard and cold,
>   It closes darkly o'er its care,
> And formed in Nature's sternest mould,
>   Is slow to feel, but strong to bear.

In the prose sketch "The Midnight Attack" (*Legends of New England*), the Indians are fiends, and no sympathy is wasted on them when the rangers wreak dire vengeance. The last sentence is pure penny dreadful: "The red men had gone to their last audit before the Great Spirit; and no sound was heard among them, save the gurgling of the hot blood from their lifeless bosoms." Nor could there be a more striking contrast than that between

Whittier's comparatively sympathetic recital of the history of the brutal colonial Indian-killer, Hannah Duston, whom Cotton Mather had glorified, and Hawthorne's bitter account of her in *Grandfather's Chair*. There are other poems, however, like "Funeral Tree of the Sokokis," in which the Indian is treated more sympathetically, and Whittier does not fail to tell us, as Conrad Richter has since told us more elaborately, that white children stolen by the Indians sometimes afterwards preferred staying with them to returning home.[24]

But *Margaret Smith's Journal* is the work which really reflects Whittier's own intelligent and humane attitude toward the Indian, and Cecil B. Williams has shown that Whittier was here entering a conscious protest not only against the colonial attitude toward the Indian but also against those historians in his own time who had defended it.

> Whittier's stress . . . on the innate goodness of the Indian, refutes Mather's portrayal of him as a child of the devil, seduced into America by the Father of Evil to keep him away from Christianity, as a *tawny pagan*, a *bloody savage*, an *infidel*, a *barbarian*, and a *rabid wolf*, employing his powwaws or sorcerers, to invoke the assistance of the devils against the settlement of the English as the Canaanites had opposed the Children of Israel.

The evidence to support Williams is abundant. Margaret feels only compassion toward the squaw nursing her baby: "I forgot everything save that she was a woman and a mother, and I felt my heart greatly drawn towards her." Again she says:

> These poor heathen people seem not so exceeding bad as they have been reported; they be like unto ourselves, only lacking our knowledge and opportunities, which, indeed, are not our own to boast of, but gifts of God, calling for humble thankfulness, and daily prayer and watchfulness, that they be rightly improved.

The sick soldier, Elnathan Stone, attacks the problem more directly:

> He had much pity for the poor savages even, though he had suffered sorely at their hands; for he did believe that they had been often ill-

used and cheated; and otherwise provoked to take up arms against us. ... Even the Indian fighters, I found, had sorrows of their own, and grievous wrongs to avenge; and I do believe, if we had from the first treated them as poor blinded brethren, and striven as hard to give them light and knowledge, as we have to cheat them in trade, and get away their lands, we should have escaped many bloody wars, and won many precious souls to Christ.

In "The Indian Question," which was published in the *Essex Gazette* the very week after "The Midnight Attack," Whittier pleads for fair play to the Indian not only on humanitarian grounds, but because, through treaty obligations, the honor of the nation is at stake. On the basis of the progress the Cherokees have already made, he argues that there can be no question of the Indian's capacity to assimilate civilization. This article was followed by another, on "Indian Relics," in which he urges that "the few vestiges which remain in our vicinity of the existence of the once formidable tribes of the Red men, should be considered as relics of more importance, than all the sanctified and consecrated ones of the Romish priesthood." Though this is one of Whittier's most disrespectful references to the Roman Catholic Church, it should still be noted that he was a pioneer in recognizing the importance of preserving Indian lore and artifacts. As we have seen elsewhere, President Jackson's Indian policy was an important element in Whittier's dislike of him. In 1830 he was incensed by the ousting of Indians from Georgia, and when the Seminole War was allowed to languish, he made even this a reproach to a President whom he had never considered good for anything but Indian-fighting and who had now shown that he was not even good for that.

Whether the President and Cabinet are conscience smitten at the abominable injustice of their proceedings, in driving these people from the homes of their fathers: and that too in direct violation of the solemn treaties—or whether they are too much taken up with their operations as *financiers* and *land speculators* to attend to the less agreeable details of an Indian war, we are left to conjecture. We doubt however whether remorse of conscience has much to do in the case, but rather suspect that a protracted war is found to be useful as a measure of finance, to drain the treasury, and prevent the operation of the bill for dividing the surplus revenue among the States.[25]

Whittier achieved a considered statement of his attitude toward the Indian and of his faith in the Indian's capacity for progress in his introduction to Stanley Pumphrey's *Indian Civilization* (1877).[26] By 1883, however, his only hope was in education and assimilation, for he perceived that with the frontier steadily moving westward, the hope of guaranteeing reservations became impossible, treaties or no treaties. "Outbreaks of Indian ferocity and revenge incited by wrong and robbery on the part of the whites will increasingly be made the pretext of indiscriminate massacres. The entire question will soon resolve itself into the single alternative of education and civilization or extermination." This was not the way it ought to be, but this was how it would be, and he had never been in the habit of crying for the moon. At the end of his life, he was even beginning to believe that the army might help to solve the Indian problem.

I have great confidence in Gen. Miles [he wrote Mrs. Fields], who is as humane as he is brave.... I am not sure that it would not be better for the Indians, also safer for the white settlers of Dakota and Nebraska, if the care and protection of the Indians could be transferred to the War Department. Our U. S. Army officers are not speculators, and would not cheat the Indian in the distribution of the Government.

Finally, it should be understood that Whittier was never so devoted to the rights of Negroes and Indians—or Europeans—that he forgot that white Americans have rights too. More than any other leading nineteenth-century American poet, he saw himself as one with those who toil. "The person who addresses you has been ranked among your numbers," he wrote in his early papers addressed "To the Young Mechanics of New England." "Called to another sphere of action, he retains a sincere regard for the welfare of his former associates, those companions of his early years whom he is proud to recognize as his friends." In *The American Manufacturer* in 1829 he saw workingmen as "trodden down and oppressed—a mark for the scorn and ridicule of the purse-proud and arrogant." In the *Essex Gazette* in 1836 he defended labor's right to collective bargaining, which was then a very live issue because Judge Edwards in New York had recently convicted certain journeymen tailors of conspiracy because they had attempted, in a small way, to establish it. During this same period, Whittier was also sympathetic toward the Working Man's Party: "It is a proud thing to see the people rising in their moral strength and proclaiming to the world that their rights as American citizens must be respected."

In his "Songs of Labor" Whittier celebrated the glory of toil and the rights of toilers before Whitman. Mordell thinks that "the husking poem, with its corn song, is the best of the group," but it seems to me that "The Shoemakers" is by far the most imaginative and the one best calculated to increase the worker's self-respect and give him a vision of his own importance and dignity.

For you, along the Spanish main
  A hundred keels are ploughing;
For you, the Indian on the plain
  His lasso-coil is throwing;
For you, deep glens with hemlock dark
  The woodman's fire is lighting;
For you, upon the oak's gray bark,
  The woodman's axe is smiting.

All this and more must be done to provide the shoemaker with materials to do his work. Through labor fact overtakes fancy.

The red brick to the mason's hand,
  The brown earth to the tiller's,
The shoe in yours shall wealth command
  Like fairy Cinderella's!

In his essay on "Mechanical Genius" Whittier wrote prose about the achievements of the worker that was almost as lyrical as his verse:

> He has built up our proud cities and pointed their spires to Heaven. He has unsealed the caverns of the earth and exposed their hidden records to the light of day. He has gone down to the sunless foundations of the sea—far down among the skeleton mariners—over whose bones the surges of a century have thundered and lifted their buried treasure to the eye of man. He has launched the proud ark of commerce upon the great deep and linked in one vast chain of intercourse the whole family of man. He has made our inland seas and our mighty rivers alive with wealth and enterprise—alive with barks that move onward without the aid of tide or breeze or oar—and he has called into practical utility the rights and privileges granted and secured by the eternal governor of all. Like the tenant of the fabled chapel of Loretto, he has traversed the illimitable air, and more powerful than Prometheus, he has called down the light without its thunder. All this has mechanical genius accomplished and a mighty, a boundless field is yet open for its further exertion.

Whittier is often thought of as having viewed the rights of man against a pre-industrial background, but such a passage as I have just quoted shows that he was not insensitive to the achievements of technology. Indeed he had less difficulty with industrialism than with mercantilism. He wondered why young men would "thrust themselves into every dark alley of the city, and shut out the blessed light of Heaven" when they could live under so much more attractive conditions as mechanics, and Bliss Perry is not the only one who has been impressed by his hostility to bankers and other mercantile leaders in such poems as "Stanzas for the Times," "The Pine Tree," and "Moloch in State Street":

> Tell us not of banks and traffics, cease your paltry pedler cries;
> Shall the good State sink her honor that your gambling stocks may rise?

And

> "Perish banks and perish traffic, spin your cotton's latest pound,
> But in Heaven's name keep your honor, keep the heart o' the Bay State sound!"

In *The Stranger in Lowell*, which dates from 1845, he is even a bit too enthusiastic over the happy lot of "The Factory Girls":

> Acres of girlhood—beauty reckoned by the square rod, or miles by long measure! The young, the graceful, the gay—flowers gathered from a thousand hillsides and green valleys of New England; fair, unveiled Nuns of Industry; Sisters of Thrift; and are ye not also Sisters of Charity, dispensing comfort and hope and happiness around many a hearth-stone of your native hills, making sad faces cheerful, and hallowing age and poverty with the sunshine of your youth and love!

He glories in the lesson taught that "from henceforth . . . woman may 'labor with her hands,' and lose nothing of the charm and glory of womanhood by so doing. . . ." "They demonstrate the economy of free and paid labor."

Yet Whittier did not really believe in the possibility of achieving Utopia by industrial means. He even resembles Thoreau when he writes that "labor, graduated to man's simple wants, necessities, and unperverted tastes, is doubtless well; but all beyond this is weariness to flesh and spirit." Nor does he overlook "the trials and disadvantages" of the position occupied by the factory girls themselves. "There have been a good many foolish essays written upon the beauty and dignity of labor, by those who have never known what it really is to earn one's livelihood by the sweat of the brow," but he dismisses this as sentimentalism. "Let such be silent."

Economic conditions are so different now from what they were in Whittier's time that it is easy to be unfair to him in discussing his stand on economic issues. He disliked strikes, which he rightly regarded as a form of industrial warfare. He would have been no happier under a tyranny of labor than he was under a tyranny of capital, for he believed, in this area of disagreement and conflicting interest as in all others, that

> Solution is there none
> Save in the Golden Rule of Christ alone.[27]

In *The Stranger in Lowell* he gives the impression that he regards the achievement of a ten-hour day in the mills as desirable but impracticable, yet he supported the Amesbury-Salisbury strike of 1852, which had the ten-hour day as one of its objectives. He is accused of having encourged young men to develop an Horatio Alger outlook, and so, in a measure, he did, but what his critics overlook is that the Alger point of view had considerable validity in his time (it retains a much more limited validity today); if this had not been so, it could never have taken the hold it did over the American imagination. He has also been blamed for declaring that intemperance, idleness, and failure to save money when wages were good, were contributing causes of poverty. But, as a matter of fact, they are, and he never pretended that they were the sole causes. One of the points at issue in the Amesbury-Salisbury strike was what we would now call the "coffee-break." Mr. Woodwell has pointed out that in those days it was actually a "beer-break," and Whittier was perfectly aware of this, but he also knew that his disapproval of beer-drinking in no sense invalidated the worker's right to a break, and that what he did with it was his business.

It might go without saying that Whittier would have had no sympathy with Communism. He feared the influence upon the American labor movement of such reformers as Fanny Wright and Robert Dale Owen, whose "unhallowed principles" repelled him. But he was equally sensitive to the danger emanating from what we now call "the radical right":

> They profess to fear the multitude—they see in every movement of masses, the germ of revolution. Every demand of the people for equal laws is agrarianism, jacobinism, insubordination and radicalism. If the people talk of the *rights of man*, they begin at once to tremble for the *rights of property*. They dislike the doctrines of the Declaration of Independence. They hold them indeed to be a "mere rhetorical flourish"—utopian and visionary—but very mischievous nevertheless, in making the "lower classes" forget their "proper place in society." What, all men equal! The shirtless hod-carrier, swallowing his whiskey, equal to the "gentleman of property and standing" discussing his claret and champagne! Nonsense!—a lie of Tom Jefferson's—that's all.

These are the people who have established the unjust militia system which requires the farmer and the mechanic to stop work periodically and "march through mud and tempest, with musket and knapsack" to defend the property of the wealthy. But actually these people welcome the riots they profess to fear.

THEY EXPECT, THROUGH THEIR MEANS, TO INTRODUCE AN ARISTOCRATIC GOVERNMENT IN THE PLACE OF A DEMOCRATIC ONE. When the riots and excesses they are now stimulating shall have become universal, and law and order shall exist only at the pleasure of a Lynch committee, or a mob—they will begin to talk of the necessity of a radical change in our Government. We must have a STRONG Government—an aristocracy to hold in check the "lower classes"—a standing army to awe them into obedience. They will point to the very tools which they now smile on and encourage, as men unworthy of the rights of suffrage, and citizenship—and to the very mobs which they now connive at and sanction, as evidence that there is a vital defect—a remediless weakness, in a democratic form of government.

In 1848 Whittier assailed the *Friends' Review* itself for branding the new French revolutionaries dangerous radicals.

They are not Agrarians or levellers, in the obnoxious sense of the term. If we understand them, they would level upwards, and remove the inequalities of the social condition by elevating the depressed and trodden-down classes by a more equal distribution of the rewards of honest labor; by making the interest of the capital and labor, of skill and muscular energy, identical; by bringing about a state of things in which the doing unto others as we would they should do to us, shall be the uniform law of the social system. Their object is certainly good and praiseworthy. Whether it can be attained, or, if so, whether the Communists have discovered the way to its accomplishment, are questions which time has yet to solve.

He did not deny that he had "reason to fear that many of the men upon whom the responsibility of the French Government rests have never passed through the deep spiritual baptism" which is the best preparation for such work, but he could still recognize in "their aims and purposes the influence of the Divine Spirit which, in all ages, has prompted and promoted the reformation of abuse in human society, and which will continue to turn and overturn until the Right is everywhere established, and the will of God is done on earth as in Heaven." [28]

III

After the war Whittier's interest in politics was much less keen than it had been; in 1881 he even told Paul Hamilton Hayne that life was now too short to read political books. He admired Garfield, and in 1882, when Senator Hoar seemed to be in danger, he went to bat for him. In a letter to James Russell Lowell, July 11, 1883, he threw out the idea of putting him up for governor if he would come home from his ambassadorship in England and run against Ben Butler, and in the fall of that same year, he addressed a letter to the colored readers of the Boston *Journal*, appealing to them "as an old abolitionist" not to permit Butler to mislead them. But the last real flare of passionate political activity—and the last striking expression of Whittier's administrative skill—came after the Massachusetts legislature of 1872 had stupidly voted to censure Sumner for the move he had made toward reconciliation between North and South by proposing that the colors of the national regiments should not carry the names of the Civil War battles in which they had been engaged. Whittier immediately set to work to get the vote expunged and succeeded just in time. Few letters can ever have given him more satisfaction than the one he sent to Sumner a month before the Senator's death: "The folly of the extra session of 1872 is wiped out thoroughly. I am especially pleased, as, like Senator Benton, on a former occasion, 'solitary and alone I set the ball in motion.'"

On the other hand, Whittier was, after the war, one thing he had never been before—a strong "party" man. Many years earlier he had written, "I never supposed that I should belong to a successful party." Now that he did, he proposed to stay there and to keep the party successful too. Before the war he had fixed it firmly in his mind that the Democratic Party was identified with treason and slavery, and even under changed conditions, he was never really able to alter this conviction. The most he would do was to refrain from voting for a Republican candidate he considered unworthy. To go beyond that, by casting his vote for the

Democratic opponent, would be "going over to the enemy." In 1872 he thought it folly for Grant to run again or for Greeley to run against him, but he would not follow even Sumner in bolting the ticket, though he defended Sumner's right to do so, and feared lest his own Republican vote should be taken as an endorsement of Republican corruption. Though he admired Tilden, he supported Hayes against him. Nor would he go Mugwump with George William Curtis and others, supporting Cleveland against Blaine. "I feel that I am now too old to change my party affiliations or to enter into any political complications" was what he told Curtis, but his real feelings about the two parties are shown in a letter he wrote G. W. Cate of Amesbury on May 7, 1880:

> I have no words of personal disparagement for the democratic nominee, and I do full justice to the sincerity and patriotism of many of his supporters, but, as a rule, the party remains as it was at the close of the war. The time has not come when it will be safe to entrust the financial interest of the country, and the welfare of the emancipated class, to a party whose President can only be elected by compromises with the greenback heresy, and the virtual suppression by fraud and violence of the vote of the colored citizens of the Southern States.[29]

Whittier's attitude toward fame also changed notably during later years. He outlived neglect. He outlived the objurgations that had been heaped upon him as an abolitionist. During his last years, his admirers almost canonized him. But if neglect had not maddened him, hysterical praise embarrassed him—the more so because he feared his life had not squared with his writings. The biographer Lytton Strachey once wittily remarked that it was almost as difficult to write a good life as to live one. Whittier could have found small comfort in such a reflection; if, as a poet, he might have understood Walter de la Mare's view that "a poem is a deed," as a devout man, he would have been shocked by the proverb which affirms that "it is a kind of good deed to say well." Sometimes he was willing to give himself the credit for good intentions, but sometimes he would not even do that.

Who, looking backward from his manhood's prime,
Sees not the spectre of his misspent time?
And, through the shade
Of funeral cypress planted thick behind,
Hears no reproachful whisper on the wind
From his loved dead?

Who bears no trace of passion's evil force?
Who shuns thy sting, O terrible Remorse?
Who does not cast
On the thronged pages of his memory's book,
At times, a sad and half-reluctant look,
Regardful of the past? [30]

Finishing his account of John Woolman's life, to be published as an introduction to his journal, Whittier felt rebuked by the "moral and spiritual symmetry" of his subject. "I would like to be a good *man*," he wrote the most fulsome of his admirers, Gail Hamilton, in 1865—"I sometimes try hard to be—but I am not. Why should thee ridicule my poor attempts at goodness, and offer mock congratulations on my success, when I sit in the dust and ashes of failure?" And when the Scottish novelist S. R. Crockett wrote him reverentially as a young man, Whittier replied simply, "I do not wish the place of teacher or leader. I have written the word which seemed right for me to utter." And he even added, "Perhaps I may have expressed myself too strongly at times." [31]

Some writers would explain the contrast between the early utterances and the late on the assumption that Whittier experienced a great change sometime in his mid-twenties, after which he put aside all thought of self and devoted himself to the service of God and His children. It may be so. I certainly would not wish to deny that Whittier grew in grace as he grew older. But it would be folly to overlook the fact that his situation had changed also. It is one thing to long for success when you are the only person in the world who really believes in your as yet undemonstrated capacities, and it is quite another to insist gently upon your unworthiness when all men speak well of you. Whittier was not an egotist—or at least he was not more an egotist than other men—but even as a poet he displayed a marked interest in autobiographical subjects (and, consequently, a marked interest in himself); the contrast between him and the almost severely impersonal Longfellow is nowhere more marked than at this point.

But he was like Longfellow in his discovery that fame cannot be had without paying a high price for it. On his eightieth birthday he had between 500 and 600 callers and 2000 letters. On his last birthday, in 1891, "the whole world came," though nobody had been invited, a steady stream from nine in the morning until dark. "I saw as few of them as I could, and laid down half the day, but I was dreadfully tired." But the birthdays did not cause the unceasing flow of letters or callers either; they only accelerated both. "My letters average twenty-five and thirty a day, and when I'm sick they accumulate; and then, when I get well, I make myself sick again trying to catch up with my answers to them." On June 6, 1874 he had 100 unanswered letters staring him in the face. Coming back from three weeks in Boston early in 1882, he found 200 letters waiting for him.

Most of his correspondents wanted autographs, but sometimes they wanted him to copy poems too, and one man angrily returned the autograph Whittier had sent because the poem he had requested had not come with it. In 1882 Whittier testily wrote one autograph seeker that Longfellow had been "driven to death" by such demands. But his admirers wrote on other subjects also; at least one man wanted matrimonial advice, to which Whittier replied that he could not give it without knowing the parties and that, in any case, matrimonial advice from an old bachelor could not be worth anything. Every time his name appeared in print it stimulated a fresh flow; in 1890 he begged S. T. Pickard not to print any more items about him in the Portland *Transcript*. One newspaper man asked a friend after him and was told that he must be pretty well since he had been seen in "Mrs. Cartland's garden," whereupon it was reported in the press that Whittier had visited "Cartland's Garden"! [32]

IV

But love is not good-will toward humanity alone; love also means women. The traditional schoolboy composition summed it up: "John Greenleaf Whittier was a Quaker. He was born in Haverhill. He never married—he hated slavery." Since it is as certain as anything of the kind can ever be that Whittier never experienced sexual intercourse, it might seem that in his case this aspect of life might well be passed over. But Mordell and others have now made so much of it that this is no longer possible.

To begin with, it is clear that Whittier liked women and was liked by them. His relationships with his mother and sister were very close; when Elizabeth died he felt as though the whole motive power of his life had been lost. He always wondered why women should trouble themselves about the "*name* of authority" in the household when everybody knew that they were in secure possession of the actuality. His mother was a strong woman, perhaps a dominating one, and his feeling that he could not bring a non-Quaker girl home to her may well have put a brake upon some of his attachments. Miss Sparhawk says that even after both mother and sister were dead, Whittier's

> first act on coming home from an absence was to go into the room in which hung the portraits of these two, and to stand before them, not only as if greeting them on his home coming, but as if also receiving their welcome to a house in which to him their presence always lingered and made it home as was no other place on earth.[33]

Of course many of his relations with women were quite free of sexual attraction in the narrower sense of the term. Women encouraged and guided him when he was young, and he encouraged and advised younger women when he was older.[34] But even very sensible females sometimes behaved as if they were not quite sensible with him, as when Mrs. Alexander asked him for a lock of his hair, which he sent, though warning her that the responsibility for such folly was hers and not his. When he was sick, even Sarah Orne Jewett wished she could come and nurse him.

Perhaps it is Nora Perry who best puts the appeal he had for women into words when she writes:

I remember years ago from the first, I had the most perfect feeling of ease and confidence with you—a feeling that I could say anything to you, and you would never, that you couldn't misunderstand. As the years have gone on, this feeling has been the same under all conditions.

Whittier's early letters contain references to many girls. When he is away from home he inquires after them and sends greetings to them. There can be no need to catalogue them here.[35] What *type* of girl he liked best is clear however:

A beautiful and happy girl,
  With step as light as summer air,
Eyes glad with smiles, and brow of pearl,
Shadowed by many a careless curl
  Of unconfined and flowing hair;
A seeming child in everything,
  Save thoughtful brow and ripening charms,
As Nature wears the smile of Spring
  When sinking into Summer's arms.[36]

It helped, too, if the hair was brown.

There are a good many pretty girls at the Athenaeum [so Whittier wrote Edwin Harriman from Boston, May 18, 1829]—and I like to sit there, and remark upon the different figures that go floating by me, like aerial creatures just stooping down to our dull earth, to take a view of the beautiful creations of the painter's genius. I love to watch their airy motions—and catch the dark brilliancy of their fine eyes, and observe the delicate blush stealing over their cheeks—but trust me my heart is untouched—cold and motionless as a Jutland lake lighted up by the moonshine. I know that they are beautiful—very, but they are nothing to me. I turn from one fair face to another, until my memory is altogether vague and indefinite—I know very well that I have nothing to do with them and, at all events, they will not be likely to have anything to do with me. There you have the history of my transgressions, if such it is, to look upon the fairest and most delicate works of God—I always did love a pretty girl—Heaven grant there is no harm in it. The worst of it is if I ever get married I must marry a Quakeress with her bonnet like a flour dipper and face as long as a tobacco yawl.

The first woman who rates specific mention is Mary Emerson Smith. She was a distant cousin, and he knew her in youth, but their real intimacy, if it can be called that, dates from the time they were fellow students at Haverhill Academy.

A bashful, ignorant boy, I was visited by the kindness of a lady who saw, or thought she saw, beneath the clownish exterior, something which gave promise of intellect and worth. The powers of my own mind—the mysteries of my own spirit—were revealed to myself only, as they were called out by one of those dangerous relations called "cousins," who with all her boarding school glories upon her, condescended to smile upon my rustic simplicity. She was so learned in the to me more than occult mysteries of "verbs and nouns" and philosophy and botany and mineralogy and French—and all that—and then she had seen something of society and could talk (an accomplishment at that time to which I could lay no claim) that on the whole I looked upon her as a being to obtain whose good opinion no effort would be too great.

There is no doubt that he was terribly in love with her. "Mary, I have loved you passionately, deeply—and you, if there is any faith in 'woman's words'—*you* have not *hated* me." Obviously she did not, but she did not love him either. At one time she promised to be a "sister" to him (apparently it really happened outside of novels), but she did not keep that promise either. Perhaps he was too serious for her and not worldly enough (she was not a Quaker), not sufficiently fashionable or sophisticated, too much the country bumpkin. Perhaps she simply did not know her own mind or was not ready to say yes to anybody. But on the whole she gives an unpleasant impression of coldness and trifling.

She married Judge Thomas of Covington, Kentucky, and became the mother of nine children. In her later years, when she was a widow, she and Whittier both saw and wrote to each other again. She had saved his old letters, though she did not know why.

When she read Pickard's biography, she seems to have been impressed by the nobility of her old lover's character as revealed in it.[37]

Evelina Bray, who also dates from Academy days, was probably a more charming girl than Mary Emerson Smith. In her old age she seems to have said, and probably believed, that she had been engaged to Whittier and that he broke it off because she was not a Friend, after which she vowed to marry the first man who asked her.[38] Mordell accepts this, and it gives him a chance to depict Whittier as jilting Evelina because he loved Mary Emerson Smith. This seems very doubtful, however. While Whittier was editing *The American Manufacturer* he walked from Salem to Marblehead one June morning to see Miss Bray. Though she did not invite him in, they walked to the old fort together and sat on the rocks overlooking the harbor; this is the incident Whittier refers to in "A Sea Dream." Whether Evelina (who became a teacher) married in pique or not, she chose unwisely, and her marriage was childless and unhappy. The Reverend Mr. Downey was a hard man and a religious fanatic, who was once stoned in New York for his violent anti-Catholic harangues. With Evelina, too, Whittier renewed his friendship in old age.

Cornelia Russ is a shadowy figure. About all we know of her is that she belonged to a prominent Hartford family and that Whittier was acquainted with her during his stay in that city. Before leaving he asked for an interview with her in a letter which is practically a declaration.[39] It is not recorded that this meeting ever took place.

Much more important was Lucy Hooper, "a noble girl—in heart as well as intellect," as he called her when she died of tuberculosis in 1841. Her background, like his, was Essex County, but she was living in Brooklyn when Whittier met her in the summer of 1837. She was an Episcopalian, an abolitionist, and a poet. Whittier encouraged her poetical ambitions and published some of her work in his paper. One night he stayed so late at her house that next day he wrote a letter of apology, explaining that since he never carried a watch, he had not realized how late it was. The material which Mordell discovered and published[40] after *Quaker Militant* may well show that Lucy loved Whittier, and it certainly shows that her sister reproached him after the girl's death, but why Mordell should hail it a triumphant demonstration of the truth of his notion that Whittier had trifled with the girl's affections is a little hard to understand.

I am not always capable of disguising my feelings, and I doubt not that our dear L. saw and understood them when I least expected it. God forgive me, if with no other than kind feelings I have done wrong. My feelings toward her were those of a Brother. I admired and loved her; yet felt myself compelled to crush every warmer feeling—poverty, protracted illness, and our separate faiths—the pledge that I had made of all the hopes and dreams of my younger years to the cause of Freedom—compelled me to steel myself against everything which tended to attract me—the blessing of woman's love and a home.

He added that all his friends complained that

at one time I am all warmth and feeling, at another cold, distant and absent. Certainly those who know me best have learned that my temperament and not my heart is at fault. I know that my habits of self-abstraction and reserve have become fixed upon me, and when I obtain the mastery over them I am very likely to go too far in the other direction. Alas, how often have my best feelings been misinterpreted, my kindness and love failed of their object and left me nothing but error and self-distrust.

The woman Whittier came closest to marrying was Elizabeth Lloyd, and here, for the first time, there was no religious barrier, for Elizabeth was a Friend, though she later turned against the Friends and became an Episcopalian. She too was a poet, and a poet of some skill. The beginning of his acquaintance with her dates from the Lucy Hooper period, but their closest intimacy occurred around 1858 after Elizabeth had been married to a man named Howell and widowed. On May 18, 1859, Whittier exhorted her to "write when thou canst—one word or ten. The very blank paper which thy hand has folded for my sake will be dear to me."

He adds that he has had more happiness through her

than I ever expected in this life. The sweet memory of the past few weeks makes me rich forever. What Providence has in store for the future I know not, I dare not hope scarcely, but the past is mine—may I not say ours—sacred and beautiful, a joy forever. Asking nothing of thee, and with the tenderest regard for thy griefs and memories, I have given thee what was thine by right—the love of an honest heart—not as a restraint or burden upon thee, imposing no obligation and calling for no solicitude on thy part as respects myself. Nobody is a loser by loving or being beloved.

As it turned out, however, the past was all he wanted, for it was he who finally broke off their love affair. On August 3, 1859 he wrote her:

If there has been any change in the letters, I am sure there is no change in the feeling which dictated them, so far as *thou* art concerned. But I ought to confess to thee that the old feeling of self-distrust, and painful consciousness of all I would be, and of all I am not, and of my inability to make those I love happy, come back to me, the stronger, perhaps, that for a time it was held in abeyance. I have grown old in a round of duties and responsibilities which still govern and urge me: my notions of life and daily habits are old-fashioned and homely: I could not for any length of time endure the restraints of fashion and society: art, refinement, and cultivated taste please me as something apart from myself.... But I cannot, dear E., be blind to the fact that thee lives in a different sphere—that thy sense of the fitting and beautiful demand accessories and surroundings very different from those that have become familiar and habitual to me. I am sure thy fine artist-nature would pine and die under the hard and uncongenial influences which make me what I am, and from which I cannot escape without feeling that I have abandoned the post of duty, without losing my self-respect, and forfeiting all right to be loved in return by those I love. These considerations, and the discouraging influence of my illness, may have affected the tone and spirit of my letters.

He went on to explain, fatuously, as it must seem to most of us, that he could not presume to thrust himself into the place of the one whose love had blessed her life, and he concluded:

For myself, I have ceased to demand what is impossible, or to quarrel with what is inevitable, for I know that the infinite Goodness *must* order all things well, for me, for thee, for all: and there are times when I am, as it were, reconciled to all things—save my own sins and follies.

She apparently asked him to destroy or return her letters, for on February 20, 1860, he wrote her: "I have obeyed thee as to thy letters—reluctantly, but with a feeling that thee had a right to their disposal. Perhaps—in the uncertainties of life—it was best." Higginson says that she later sometimes spoke harshly of him. According to Martha Hale Shackford, Whittier himself told Gertrude Cartland that Elizabeth was the only woman he had ever loved. "When asked why he did not marry her he said that because his mother and his sister were dependent on him he could not afford to marry." But his mother had died in 1858.

It has sometimes been conjectured that Lucy Larcom loved Whittier. If she did, she kept it strictly to herself. Among all the literary ladies he encouraged, the only one who permitted herself privileges with him was the exuberant Gail Hamilton, who addressed her letters to "Dearly Beloved," "Dear Angel," "My dear Sheikh," and "Dear little Darling." Depending upon the interpretation, Gail Hamilton's letters are either too playful for real passion or else the whimsicality is worn as a cloak for passion.

1874: I have your last living picture . . . standing before me on my mantle-piece—a thing of beauty and a joy forever. You know, you know you are handsome; that is what spoils you and makes you take on airs and stay at home all the time, because no one else's house is good enough for you.

1878: Why don't you write to me? Why don't you come to see me? Why don't you say you love and admire me? Because you have perched on Oak Knoll, and are lapped in luxury, and petted to death by your cousins, and are nothing in the world but a sleeping beauty! When you were in Amesbury you seemed definite and local, but now I have lost you out of Amesbury, and I don't find you anywhere else.

1884: Dear Angel: Is it your birthday? Thank Heaven you were born! Thank Heaven a thousand times more that you will never die; for the kingdom of heaven is within you.

Whittier was both shocked and flattered. "Through all the fun and bantering and unreason of thy letter, I discern the true, good and noble woman, whose friendship has been so much to me. I am quite willing to be laughed at or criticized by her." He often thought her too sharp in what she wrote for publication, and he was quite out of sympathy with her in her attack on Fields.[41] Yet she says that once when she arrived at his house, "he jumped up and came to me with both hands extended, 'Why, it is Gail Hamilton,' and then we all three [the third was his sister Elizabeth] walked into Paradise, shut the gate, and threw away the key." [42]

What does it all add up to, then, as to Whittier's attitude toward love, in general and for him in particular? There are contradictions of course. He tells us that love never lasts more than a fortnight with him, but he also tells us that his heart is softer than he dares expose. He tells us that he was a bachelor from principle (he does not stipulate what principle), and he also tells us that he was a bachelor by accident. He and Theodore Weld once made a joint vow of bachelorhood, but this meant nothing whatever to Weld when he wished to marry Angelina Grimké, and it cannot have meant much to Whittier either. When the poet heard that Moses Cartland was to be married, he wrote him a letter in which he blew hot and cold together, not uncharacteristically misquoting Shakespeare and misassigning the horribly garbled quotation: "No dreading of it: 'If 'twere done 'twere well done if it be done quickly,' Hamlet says."

He was chivalrous toward women, but there are vicious women in his writings, especially in *Margaret Smith's Journal* and "My Summer with Dr. Singletary." Though he has few erotic references, he does not really give the impression of prudishness. His mind and his principles reject beauty uncoupled with fine character, but he knows that love has power: it is, he says, the real witchcraft of these latter days. He was emphatically a family man, and he had no sympathy with religious asceticism. He was even aware of a meeting-ground between eroticism and religion, and the mingling of the sacred and secular did not trouble him.[43] His congratulations to friends about to be married were generally hearty. He did not approve of long engagements, and in later years he was fond of rallying young girls on the importance of getting themselves married quickly and not waiting for Providence to arrange it for them. When the announcement came that Elizabeth Stuart Phelps was to be married to a man much younger than herself, he said he could not have been more surprised if he had heard that she was going on the stage, but he sturdily continued to maintain that she had a perfect right to seek happiness in her own way. According to at least one letter to Celia Thaxter, he even liked literary ladies better when they combined writing with domesticity.[44]

Certainly there is no underrating the power of love in his poetry, and it is surprising how often he treats the theme of unsuitable love, "misgraffed in respect of years" or leaping over the barriers of rank, race, and creed. Even "The Knight of St. John," who broke his religious vows for love, is sympathetically presented.

"I tell you love has naught to do
With meetness or unmeetness.

"Itself its best excuse, it asks
No leave of pride or fashion
When silken zone or homespun frock
It stirs with throbs of passion."[45]

And again:

Oh, rank is good, and gold is fair,
And high and low mate ill;
But love has never known a law
Beyond its own sweet will![46]

One fine, though somewhat uncharacteristic, poem, "The Henchman," is much in the spirit of the Cavalier poets.

My lady walks her morning round,
My lady's page her fleet greyhound,
My lady's hair the fond winds stir,
And all the birds make songs for her.

And so on to the end, ten stanzas later:

No lance have I, in joust or right,
To splinter in my lady's sight;
But, at her feet, how blest were I
For any need of hers to die!

Why, then, did Whittier not marry? He once jocosely stated that he would not have anybody who would be willing to have him, but the obvious, serious obstacles have all been stated already: poverty, poor health, his obligations to his family, and in some cases, the religious barrier. These obstacles were both real and great, but it must be added frankly that they would probably not have deterred him had he really wished to marry. Whatever desire in that direction he may have had was obviously not strong enough to surmount the obstacles.

He once said, "Matrimony was never a success in my family," and it is true that a considerable number of Whittiers married late or unhappily or not at all. He also said that he would have made a good husband if he had been caught young. But he was not caught young, and it is clear that in his later years he did not really wish to change his state. Having failed to marry a wife, he did not wish to marry a nurse. He could say that "even sorrow shared and sympathized with is better than the solitary joy which begins and ends with one's self," and he could put a lady visitor to work with him in the kitchen making currant jelly! Yet despite all his bias toward domesticity, he was not really the marrying kind.

In a way the schoolboy came closer to getting it right than any of the rest of us: "John Greenleaf Whittier was a Quaker. He was born in Haverhill. He never married—he hated slavery." Whittier did not lack passion, but he lacked the disposition to surrender himself to it. The reasons why many bachelors wish to retain their freedom meant nothing to him, but he wanted his freedom for all that. He was an artist and he was a pilgrim, and neither quite belongs to the world which marries and gives in marriage. At the end as in the beginning he marched to a far-away music.

CHAPTER THREE

BEAUTY AS GRACE AND SNARE

I

Before Whittier can be examined as a writer, something must be said about his reading. Some critics who ought to have known better have said that he did not care for literature; others have even called him "anti-intellectual." Both statements, as we shall see, are nonsense. The modern writer who has no literary inspiration behind him is a little like the hoop-snake; it is always somebody else who has seen him, but one has never seen him oneself. Burns, Mark Twain, Hemingway, and many others—one by one, the non-literary backgrounds hypothesized for them have vanished upon examination.

The scarcity of books in the household in which Whittier grew up is an old story to every reader of *Snow-Bound:*

> The Almanac we studied o'er,
> Read and reread our little store,
> Of books and pamphlets, scarce a score;
> One harmless novel, mostly hid
> From younger eyes, a book forbid,
> And poetry, (or good or bad,
> A single book was all we had,)

Where Ellwood's meek, drab-skirted Muse,
A stranger to the heathen Nine,
Sang with a somewhat nasal whine,
The wars of David and the Jews.

The novel was *The Pirate* by Sir Walter Scott. The poetry was Thomas Ellwood's *Davideis* (1712). The fact that Whittier could never find much merit in it, Quaker product though it was, tends to controvert the popular view that he based his literary judgments solely on the capacity of the book in question to inspire edification.

When he was fifteen or sixteen, Whittier produced a versified and classified catalogue of the books in the family library:

NARRATIVES

How Captain Riley and his crew
Were on Sahara's desert threw.
How Rollins to obtain the cash
Wrote a dull history of trash.
O'er Bruce's travels I have pored,
Who the sources of the Nile explored.
Malcolm of Salem's narrative beside,
Who lost his ship's crew, unless belied.
How David Foss, poor man, was thrown
Upon an island all alone.

RELIGIOUS

The Bible towering o'er the rest,
Of all the other books the best.
Old Father Baxter's pious call
To the unconverted all.
William Penn's laborious writing,
And the books 'gainst Christians fighting.
Some books of sound theology,
Robert Barclay's "Apology."
Dyer's "Religion of the Shakers,"
Clarkson's also of the Quakers.

Many more books I have read through—
Bunyan's "Pilgrim's Progress" too.
A book concerning John's baptism,
Elias Smith's "Universalism."

JOURNALS, LIVES, &c.

The Lives of Franklin and of Penn,
Of Fox and Scott, all worthy men.
The Lives of Pope, of Young and Prior,
Of Milton, Addison, and Dyer;
Of Doddridge, Fénelon and Gray,
Armstrong, Akenside, and Gay.
The Life of Burroughs, too, I've read,
As big a rogue as e'er was made;
And Tufts, who, I will be civil,
Was worse than an incarnate devil.[1]

"The Bible towering o'er the rest" and Bunyan were about all that could have been counted upon to form the boy's literary taste, though he doubtless learned something of poetry from the biographies of the poets, which must have included some quoted verses. The Quaker books made no literary pretensions, but for that very reason they taught him simplicity and sincerity of style. The travel books began feeding a never-satiated lifelong hunger for vicarious exotic adventure. But the most startling entries are the biographies of the two New England rogues, Stephen Burroughs and Henry Tufts, who must have felt strangely ill at ease in a collection where even a novel by Scott was suspect. Yet they helped tie Whittier to his New England background and to the life of the common people in it. To the predestined writer, nothing comes amiss.

Compared to the library in which Oliver Wendell Holmes "tumbled about" in his youth, Whittier's resources were not many. But his situation might easily have been worse than it was. Dr. Elias Weld had a library, and in his introductory note to "The Countess," Whittier was to make grateful acknowledgment for the use he had had of it. (Like the young Lincoln, he would walk any distance to borrow a book.) Later, in Haverhill Academy days, he was to have access to other libraries. There was good poetry, too, in Lindley Murray's *English Reader* and Caleb Bingham's *American Preceptor*, much better poetry than most American boys and girls encounter today at the same level. "The African Chief" in Bingham seems early to have turned his mind in the direction of abolition. But in the beginning, the connotations of fine poetry were even more important than its denotations, and he has testified that

> the solemn organ-roll of Gray's "Elegy" and the lyric sweep and pathos of Cowper's "Lament for the Royal George" moved and fascinated me with a sense of mystery and power felt rather than understood.... Freighted with unguessed meanings, these poems spake to me, in an unknown tongue indeed, but like the wind in the pines or the waves on the beach, awakening faint echoes and responses, and vaguely prophesying of wonders yet to be revealed.

Such learning as Whittier acquired was mainly literary and historical. In his time, scientific education lay largely in the future. That he was learned in the colonial period of New England history and culture and in later scholarship relating to it, Cecil B. Williams's study of *Margaret Smith's Journal* has made abundantly clear. Pollard finds traces of Coleridge, Domitian, Lavater, Pliny, Seneca, Swedenborg, and the phrenologists Gall and Spurzheim, in a single sketch, "The Nervous Man." In 1834 Whittier wrote Elizur Wright that he was studying constitutional law and political economy, and his writings on slavery prove that he did this.

He studied French at the Academy, but since he once asked Mrs. Fields to translate a French review of one of his works for him, he can hardly have read it with ease. He quotes Achille Murat in the original in one of his anti-slavery papers, and Higginson says [2] that he translated one or two simple French poems. He occasionally quotes Latin in his letters and in at least one poem.[3] There is a letter to Thomas Tracy, in which he thanks him for lending him German books, adding that he now has others also and that he is planning to renew his study of German. He made a translation of Goethe's ballad, "Der Erlkönig."

It should go without saying that a man thus limited linguistically might be expected to do most of his reading in English and American literature. The Bible would, of course, be an exception, but that, too, was an English book so far as Whittier was concerned. James Stacy Stevens counted 816 passages in Whittier's poems "which come from the Bible directly or indirectly." [4] He refers again and again to "Thy will be done," the waters of Shiloah (Isaiah 8:6), for which he employs variant spellings, the dews of Hermon, the hem of Jesus' garment, the seamless robe, the letter and the spirit, and the burning bush.

But he also read, in translation, a reasonable amount of the sacred literature of the non-Christian East. He was greatly impressed by the *Bhagavad-Gita*, which he borrowed from Emerson in 1852. In "Our Dumb Relations" he retells a story from the *Mahabharata*. The amount of material which Whittier takes from Oriental sources (as in "Miriam" and "The Over-Heart"), compares very well with Emerson's in its extent, but Whittier always shows a tendency to christianize his materials.[5] One non-religious work of Oriental origin was important to him as it was to most of the readers of his time, and he and his brother remembered *The Arabian Nights* even while they were digging out after the storm of *Snow-Bound:*

we had read
Of rare Aladdin's wondrous cave,
And to our own his name we gave,
With many a wish the luck were ours
To test the lamp's supernal powers.

Homer, Virgil, Sophocles, Pliny, Seneca, Apuleius, and Tibullus are among the classical writers referred to. One reference to Plato is of interest:

I pray the prayer of Plato old;
God make thee beautiful within,
And let thine eyes the good behold
In everything save sin! [6]

Margaret Smith's Journal contains a large number of classical references, but the only really significant discussion of classical literature in Whittier is the long consideration of Horace in "My Summer with Dr. Singletary." [7]

Among the Italians, Whittier refers a number of times to Dante; in Longfellow's translation at least, he seems to have liked the "Purgatorio" better than either the "Inferno" or the "Paradiso." [8] He speaks of both Ariosto and Boccaccio; his references to the *Decameron* are not significant, but it is interesting that he achieves them without a moral shudder.

Molière, Montaigne, and Pascal are among the Frenchmen referred to. One of his papers takes an epigraph from *The Song of the Cid*. He admired Sainte-Beuve's psychographs. But his favorite French writers were undoubtedly de Tocqueville, whose *Democracy in America* he judged, not entirely for literary reasons, "one of the best books of the century," and Bernardin de St. Pierre's "wonderful story" of *Paul and Virginia:*

> His simple tale of love and woe
> All hearts had melted high or low;–
> A blissful pain, a sweet distress,
> Immortal in its tenderness.[9]

In German, Fouqué's *Undine*, appealing to the same taste, was also greatly loved. He speaks of Novalis and of Lessing, of whom Lucy Larcom's work reminded him, and Miss Eastburn thinks [10] "The Witch of Wenham" echoes Heine's "Die Lorelei" in the lines:

> She weaves her golden hair, she sings
> Her spell-song low and faint.

With the king of German literature, Goethe, Whittier had trouble, which is not surprising, since even the much more scholarly and cosmopolitan Longfellow had the same experience.[11] In Whittier's 1858 lines "To James T. Fields" there is a very uncomplimentary reference to Goethe:

Better his lot whose axe is swung
  In Wartburg's woods, or that poor girl's
  Who by the Ilm her spindle whirls
And sings the songs that Luther sung,

Than his who, old, and cold, and vain,
  At Weimar sat, a demigod,
  And bowed with Jove's imperial nod
His votaries in and out again!

Yet the year before Whittier had written Fields himself that he now had "for the first time an adequate idea of Goethe's genius." Frank Stearns says that after reading Bayard Taylor's translation of *Faust*, Whittier asked what explanation Goethe's admirers "could make for the strange, and extraordinary characters in the second part." But when *The Independent* printed what Whittier regarded as an unfair review of Taylor, he protested vigorously:

Faust is a classic,—not a model Christian poem,—but quite as much so as Dante's *Inferno*, *Purgatorio*, and *Paradiso*—and I cannot think a man ought to be denounced for translating it. Besides it seemed to me that the translation is in many respects the best ever made. And such, I think, is the judgment of eminent critics here and in Europe.

The protest was certainly in order, but the comparison between the two works on the score of their relative christianism is absurd, and Whittier surely had no basis in his own knowledge for judging the value of the translation.

Scandinavian folklore and mythology interested him (he published a paper on "The Poetry of the North"), and Pollard says he read some Gogol, Pushkin, and Tolstoy, including *War and Peace*.

Whittier's references to English and American writers cannot all be noted here. In his notion that Shakespeare and Milton were the king figures he was orthodox.[12] "Blind Milton approaches nearly to my conception of a true hero." About this there is nothing remarkable, both men being what they were. It may seem surprising, however, that Whittier should express more enthusiasm for the prose than for the poetry. "Milton's prose has long been my favorite reading. My whole life has felt the influence of his writings." Part of the explanation must surely be that it was in the prose that Milton contended directly for what Whittier believed in. Obviously the *Areopagitica* was important to him in his own battle for a free press, which was a very important part of the anti-slavery struggle.[13] Of course this does not mean that he was indifferent to Milton's poetry or that he did not sense its quality. In his tribute to Burns,

> The mournful Tuscan's haunted rhyme,
> And Milton's starry splendor!

are cited as examples of the loftiest reaches of poetic achievement, beyond Burns's (and obviously Whittier's) grasp, but when he excludes "tedious extracts from dull plays and weary epics" from *Songs of Three Centuries*, he sounds a little like Poe, who is himself represented in the anthology only by "The Bells." "The Slave Ships" carries an epigraph from "Lycidas," and "The Waiting" may well have been influenced by

> They also serve who only stand and wait.

The inscription Whittier wrote for the Milton memorial window in St. Margaret's Church, London, is in a lofty strain for him, though here again he stresses public service above poetic achievement:

> The new world honors him whose lofty plea
> For England's freedom made her own more sure,
> Whose song, immortal in its theme, shall be
> Their common freehold while both worlds endure.

There are numerous references to Milton in Whittier's papers on Andrew Marvell and Thomas Ellwood (his Quakerism gave him a special interest in the seventeenth century), and one can only wonder why he did not dedicate an independent essay to the master himself.

In contrast to Chaucer and Spenser, whom he largely missed, Shakespeare would seem to have come off rather well with Whittier, for not only his literary works but even his political and anti-slavery writings bristle with Shakespearean echoes and references. Mrs. Marcy found that his favorite plays for quotation were *A Midsummer Night's Dream*, *The Winter's Tale*, *The Tempest*, *Henry IV*, Parts I and II, *Julius Caesar*, *Macbeth*, *Hamlet*, and *Othello*. She thought that "his numerous allusions to Falstaff come strangely from the ascetic Quaker," but added that "Whittier was gifted with a pronounced sense of humor, to which the fat, but not fat-witted knight evidently appealed." In an 1840 letter to Elizabeth Lloyd, Whittier refers, rather surprisingly, to *Titus Andronicus*. There is an 1844 letter to the Boston *Times*, on a political subject, in which he manages a double reference to Shakespeare:

> Judging from the tone of the article which has been copied into the *Times*, it seems very probable that, if I should chance to fall into the hands of the truculent editor and his correspondents, I should share the fate of the Roman Cinna, and be "hanged for my bad verses." There are doubtless Dogberrys enough in the land of Lynch law to prove satisfactorily that opposition to Texas annexation is "flat burglary."

There is also an 1870 letter to Fields, in which, lamenting the onset of age and the thinning of the ranks of his generation by death, he (no doubt intentionally) misquotes or rather plays a variation upon Falstaff: "There are but few of us good fellows left, and one of them is not fat but lean, and grows old."

There is nothing worth referring to on Spenser. Chaucer is grouped with Shakespeare in the lines Whittier wrote for the Haverhill Library opening in 1875:

> Here Greek and Roman find themselves
> Alive along these crowded shelves;
> And Shakespeare treads again his stage,
> And Chaucer paints anew his age.

In his "Greeting" to Harriet Beecher Stowe at her seventieth birthday party, he told her that her *Oldtown Fireside Stories*

> Are racy as the legends old
> By Chaucer or Boccaccio told.

I should think "The Squire's Tale" must have been Whittier's favorite, for he refers to it, though without naming it, in both *Margaret Smith's Journal* and *The Supernaturalism of New England*, and he also wrote a poem about it.[14] As for the "racy" stories (in a different sense, surely, than those told by Mrs. Stowe), I should guess that they had considerable influence upon Whittier's attitude toward Chaucer, for in 1870 he wrote Celia Thaxter that William Morris was "Chaucer improved and made decent—wonderfully sweet and pleasant reading." [15]

After that, there is nothing of consequence about any English poet until we come to the Romantics and their predecessors. In the Preface to *Songs of Three Centuries*, Whittier admitted his predilection for nineteenth-century poetry freely, declaring that the future would rank it even more highly than he did.

I have found only one significant reference to Blake, but it shows considerable sense of his quality: "The man was a marvel—perhaps a great deal more sane than most of us—ever reaching out from the shows and shadows of time and sense to the things unseen 'by the outward eye' which are eternal." There is a very sympathetic early poem "To the Memory of Chatterton":

> The cold and heartless bigot may
> Thy closing scene in gloom array,
> Thy name to hate and scorn consign,
> But who shall say what guilt was thine?
> The misery of thy life to scan
> And judge thy crime is not for man.[16]

Tom Moore is sometimes scolded for what Whittier considered his licentious tone, but there is an 1879 letter to John Boyle O'Reilly, declining an invitation to a banquet, in which Whittier includes what is virtually a roll-call of the Irish poets (all of whom he expects to be there in spirit), culminating in passionate praise for Moore as a friend of America and "the advocate of liberal political principles and rational liberty."

When we come to the great Romantics we draw a mixed bag of critical notices from Whittier. Though "The Rattlesnake Hunter" suggests that he may have known "Lamia," he had no appreciation or understanding of Keats. He criticized Wordsworth's "puerility," but he also praised him as the author of

> the sweetest lays
> Our Saxon tongue has known.

Coleridge he quotes often, sometimes in the anti-slavery writings.[17]

Shelley Whittier attacked fiercely for profligacy and infidelity in the *Essex Gazette* in 1830, and when he was criticized for this he valiantly stood his ground, even implicating Mrs. Shelley [18] in his condemnation as "the daughter of the licentious, the profligate and shameless Mary Woolstonecraft." Apparently he did not know how to spell Mary Wollstonecraft's name, and he does not seem to have known much about her either. Toward Shelley's first wife, Harriet Westbrook, he was fortunately more charitable, anticipating briefly some of the lines of Mark Twain's famous defense of her.[19] Yet Whittier often quotes Shelley, and ultimately he ranked him, as a poet, ahead of Byron.

Byron's own fascination for Puritans is, of course, one of the phenomena of literary taste, and Whittier succumbed as abjectly as the Beechers. When Byron died,

> The pride, the shame, the wonder of his age,

Whittier's elegy mingled moral disapproval with extravagant admiration,[20] but when the noble bard's cynicism was echoed by other writers—even in a milk-and-water form, as by Nathaniel Parker Willis—Whittier was always shocked.[21] Moore's biography of Byron was a shock too:

> I have read Byron's own relation of himself with sorrow—with deep anguish. That a man of such genius could be degraded to affectation

and vanity and unbelief and wickedness is humiliating—is revolting and dreadful. How could he so wilfully stain the brightness of his birthright? ... But it is vain to attempt to account for the aberrations of genius. In its best estate it is united with sensibility, and pride, and anger, and all the weakness of human fallibility. Feeling barbs its arrows and ambition casts them with a fatal aim; hatred incites the contest, and hope often protracts it to an awful termination.

Yet, though genius does not excuse vice but rather aggravates the offense, Byron was still "the master spirit of his time," and Whittier could not but "admire ... almost worship," his genius.

One cannot but feel that Byron's personality must have been an important element in this appeal. Perhaps, like Ethel Colburn Mayne, Whittier was drawn to the noble bard by his "enthralling humanity." The saints are often fascinated by sin (in a sense they could not get along without it), and they are always better able to cope with it when the sinner admits his sinfulness, as Byron did, though his confession often sounded strangely like a boast, than when he justifies it or explains it away in terms of some set of standards peculiar to himself, as Shelley was inclined to do. Moreover, it must be understood that there were definite limits to Whittier's infatuation even when he was most enthralled. Writing to Jonathan Law in 1832, at a time when he had become "such a melancholy person that the risible muscles of my face relax only in sympathy," he wondered "how it would do for me to turn down my shirt collar and rail at the world like Byron," but he rejected the idea on the ground that "I should catch a sore throat, and this great, lubberly, ill-mannered lout of a world would only laugh at me."

Like most readers of his time, Whittier thought Tennyson the greatest modern poet, but both *Maud* and *Idylls of the King* disappointed him, the first as "a mawkish, morbid love-story, utterly destitute of lofty purposes," and the *Idylls* because though "full of beautiful, sensuous pictures," they were "not great and deep and earnest and loving like *In Memoriam*." He may well have thought better of the King Arthur poems later; at least he quotes from them as he does from Tennyson's other poems also. Perhaps the most interesting quotation is a rather indirect one in 1885: "For myself, I would not exchange a decade of my own life for a century of the Middle Ages, or a 'cycle of Cathay.'" His prose sketch, "David Matson," first published in *Our Young Folks*, describes a real-life Enoch Arden.[22]

Though Whittier does not have many references to Matthew Arnold, he expressed great regret when he died, and Mrs. Fields assures us that Whittier knew Arnold, "as it were, 'by heart,'" long before he met him. When he encountered some extracts from Swinburne's "Atalanta in Calydon" in 1865, he thought they presaged the coming of a great poet, but I have found nothing to follow this up. The great Victorians to whom he did not respond seem, oddly enough, to have been the Brownings, whose intense christianism might have been expected to win him in spite of all other objections. *Men and Women* struck him "like a galvanic battery in full play," and Higginson could not remember his ever speaking of Browning. He commended Longfellow's *The Seaside and the Fireside* to "all those whose ears have been tortured by Browning's burlesque of rhythm." Mrs. Browning's *A Drama of Life* he reviewed favorably when she was still Miss Barrett, but he thought *Aurora Leigh* "not comfortable reading." It is tempting to find Browning's influence in the dramatic monologue of "Cassandra Southwick," but the early date (1843) makes this seem improbable.[23]

So far as Whittier's own literary career was concerned, the poet of poets was Robert Burns. It may be doubted that any other verse-maker ever lay so close to his heart. It was the schoolmaster Joshua Coffin who read Burns's poems aloud one night to the enraptured boy and his doubtless somewhat less enraptured family, and who then, realizing what he had done for his pupil, offered to leave the book with him. The boy had already, it seems, heard some of the songs from a "pawky auld carle" who rehearsed them in exchange for bread and ale as he wandered through the country. But the real awakening came with Coffin, and S. T. Pickard does not exaggerate when he writes: "A fire was that evening kindled upon an altar that grew not cold for seventy years."

Whittier himself has described what his discovery of Burns meant to him—how he turned away from the meaningless, dreary romanticism and sensationalism that had until now engrossed him and began to apprehend the significance of the common human experience all about him.

> New light on home-seen Nature beamed,
>   New glory over Woman;
> And daily life and duty seemed
>   No longer poor and common.
>
> I woke to find the simple truth
>   Of fact and feeling better
> Than all the dreams that held my youth
>   A still repining debtor.
>
> Why dream of lands of gold and pearl,
>   Of loving knight and lady,
> When farmer boy and barefoot girl
>   Were wandering there already?
>
> With clearer eyes I saw the worth
>   Of life among the lowly;
> The Bible at his Cotter's hearth
>   Had made my own more holy.[24]

In the last stanza quoted literature comments upon and interprets the meaning of the reader's own life.

At first, of course, Whittier supposed that, having been inspired by Burns, he must write like Burns—on Scottish subjects or in Scottish dialect—and some of his imitative pieces are not bad examples of their kind. Certainly "Kathleen" (which is Irish, not Scottish) is an excellent ballad.[25] He even reformed one of Burns's failings for him in a Scottish dialect poem, "The Drunkard to His Bottle." [26] It would not be correct to say that Whittier wrote no more sensational, conventionally "romantic" pieces after discovering Burns, nor that all his imitations, in the bad sense, were early. Nevertheless, he had made an important discovery, and as time went on, he learned increasingly that the way to use it was to be as American, and even as Essex County, as Burns had been Scottish.

He was always conscious of Burns's shortcomings—sometimes, perhaps, even priggishly.

And if at times an evil strain,
  To lawless love appealing,
Broke in upon the sweet refrain
  Of pure and healthful feeling,

It dies upon the eye and ear,
  No inward answer gaining;
No heart had I to see or hear
  The discord and the staining.

Let those who never erred forget
  His worth, in vain bewailings;
Sweet Soul of Song! I own my debt
  Uncancelled by his failings.

Whittier exercised Christian charity toward Burns, and he deserves credit for this, but Burns had important advantages on his side. One can sympathize with Whitman, who used to wonder why Whittier was so much less charitable toward what he considered his failings than he was toward those of Burns. Whittier forgave General Gordon for being a soldier because he was also an earnest Evangelical Christian and an enemy of the slave traffic, and it is clear that he had a fellow-feeling for Burns, who grew up in surroundings similar to his own, who shared his political and emotional democracy, and who, like him, revolted against an inhuman religion. "Burns was not a Quaker—he had his faults—but he did a noble work for Scotland and humanity. He sweetened an atmosphere bitter with Calvinism." We all take our allies where we find them, and such are the limitations of human imagination that it is always easier to forgive those in whom we can, in one aspect or another, discern some likeness of ourselves. "He lives, next to Shakespeare," he told Mrs. Fields of Burns, "in the heart of humanity." "We admire others," he wrote the Burns Club of Washington; "we love him." As late as 1885 he urged Lowell to devote a lecture to him:

Somehow I have come to look upon him as the true world-singer—the very Father of Songs as the Orientals would say. The great poets seem to me to be Chaucer, Spenser, Shakespeare, Milton (I have almost said Dryden), Burns, and Shelley.[27]

Of the non-fiction prose writers of England, "dear Charles Lamb" is probably the one to whom Whittier refers most affectionately, but Edmund Burke is the one who influenced him most. Burke colored not only his political convictions but also his prose style as a controversialist, especially in *Justice and Expediency*, and Pollard noted that the set of Burke is the most heavily marked of all the books in the Whittier library at Amesbury. He admired Ruskin, and De Quincey directly inspired the curious sketch of "The Opium Eater." He considered Macaulay brilliant but less trustworthy than Edwin Percy Whipple, and when the historian was defeated for Parliament in 1847, Whittier rejoiced and denounced him as having sold his gifts into the service of oppressors.[28] He seems to have read Carlyle's *Sartor Resartus*, *The French Revolution*, and *Past and Present* with much interest, but the "hero-worship" of *Letters and Speeches of Oliver Cromwell* seemed to him a form of devil-worship, and his attack on Carlyle's brutal racism in "An Occasional Discourse on the Negro Question" was all-out. His first reaction to Jane Carlyle's letters was unfavorable, but he later came to think of her as a noble woman who was far too good for her husband.

Bunyan, the only fictionist to whom Whittier ever devoted a whole considered essay,[29] enthralled him from his youth. He is both shrewd and sophisticated when he writes of Bunyan:

His vivid but disturbed imagination lent new terrors to the awful figures by which the sacred writers conveyed the idea of future retribution to the Oriental mind. [This is no Fundamentalist or literalist interpretation of Scripture.] Bunyan's World of Woe, if it lacked the colossal architecture and solemn vastness of Milton's Pandemonium, was more clearly defined; its agonies were within the pale of human comprehension; its victims were men and women, with the same sense of corporeal suffering which they possessed in life; and who, to use his own terrible description, had "all the loathed variety of hell to grapple with; fire unquenchable, a lake of choking brimstone, eternal chains, darkness more black than night, the ever-lasting gnawing of the worm, the sight of devils, and the yells and outcries of the damned." [And this is not the comment of a writer incapable of relishing literary realism.]

Later in the essay he tries to trace a relationship between characters and incidents in *The Pilgrim's Progress* and Bunyan's own experience.

In early days, as has been noted, Whittier and his sister read *The Pirate* surreptitiously—

> One harmless novel, mostly hid
> From younger eyes, a book forbid.

Since *The Pirate* is far from representing the height of Scott's bent, one would be disposed to see both of them as predestined Scottians. As a matter of fact, however, Whittier gave Scott a much less generous hearing than he was to accord either Dickens or (surprisingly) Sterne, whom, in his day, many more sophisticated persons regarded as a merely prurient writer. In 1829, though already sure that Scott was greater in fiction than in poetry, and obviously unwilling to criticize him severely, Whittier was yet disturbed that his writings had

> a tendency to subvert some of the purest principles of christian morality. They breathe a war-like spirit—they carry the dazzled reader back to the stirring days of chivalry, and the engrossing interest of the crusade. Our sympathies are enlisted frequently on the wrong side, yet we cannot avoid it, for a fascination is around us—the fascination of glowing narrative, and masterly delineation of character. . . . We do not impugn the motives of Scott. He has doubtless endeavored to bring forth his heroes, as the faithful representatives of their times; but the darker and more repulsive portions of their character have been softened with the too charitable light of romance.[30]

None of this seemed to trouble him, however, when he reviewed a new edition of the "Waverley Novels" in *The National Era* in 1852:

We are sure to speak for thousands, when we welcome these charming volumes. We have experienced real pleasure in turning over their clear pages, and remembering how they bewitched us years ago. We love to linger over some familiar scene, and think how our heart beat with the wildest romance as we gave ourselves wholly to the sweet glamour of the story.[31]

Whittier does not actually say very much about Sterne, but he refers to him affectionately again and again. When, in 1832, he began work on his aborted conciliatory slavery novel, he adopted a style "about half-way between the abruptness of Laurence Sterne and the smooth gracefulness of W. Irving." I am sure his favorite quotation must have been "I like it hugely" from *Tristram Shandy;* I think I have met it in him more often than any single quotation from the Bible itself.

About Dickens he says much more. At the beginning he had reservations here also.

... much as I admire his genius, there are some things in his writings which I cannot approve. Yet, he is doing good I believe: his works have uniformly a kindly and philanthropic character—in the lowest and most sinful he sees something of good; he recognizes the universal brotherhood of the human family.

Later we hear nothing of the reservations, and he is often reminded of Dickens and his characters by events in his own life or in the lives of those whom he encounters. He was inclined to think that Dickens did not exaggerate obnoxious American types in *Martin Chuzzlewit.*

When Dickens came to America in 1867, Whittier, despite his horror of crowds and late hours, asked Fields to get him a ticket for one of his readings, then decided he couldn't go, and finally went after all. He had already dreamed of the novelist, "surrounded by a mob of ladies, each with her scissors snipping at his hair, and he seemed in a fair way to be 'shaven and shorn' like the Priest in the House that Jack built." What he really saw was, as he described it to Celia Thaxter, quite different:

I have "made an effort," as Mrs. Chick would say and have heard Dickens. It was his last night in Boston. . . . We waited some half hour a slight brisk man tripped up the steps, sparkling with ring and chain—tight vested wide bosomed, short dress coat, white choker, tight pantaloons enclosing, as the Prairie girl said of Judge Douglass'—"a mighty slim chance of legs!" Somehow a slight reminder of his own Sim Tappertit in Barnaby Rudge. Face marked with thought as well as years—head bald or nearly so—a look of keen intelligence about the strong brow and eye—the look of a man who has seen much and is wide awake to see more. I don't think he shows the great genius that he is—he might pass for a shrewd Massachusetts manufacturer or an active N.Y. merchant. But his reading is wonderful, far beyond my expectations. Those marvellous characters of his come forth, one by one, real personages as if their original creator had breathed new life into them. You shut your eyes and there before you you know are Pecksniff and Sairy Gamp, Sam Weller and Dick Swiveller and all the rest. But it is idle to talk about it: you must beg, borrow, or steal a ticket and hear him. Another such star-shower is not to be expected in one's life-time. After his reading I called on him with Longfellow and the Fields.

In another letter, to Gail Hamilton, he enlarged on the record:

I heard Charles Dickens read the other night. It is difficult to detach the reader from the writer, but both together are absorbing. My eyes ached all next day from the intensity of my gazing. I do not think his voice naturally particularly fine, but he uses it with great effect. He has wonderful dramatic power—a command over his face which recalls the old stories of Garrick. He reproduces, recreates almost the characters with whom his pen has made you familiar. I like him better than any public reader I have ever before heard. He has less mouthing and unnaturalness.[32]

When, not long afterwards, the great novelist died with such cruel suddenness, Whittier was sincerely grieved. On June 13, 1870 he wrote Mrs. Fields:

I know thee must be greatly pained by the sad news of the death of Charles Dickens. Is it possible that that wonderful creative life is now but a memory?—That that marvellous hand has forever lost its cunning?

So they pass away—the great and good ones, who made themselves so dear and necessary to us!—Where are they?—What are they?—Shall we who are following them into the darkness and silence never meet them again?

Thee and thy husband who have had the privilege of calling him friend have, at least, the satisfaction of knowing that his earthly life was made happier by your kindness and love.

What a brief and sad life that would be if it did not include the possibilities of a love which takes hold of eternity!

I have found nothing on Thackeray save the statement that Charles Reade, despite some coarseness, is second only to Dickens, Thackeray, and George Eliot. He thought Bulwer's *Falkland* dangerous because the reader's sympathy was irresistibly commanded by the lovers. "It is not in human nature to resist such appeals as those of the seducer—it is not in man to resist such love—such wild fondness as that of the seduced." He considered Gwendolen Harleth in *Daniel Deronda* an achievement but did not care for Mirah Cohen. Kingsley and George MacDonald appealed to him because he was like-minded with them in many ways, and in both cases the appeal of the book was reinforced by that of the personality when reader and writer met. We should not be surprised that he thought Shorthouse's *John Ingelsant* "wonderful" nor Mrs. Humphry Ward's *Robert Elsmere* "unsettling," nor even, perhaps, that having read *A Little Pilgrim in the Unseen*, by that considerable Victorian artist Mrs. Oliphant, he should have preferred it to Dante's picture of heaven, which he described as that of "an old man sitting eternally on a high chair, and concentric circles of saints, martyrs, and ordinary church members, whirling around him in perpetual gyration, and singing 'Glory.' " His most insensitive judgment of a Victorian novel was undoubtedly that of *Wuthering Heights*, in which he found "great strength and power" and "an important and salutary moral" but "no beauty"!

It must not be forgotten that Whittier's readings in American literature were largely readings in contemporary literature, and that much of it was done in the books of those who were known to him personally.[33] He knew all the "great" New England writers of his time, though he certainly knew Hawthorne and Thoreau less than the others. As for their non-New England peers, he makes a genuflection toward Bryant every now and then, or quotes from him, but this does not seem very significant. I doubt that he had much sympathy with Poe, though he quotes from "The Haunted Palace" in one of his sketches, and it has been said that he was fond of repeating "Annabel Lee" and "The Raven" in later years.[34] He mourned the early death of Edward C. Pinkney, and in early years at least he regarded James Gates Percival as a "singular and high-minded Poet" and "a genius of Nature's making." I do not believe that his apparent admiration for the verses of Mrs. Sigourney, during his Hartford period, should be held to militate against his critical judgment. She was at the time a great figure in Hartford, she was kind to him, and he would have had to be a churl to behave other than as he did. In spite of the graceful verses he wrote for her memorial tablet, there is no reason to suppose that the mature Whittier was unaware of her limitations:

> She sang alone, ere womanhood had known
>   The gift of song which fills the air to-day:
> Tender and sweet, a music all her own
>   May fitly linger where she knelt to pray.[35]

Whittier considered Emerson the greatest of American writers, though there were times when both Hawthorne and Holmes seemed to be pushing him a little for the title: "I regard Emerson as foremost in the rank of American poets; he has written better things than any of us." Whittier's birthday tribute of 1882 declares that "no living poet of the English-speaking tongue has written verses bearing more distinctly than his the mark of immortality," and Miss Sparhawk quotes him as having said that "Emerson is the one American who will live a thousand years." He told Edmund Gosse that Emerson was "the noblest human being I have known" and Longfellow "perhaps the sweetest." When somebody said that Emerson's unorganized prose style suggested "the shooting forth of stones from a sack," Whittier was unperturbed because he thought they were all precious stones. Somewhat more playfully, perhaps, he once wrote Celia Thaxter that if anybody was to be worshipped it ought to be Emerson, because "he *bears* it so admirably." Whittier was sometimes distressed by Emerson's not taking a more distinctively Christian stand on certain points, but he seems never to have held this against him, nor to have valued his company less on this account. "Emerson was a delightful companion," he recalled, "and was often here. No matter who remained, when he left, there was a void." [36]

His first reaction to Thoreau, on the other hand, was mixed, and decidedly less tolerant:

> Thoreau's *Walden* is capital reading, but very wicked and heathenish. The practical moral of it seems to be that if a man is willing to sink himself into a woodchuck he can live as cheaply as that quadruped; but after all, for me, I prefer walking on two legs.

This was substantially Lowell's attitude toward Thoreau, but Whittier did not hold to it permanently. In an 1873 letter to Emerson he spoke of "that wise, wonderful Thoreau," and in 1875 he wrote: "What a rare genius he was! To take up his books is like a stroll in the woods or a sail on the lake—the leaves rustle and the water ripples along his pages." In 1886 he went so far as to say that he had "loved" both Thoreau and Emerson.

With the other great literary man of Concord, Hawthorne, Whittier never made anything like a vital contact; Hawthorne, said Whittier, never seemed to be doing anything, yet he did not like being disturbed at it. The novelist, on his part, professed to like Whittier as a man, though he cared nothing for his writings, but apparently he was in his most difficult and standoffish mood when Whittier called on him. Whittier never held it against him in any way. He had recognized Hawthorne's talent as early as "Sights from a Steeple," and he never changed his mind. In 1860 he declared that Hawthorne's legendary tales had awakened "his own poor efforts," and on other occasions he called him the greatest master of English prose and Addison's superior as a stylist and said he thought it not unlikely that he would outlive every other writer of his time. There may or may not be significance in the fact that we have no specific praise from Whittier for *The Scarlet Letter*, but he found a "good deal of wisdom" in the essay "Chiefly About War-Matters" which so enraged most Northern patriots when the *Atlantic* printed it in July 1862.

Whittier wrote two poems in honor of Lowell; no doubt he felt especially close to him because, like himself, though less intensively, Lowell engaged in anti-slavery agitation. In 1850 he hailed him as "one of the strongest and manliest of our writers—a republican poet who dares to speak brave words for unpopular truth" and praised him for having "happily overcome a slight tendency to mysticism and metaphysics" evident in his earlier work. Whittier was not sure that Lowell always concerned himself sufficiently with the "niceties of diction and metaphor," but apparently he never resented Lowell's criticism of him in *A Fable for Critics.* In 1866 he praised *The Biglow Papers*, giving no indication that he valued the pro-Civil War Second Series any less than the anti-Mexican War First Series; the next year, in *The Tent on the Beach*, he called Lowell "our new Theocritus." Whittier also rated Lowell very high as a critic, seeing him, in this aspect, as Matthew Arnold's peer.

Longfellow was a more complicated case. Everything Whittier ever said about him was more than friendly, though the two were never close. He praised *The Seaside and the Fireside* as illustrating "the careful moulding by which art attains the graceful ease and chaste simplicity of nature." *Tales of a Wayside Inn* he thought as good as either Chaucer or Boccaccio, and the "Morituri Salutamus" was "a little sad, but full of 'sweetness and light.' " He wrote a poem in Longfellow's praise, "The Poet and the Children," and the letter he sent him upon his seventy-fifth and last birthday could hardly have been better:

> . . . I cannot let the occasion pass without expressing my gratitude for the happy hours I have spent over thy writings, and the pride which I share with all Americans in view of thy success as an author and thy character as a man. It is permitted to but few in this world to

reach a position so honorable as that which thee occupy or to enjoy so widely the love of their fellow men.[37]

Whittier's only extended published critique of Longfellow is that of *Evangeline,* which begins, "Eureka! Here, then, we have it at last,—an American poem, with the lack of which British reviewers have so long reproached us." [38] Though he had feared that the hexameters might create a problem, he thought their use justified by the event. Yet if I had been Longfellow, I am not sure that I should have felt flattered by the statement that "the story of *Evangeline* would have been quite as acceptable to the public taste had it been told in the poetic prose of the author's *Hyperion*."

I would not for a moment suggest that there was any insincerity in anything that Whittier felt or said about Longfellow, but I do think that he used the Cambridge poet, in his great popularity, as a kind of measuring-rod of what he wanted for himself. In 1850, as Joseph E. Ernest, Jr. has observed, he wrote Fields that a projected book would be about the length of a recent book of Longfellow's. In 1863 he inquired whether some one could not be found to write such a review of *In War Time* as George William Curtis had recently given *Tales of a Wayside Inn* (to which, incidentally, the idea of *The Tent on the Beach* may well have been indebted). Pleased with Underwood's study of Longfellow, he suggested that the author might follow it with studies of Lowell, Holmes, and himself. When he read Charlotte Fisk Bates's Longfellow anthology, he wished she could do the same for him, and when Longfellow's "Blue and Gold" edition appeared, he wanted one too. "Do not dream for an instant that I could be jealous of any good words for Longfellow," he wrote Paul Hamilton Hayne in 1880. "That would be too much like Dick when the cat gets noticed." But the very disclaimer shows that the idea had crossed his mind.

The great contemporary to whom Whittier felt closest personally was Oliver Wendell Holmes, who was also the only one of the group who outlived him. To Holmes he paid considered poetical tribute on his eightieth birthday and again in 1892, in what may well have been the last poem he ever wrote. Sometimes, to be sure, he had reservations even about Holmes. In 1849 he did not think "The Ballad of the Oysterman," "The Comet," and "The September Gale" quite in good taste. He told Elizabeth Lloyd that *Elsie Venner* "fascinates and repels me, like the evil influence of the snake it describes," and as late as 1867 he found "a one-sided exaggerated presentation of one of the 'mixed elements' of our strange natures" in *The Guardian Angel.* Ultimately, however, all reservations were swept aside. *The Autocrat of the Breakfast-Table* made Boston Common "henceforth classic ground." When Wyatt Eaton came to paint Whittier, and the poet learned that he was not painting Holmes too, he was shocked. "Why, Holmes is, in many respects, the greatest of us all." And when, in 1884, *The Critic* asked him for a birthday tribute, he declared that "if Dr. Holmes does not, at the present time, hold in popular estimation the first place in American literature, his rare versatility is the cause." Holmes's religious "liberalism" ran ahead of that of both Whittier and Harriet Beecher Stowe, but such was his personal charm and warmth that apparently neither of them was troubled.

One other poet, not commonly placed there, Whittier tried to elevate to "the front rank of the poets of his time"; this was Bayard Taylor. Indeed he once told Mrs. Fields that he loved Taylor so much that he could never bear to criticize his verses. The complete absence of reservation is a little surprising, for though Taylor had a Quaker inheritance, he was not himself a Quaker, and one might have thought there would be a good deal about him that must rub Whittier the wrong way.[39] He was very enthusiastic about *Deukalion* and about *Lars,* which he ranked with both *Evangeline* and *Hermann und Dorothea,* and he said that *The Story of Kennet* (which is certainly a very charming novel), contained "as good things as there are in the English language." He paid poetic tribute to Taylor in *The Tent on the Beach* and "The Last Walk in Autumn," and when the world traveler died, he sent a prose statement to be read at the memorial meeting in Tremont Temple.

Unfortunately for his reputation, Whittier failed to achieve a similar tolerance toward a poet whom posterity has chosen to remember as much as it has forgotten Taylor—Walt Whitman, and his coldness seems the more unfortunate in view of Whitman's always generous and admiring attitude toward him. Whether or not it is literally true that he burned his complimentary copy of *Leaves of Grass*, he omitted Whitman entirely from his anthology, *Songs of Three Centuries*, nor did he mention his poetry even when acknowledging eightieth birthday greetings. He did say a good word for Whitman's Civil War work and his "tribute" to Lincoln, but without specifying which poem he had in mind.

When he was asked to contribute to a fund to buy a horse and buggy for the lame Camden poet, Whittier complied but carefully stipulated that he was performing a work of charity, not expressing admiration for Whitman's poetry. To guard against misrepresentation, he even wrote a letter on the subject to the Boston *Transcript*, then apparently decided not to mail it. Later, when the *Herald* asked him to head a subscription list to buy a house for Whitman, he sent a contribution but refused his name, somewhat tartly commenting to Mrs. Fields that he had already had a share in buying Whitman a carriage, which was more than he had himself. Whitman regretted Whittier's attitude toward him, which he regarded as the fruit of misunderstanding, but did not blame him for it. "We would not travel well harnessed to the same rig." [40]

He was more generous to others with whom he had—or might easily have had—ideological differences, including the Georgia poet, Paul Hamilton Hayne, with whom he enjoyed a warm post-War friendship; he even rejoiced Hayne's heart by going back to praise "the laureate of the Confederacy," Henry Timrod, whose later poems he called "very powerful and impressive," "notwithstanding their hostility to my own section." "He had the true fire within." [41] Whittier encouraged a great variety of younger poets, some of whom, like Alice and Phoebe Cary, were almost protégées. He was very fond of Thomas Bailey Aldrich, and particularly of "Memory" and "Identity." [42] He considered Edmund Clarence Stedman's "Corda Concordia" "the best occasional poem of the last quarter of a century" and "The Discoverer" "one of the most striking and powerfully suggestive poems of our time," and he admired "The Fool's Prayer," by Edward Rowland Sill, though he thought it "not quite simple and natural" enough. He certainly showed considerable tolerance when he wrote of the eccentric Joaquin Miller that "I think his strong point is color, which is really wonderful to a drab Quaker like myself." He was tremendously enthusiastic about Julia Ward Howe's *Passion Flowers* in 1853 ("It is a great book—it has placed thee at the head of us all"), partly, perhaps, because of "its noble aims, its scorn and hate of priestcraft and Slavery." He told Fields that it was "really great," having "as many fine passages as Alex. Smith—and is truer, nobler in every way," and he also wrote Mary Russell Mitford in its praise. It seems odd, however, that he should have added, to Mrs. Howe herself, "I dare say it has faults enough, but thee need not fear on that account." [43]

Passing from poetry to fiction, Whittier wrote a paper about Brockden Brown's *Wieland*,[44] in which I think the author is overpraised, but this is my feeling about criticism of Brown in general. He also praised John Neal's *Rachel Dyer*. He must have read nearly all his noteworthy contemporaries, for he consumed vast quantities of fiction. He did not care for Cooper's "females" and, as we have seen, he thought his Indians much too Ossianic. Cooper lacked both "skill in metaphysical matters" and knowledge of the intricacies of the human heart. His strength lay in "description of outward and tangible matters"; to make a perfect novelist, this would have had to be coupled with Brown's "metaphysical and searching spirit." Whittier's hatred of slavery and his relish for a good story being what they were, it was inevitable that he should be enthralled by *Uncle Tom's Cabin*—

> What a glorious work Harriet Beecher Stowe has wrought! Thanks for the Fugitive Slave Law! Better for slavery that law had never been enacted, for it gave occasion for *Uncle Tom's Cabin*—

and his knowledge of early New England being what it was, it was equally inevitable that he should relish *Oldtown Folks*, but his favorite Stowe novel was *The Pearl of Orr's Island*[45]—"the most charming New England idyll ever written." So far as I know, Whittier criticized Mrs. Stowe only twice. He objected to her characteristic vagueness in time and place relations, writing Lowell after the *Atlantic* had begun serializing *The Minister's Wooing* that

> Mrs. Stowe's story opens admirably. I wish, however, she would give more local coloring and atmosphere to her picture, so that we may know what part of the world we are in, in what age, as respects costume etc. and what climate. In other respects the tale is very striking in its promise.

Later he resented the criticisms which were made of her after her defense of Lady Byron, but he also thought she ought not to have published it, probably because it shocked him to find a woman discussing such horrendous matters publicly.

There is no actual evidence of a meeting between Whittier and Mark Twain, though they were, of course, in the same room at the Whittier Seventieth Birthday Dinner. Joseph E. Ernest, Jr. speaks of an 1887 letter of Whittier's to Horace Currier in which he speaks of Mark Twain's books as if he had read them all. One of the oddest things about Whittier's literary references is that I have nowhere found any mention of Henry James. But he seems to have read all the novels which William Dean Howells published during his lifetime, even overcoming his dislike of serialization to devour them more quickly. *An Imperative Duty* interested him for its treatment of miscegenation ("I am anxious to see how he solves the terrible problem which socially as well as politically confronts us"), and he was fond of "that saint of the rather godless sect of dynamiters," Lindau, in *A Hazard of New Fortunes*. He liked Bret Harte when he met him in Boston, and does not seem to have resented his parody of "Maud Muller."[46]

Of the many women writers whom he encouraged in his later

years, Sarah Orne Jewett was, by all means, the finest. Mrs. Fields says that Whittier "was as fond" of her "as of a daughter, and from their earliest acquaintance his letters are filled with appreciation of her stories." In 1879 he wrote her that he had read *Deephaven,* then only two years old, "over half a dozen times, and always with gratitude to thee for such a book—so simple, pure, and so true to nature." In 1882 he wrote a charming poem "Godspeed" to her and Mrs. Fields when they sailed for Europe. Yet I am not sure that he himself would have placed her higher than Elizabeth Stuart Phelps. Though he admitted "peculiar mannerisms" even in such "a very admirable story" as "The Madonna of the Washtubs," he considered Miss Phelps "one of the few upon whom has been bestowed the mysterious and awful gift of genius, and the fewer still who strive to use that gift for the glory of the Giver and the welfare of men." When *Sealed Orders* was published, he told her that it was the finest collection of the kind "since Hawthorne's Twice Told Tales," adding that "morally and spiritually thine is far better than his."

Whittier recognized the gifts of both F. Marion Crawford and Margaret Deland at the very beginning of their careers. *Ramona,* by Helen Hunt Jackson, he found almost too powerful to bear. "I cannot now read such sad things with safety." He testified to his interest in George W. Cable by calling upon him and inviting him to Danvers when he came to Boston to read in 1883. Two years later he called him "a noble fellow—more than a genius—a true good man. Ten righteous men like him would save the South." In view of his enjoyment of popular fiction in general, his attitude toward *The Lamplighter* (1854) by Maria Cummins seems pernickety. "It vexes me," he wrote Lucy Larcom, "to see such a work . . . having such a run, when you cannot remember a single sentence or idea in it." On the other hand, he would seem absurdly to have overestimated Mrs. E. D. E. N. Southworth, one of the most successful of Hawthorne's "damned mob of scribbling women." Her first novel, *Retribution,* reminded him of *Jane Eyre* in its "strength and sustained intensity," but he thought it surpassed Charlotte Brontë in inculcating "an important moral lesson." Perhaps this should be discounted somewhat on the ground of Whittier's eagerness to encourage a brave and needy woman whom he knew and liked, and who, just then, needed all the encouragement she could get. Besides, as we have seen, the Brontës were always one of his blind spots.

II

The writing impulse was present with Whittier as early as it was with Bryant, though unlike Bryant he did not early produce works of high quality. He began scribbling verses on his slate, and at least one of the early pieces sheds considerable poignant light on the kind of boy he was:

And must I always swing the flail,
And help to fill the milking pail?
I wish to go away to school;
I do not wish to be a fool.

"At the age of twenty-five," says Mordell, "he had written and published more than had his idol Robert Burns at that age." [47]

Because he began writing before he had anything to say, he imitated everybody he read. His mother suggested "that he write of some striking event in the past that had come under his observation," but the only thing he could think of was the great wind storm of 1815. Nevertheless, it is clear that the desire for self-expression was irresistible, and in his unbookish milieu this is striking testimony that he had been made for his work. "I have had no leisure . . . for the polishing of my rhymes," he once wrote Fields, "I suppose under such circumstances I ought not to have made any, but *I could not help it.*"

Yet there were times when he disparaged poetry altogether. Once he calls even the imitation of nature "her mockery, Art." In 1830 he exclaims: "God forbid, that we should quarrel with Willis, for writing poetry, (thankless and unprofitable as the task, or pleasure of it, may be,) for we acknowledge, with due humility, that we have been foolish enough to attempt as much, ourself, for which sin we hope to be forgiven by the public." And ten years later he described his own early poems as

> Record of time misspent—of mind abused—
> Of God-given powers in Folly's service used!

But possibly he might not have felt that way if they had been better poems.

In 1870 he wrote L. D. Lewelling, who had sent him some verses:

> As regards poetry, let me here say that to make it the end and aim of life seems to me an unprofitable endeavor. I do not undervalue a literary reputation; but *it* alone can do little towards making any one happy. The literary life has great temptations.

Without seeing the verses and knowing what Whittier really thought of them it is difficult to tell just how much this should be discounted, and over against it we must place the fact that he probably encouraged more young writers than any other of the great New England literary figures. "More and more," he wrote Celia Thaxter in 1875, "I congratulate myself on my share in urging thee to 'exercise thy gift,' as we Friends say." But unless we are to take it as mere self-depreciation, what he wrote William Allinson in 1857, when Allinson named his son after him, cannot be similarly discounted: "I can only hope the newcomer may prove a better man than his namesake—cultivate his Jersey acres in peace and goodwill and never let himself turn to writing poetry." In 1884, too, he wrote to a correspondent in whose work he saw promise that he would "advise no young man to *depend* upon poetry. A profession or trade is needed: and brave work must be done in a world of need and suffering." And there is an 1878 letter in which he even declares: "For myself I regard good prose writing as really better than rhyme; at any rate I prefer to read it; and the public at large certainly do."

Whittier's poetic theory, so far as he had one, was determined by the interaction of his temperament and his convictions. He was "a dreamer born," whose "eye was beauty's powerless slave," but had he stopped there, he would not only have found himself ignoring the basic Quaker tenet that the only safe guide to life must be sought in the depths of the worshipper's own soul, illuminated by contact with the Supreme Light which is God, but he would also have been left open to the age-old Christian reproach of "worldliness." He was always sufficiently devoted to beauty to resent the charge that Friends—and Puritans generally—were hostile to it.

It has been the fashion of a class of shallow Church and State defenders to ridicule the great men of the Commonwealth, the sturdy republicans of England, as sour-featured, hard-hearted ascetics, enemies of fine arts and polite literature. The works of Milton and Marvell, the prose-poem of Harrington, and the admirable discourses of Algernon Sydney are a sufficient answer to this accusation.

And he tells his fellow Quakers that

If we are not free, generous, tolerant, if we are not up to or above the level of the age in good works, in culture and love of beauty, order and fitness, if we are not ready recipients of the truths of science and philosophy,—in a word, if we are not full-grown men and Christians, the fault is not in Quakerism, but in ourselves.

Does this mean, then, that Whittier saw beauty—and the creation of beauty in art—as an end in itself? For a time, under Coleridge's inspiration, he was tempted to believe just that, but this was not his permanent view. He never underestimated the power of the imagination. In the sense that he knew life would be a poor thing without it, he may even be said to have viewed it as a positive good. But it was still a good that might easily be perverted. What he really believed in was

Imagination, held in check
To serve, not rule, thy poisëd mind,

the kind of imagination that guided Bunyan when he wrote *The Pilgrim's Progress,* with "his powerful imagination . . . under the direction of reason and grace." When reason and grace were absent, imagination might easily lead to evil thoughts and feelings. "There would be a strong temptation attending the process of poetical composition to give imagination the legitimate place of truth; to make boldness and originality the primary objects at the expense of virtuous sentiment and religious feeling." This, in Whittier's view, was what happened with Byron and Shelley, and this is why, though recognizing their superior genius, he sometimes found them less satisfying reading than Mrs. Hemans or a dozen other ladies (he seems to have felt that women were somehow less subject to this temptation than men). So when Thomas Bailey Aldrich adversely criticized *Within the Gates*, Whittier, despite his affection for Aldrich and his own lifelong poetic striving, could write to its author, Elizabeth Stuart Phelps, "It is beyond A's range of vision. His feet are in the earth. He believes in Art."

He could not connect the idea of beauty with anything that was morally exceptionable.

> Beauty is goodness; ugliness is sin;
> Art's place is sacred; nothing foul therein
> May crawl or tread with brutal feet profane.[48]

Actually, in his eyes, beauty needed a double consecration. On the one hand, it must aspire toward "the beauty of holiness, of purity, of that inward grace which passeth show," and, on the other, it must embrace the consecration of duty, of service, and become "the bride of use." Whittier did not deny the legitimacy of love poetry, for example, but he did insist that it must concern itself with the spiritual being of the beloved and not get stranded on the shoal of what was merely the physical attraction of her person. In his view, to fail at this point was to tumble into the sentimentalism which had engulfed Moore, Willis, and other writers, and Whittier, who agreed with Meredith about feminism and comedy, was one with him again in his conviction that sentimentalism and sensualism sprang from the same root.

As to the moralism, there can be no question that for Whittier the primacy of righteousness was axiomatic. Sometimes, to be sure, he was inclined to feel that great poetry was an end in itself, though even then he insisted that minor poetry (like his own) must have an ethical justification:

Art's perfect forms no moral need,
  And beauty is its own excuse;
But for the dull and flowerless weed
Some healing virtue still must plead,
And the rough ore must find its honors in its use.[49]

But he did not keep to this. In *The Tent on the Beach*, the Traveller (Bayard Taylor) is made to admonish Whittier that

. . . Art no other sanction needs
  Than beauty for its own fair sake,

and that the "austere school" to which Whittier himself adheres has necessarily constrained his art, but the poet replies that this is better

Than bolder flights that know no check,

that

The liberal range of Art should be
The breadth of Christian liberty,

and that "the inward monitor" must be obeyed. In making selections for *Songs of Three Centuries*, though allowing "a large tolerance of personal individuality manifesting itself in widely varying forms of expression," Whittier still "somewhat scrupulously endeavored to avoid in my selections everything which seemed liable to the charge of irreverence or questionable morality," and in 1852 he was even willing to allow Elizabeth Nicolson and Enoch Lewis to alter some of his pieces in order to make them more Quakerly in an anthology intended for Friends:

I regret—and deeply too—all that I have written which is not in spirit and in the letter consistent with principles and testimonies which I love and regard as vital to the interests of humanity, and the cause not of Quakerism alone but of "pure religion and undefiled."[50]

"What avail great talents if they be not devoted to goodness?" "A long poem, unconsecrated to religion and humanity, would be a criminal waste of life." "The humblest follower of the meek and lowly Redeemer is more to be envied than a Voltaire, a Rousseau, or a Byron. . . ." These are typical utterances, and he would not, I think, have repudiated them at any period. It is not surprising, then, that he should have written Lydia Maria Child: "I read anything thee may write,—not only for its literary qualities, but because I know a true and noble woman stands behind it,"[51] or that, losing critical sense altogether, he should declare that "A Psalm of Life" was "worth more than all the dreams of Shelley, and Keats, and Wordsworth." Nor should it occasion surprise when he draws morals from nature (as in "The Lakeside") or tacks them on—I am deliberately stating his practice at its worst—at the end of a narrative or reflective poem (as in "The Legend of St. Mark" or "The Barefoot Boy").

Yet George Arms finds that Whittier was not essentially a didactic poet, citing as evidence "Proem" and the "Dedication" to *The Tent on the Beach*, and there is much to be said for this view. Whittier himself says that

> The chief defect of the poetry of Transcendentalism is that it is too philosophical. Its largest intent is ethical or religious and not artistic. Beauty is not its chief inspiration, but thought. . . . It is not written to please, but to convince. It contains a gospel and not an appeal to the imagination. . . . These poets are not singers, but preachers. . . .

And once he told Celia Thaxter that one of her poems was "too good, too preachy, like some of my sermons!" The moralizing in "The Barefoot Boy" is bad, not because moralizing itself is bad but because it is not integral; it does not grow out of the poem but is superimposed upon it.[52] In "Cassandra Southwick," on the other hand, Whittier solves the problem of moralizing, or, rather, transforms it into interpretation, through the use of the dramatic monologue. Nothing that Cassandra feels can be alien to the poem; even the otherwise objectionable unshaded and melodramatic presentation of the Puritan persecutors is justified by the fact that we view them only through the eyes of a girl who could hardly, at the moment, have been expected to be dispassionate about them. As a record of her experience, the theophanic moment which begins with

> Oh, at that hour the very earth seemed changed beneath my eye [53]

is quite at home in the poem, and it is completely natural that, having experienced it, she should break out into

> Thanksgiving to the Lord of life! to Him all praises be,

and all that follows. But if any of this had been presented as the *poet's* comments on the situation, it would have been intrusive, pietistic, and unconvincing.

Moreover, if Whittier's views about art inclined toward moralism, they also inclined toward realism. He excused his writing of "Amy Wentworth" in wartime on the ground that it provided a necessary relief for the terrible strains of the hour, but he could not have rested permanently content with that, for he was passionately devoted to art and duty alike, and no man can serve two masters unless their interests can be made one. Like Milton, Whittier wanted poetry to be simple, sensuous, and passionate. The reason he disliked metaphysical poetry was that he thought of it as not rooted in life but only in thought, and, for the most part, in thought derivative, unconnected with the poet's own living. At an early age, he felt the need of "Yankee pastorals" and set to work to supply them for the region he knew best. It was his view that natural beauty and human emotion were as accessible to Americans as to any other people. Thanksgiving, "apple-bees, huskings, berry pickings, summer picnics, and winter sleigh-rides," "school loves and friendships, courtings and match-making," and the universal "keen struggles of gain, the mad grasping of ambition,—sin and remorse, tearful repentance and jolly aspirations"—all this was poetic material quite as authentic as anything that was available to Homer.

Such materials could only be used effectively by him who should make himself "part and parcel" of the life he described.

This Whittier, at his best, clearly achieved. His imagination recaptured past experience—"the faded color of Time's tapestry"—and revealed the beauty of common things, and it is this achievement upon which his claim to a place in American poetry must finally rest. He did not close his eyes to ugliness. If *Snow-Bound* is the great idyll of New England farm life, the remarkable "Prelude" to "Among the Hills," with its "bookless, pictureless" interiors, inhabited by

> Shrill, querulous women, sour and sullen men,
> Untidy, loveless, old before their time,
> With scarce a human interest save their own
> Monotonous round of small economies,
> Or the poor scandal of the neighborhood,

anticipates by many years what Hamlin Garland was to do for a Midwestern locale in *Main-Travelled Roads*. Yet *Snow-Bound* remains, for Whittier, a greater achievement than "Among the Hills," because, like Robert Frost, he was at heart the kind of realist who liked his potato "brushed clean." He did not have to offer "a good deal of dirt with his potato to show that it is a real potato."

Desmond Powell, then, was mistaken when he wrote that Whittier thought of art as an escape from life. "He believed poetry should be something plaintive and sweet," writes Powell, "which would charm the world away from its memory of bitter things. That is why he so loved Spenser and Sidney, who live apart in a dream world of their own." [54] But he didn't particularly, and even if he had done so, Mr. Powell's case would not be greatly strengthened, for his is an excellent statement of what Spenser and Sidney did not do. For all that, Whittier could hardly ever stand, in a gallery of "representative men" as "The Poet." As the Emerson whom he so much admired wished to be no "writer" but a "man writing," so he insisted upon being a man and not a mere verse-maker. Hyatt H. Waggoner exaggerates somewhat, but his exaggeration is helpful and illuminating, when he writes:

With at least a part of his mind Whittier did not finally believe in poetry. His work aspires, Quaker-like, to silence. His attitude toward poetry was as ambivalent as his attitude toward nature: could nature be trusted to lead us to God, could words be trusted to communicate? ... His profound distrust of the "cumberings" of form and creed in religion is parallel with and related to his distrust of the symbol in poetry.[55]

III

Whittier once said, "Everything is labor to me. I don't know any easy writing," but the facts hardly bear this out, for he had tremendous facility; indeed his poems might well have been better if they had not come to him quite so easily. It was his opinion that occasional verse was fatal to everybody except Dr. Holmes —apparently he himself was asked to write a poem for the death of Longfellow and found it impossible to do so—but he seems to have been able to scribble occasional verses for his friends and letters in verse almost *ad infinitum*, and the reader of the section called "Whittier's Uncollected Poems" in S. T. Pickard's *Whittier-Land* can hardly be expected to avoid feeling that Whittier could write something on any subject at any time.[56]

Frances Sparhawk, who knew Whittier well, says that he always had to think with a pen in his hand and that he often saw the persons and places he wrote about before him while he wrote. It is certainly true that his imagination was more visual than aural. When he was asked to write some verses for a Colorado bas-relief representing the last Indian and the last bison, he said that he could not see the work in its setting clearly enough to be able to do this, but when his attention was directed to a photograph he possessed of "The Lion of Lucerne," he was able to produce the quatrain without difficulty. Yet it is clear that he sometimes composed orally, saying his lines aloud as they came to him, and afterwards writing them down, in an almost illegible script, on old scraps of paper, the backs of letters, and even the margins and fly leaves of books. Robert Rantoul reports Whittier's having told him that "in the white heat of literary production, words failed him to such an extent that he was sometimes in terror lest the vision he saw so clearly should vanish before it could be fixed on paper." Fortunately he had great power of concentration and could write without difficulty in a family group.[57] Once at least, a poem, "What of the Day?" "came" to him with such suddenness that he himself did not understand it.

> I wrote that poem two years before the Civil War broke out. I was in my garden one morning, when I dropped my hoe and went to my desk and wrote it. I read it over several times and said, "What does it mean?" I opened my drawer and put it out of my sight, and there it remained for two years, when I published it.

"Laus Deo," too, represented James's "suddenly determined absolute of perception," for Whittier conceived the entire poem one morning in meeting, and he had only to set down the lines after returning home, and "Barbara Frietchie" was written immediately after Mrs. Southworth had related to him the incident upon which it was based. On the other hand, "Skipper Ireson's Ride" had a phenomenally long period of gestation: Whittier heard the story in 1828, tried to write it and failed, and did not produce the ballad we know until a generation afterwards.

Whittier's use of oral tradition was acknowledged in the introduction to *Snow-Bound*, and his narrative poems derive from many tales of many lands. In 1832 he wrote Sarah Josepha Hale:

> There is a fine opening now for a spiritual novel-writer—one who will take an original path and maintain it—I do not think myself competent for it now—but I have an idea of publishing a series of sketches in the manner of Irving's—distinct enough however from him in style—sketches which shall illustrate some of the superstitions and peculiarities of our New Englanders—some of a grave and some of a lighter character.

Just what he had in mind when he wrote this letter it would be hard to say, for this would seem to be exactly what he *had* done in his *Legends of New England*, published the previous year. Except, of course, that that work had contained little "of a lighter character," nor was its tone quite so detached or scholarly as this letter would suggest. The truth of the matter seems to have been that at the outset, the Quaker poet, like the Fat Boy in *Pickwick*, wanted to make the flesh crawl, and he evidently enjoyed the crawling sensation in his own flesh also. His early work abounds in violence and garish supernaturalism, as in these passages from "Lines Written on Visiting a Singular Cave in Chester, N.H., Known in the Vicinity by the Name of 'The Devil's Den' ":

'Tis said that this cave is an evil place–
The chosen haunt of the fallen race;
That the midnight traveler oft hath seen
A red flame tremble its jaws between,
And lighten and quiver the boughs among,
Like the fiery play of a serpent's tongue;
That sounds of fear from its chambers swell–
The ghostly gibber, the fiendish yell;
That bodiless hands at its entrance wave,–
And hence they have named it THE DEMON'S CAVE!

Yet is there something to fancy dear
In this silent cave and its lingering fear,–
Something which tells of another age,
Of the wizard's wand, and the Sybil's page,
Of the fairy ring and the haunted glen,
And the restless phantoms of murder'd men,
The grandame's tale and the nurse's song,
The dreams of childhood remember'd long;
And I love even now to list the tale
Of the Demon's Cave, and its haunted vale.

Fortunately for his reputation, Whittier did not long continue to write such verses, but vestiges of his early Gothicism still clung to him. He did not quite approve of his own treatment of a heartbreaking local tragedy in "Suicide Pond," yet at one time the inclusion of this very morbid poem in his collected works was seriously considered. In 1873 he was much interested in the double murder at the Isles of Shoals which his friend Celia Thaxter wrote up.[58]

What a strange, wonderful story it is! The imagination of man never conceived anything more dreadful than its grim reality. What a weird, awful interest will for all time invest that island! It will be haunted by those murdered women; and in future midnights the light of Wagner's lantern will glimmer along the shore in search of another victim.

Along this same line, William Stetson Merrill tells of an amusing encounter with Whittier on a camping trip. When the old poet spied a hunting knife in the belt of one of Merrill's young companions, he asked to see it. "This reminds me of the knives the Norwegians are said to use when they fight duels. The two men are tied together around the waist. Knives are given them and they slash at each other." The boys, who did not know that he had just read a description of such a fight in Bayard Taylor's *Lars*, were somewhat shocked and amused at "a poet and a Quaker" choosing this to say to them at their only meeting.

The pieces included under the heading "Narrative and Legendary Poems" in Whittier's collected works are laced with references to legends of many lands, derived from reading and from oral tradition, and woven together into a seamless robe that was all the poet's own. It would be difficult to find a more disarming combination of literary sophistication with innocent wide-eyed wonder than is afforded by that fine ballad, "The Double-Headed Snake of Newbury":

Cotton Mather came galloping down
All the way to Newbury town,
With his eyes agog and his ears set wide,
And his marvellous inkhorn at his side;
Stirring the while in the shallow pool
Of his brains for the lore he learned at school,
To garnish the story, with here a streak
Of Latin, and there another of Greek:
And the tales he heard and the notes he took,
Behold! are they not in his Wonder-Book?

Stories, like dragons, are hard to kill.
If the snake does not, the tale runs still
In Byfield Meadows, on Pipestave Hill.
And still, whenever husband and wife
Publish the shame of their daily strife,

And with mad cross-purpose, tug and strain
At either end of the marriage-chain,
The gossips say, with a knowing shake
Of their gray heads, "Look at the Double Snake!
One in body and two in will,
And Amphisbaena is living still!"

By this time, too, Whittier had come to feel that legendry was valuable as a kind of antidote to the growing materialism of the world around him. "I am glad thee are working in the line of these old stories," he wrote a correspondent in 1889. "We need them all in this matter of fact age."

The sources, as has already been suggested, were manifold. In fact, literary sources often turn up even for that which would seem to have been most deeply rooted in his own experience. Obviously the title of "Ichabod" derives from the Bible, but Whittier may also have been inspired by Lowell's query in the *National Anti-Slavery Standard:* "Shall not the Recording Angel write *Ichabod* after the name of this man in the great book of Doom?" and a literary source has even been suggested for "The Barefoot Boy."[59] Washington Irving's miscellanies and John G. C. Brainard's collection of Connecticut traditions certainly influenced *Legends of New England;* Brainard is quoted on the title page. Cecil B. Williams's account of the sources of *Margaret Smith's Journal* and the use Whittier made of them is comparable in its way to Walter Blair's study of *Huckleberry Finn* and Albert Morton Turner's of *The Cloister and the Hearth.*[60]

Not infrequently Whittier even echoes his reading in phraseology, drawing freely upon contemporary literature, among other sources, and the writings of the men he knew.

The clustered spires of Frederick stand
Green-walled by the hills of Maryland

in "Barbara Frietchie" was clearly derived from "My Hunt after the Captain," by Oliver Wendell Holmes, which had appeared in *The Atlantic Monthly* as recently as December 1862. "The last bud on thy household tree" in "Daniel Wheeler" would seem to come from "The Last Leaf," and "Oh, tear the gorgeous emblem down" in "The New Year" is very close to "Ay, tear her tattered ensign down" in "Old Ironsides." The title "An Artist of the Beautiful" differs from that of one of Hawthorne's stories only in the first article, and "The Wife" was certainly suggested by Irving's piece of that title in *The Sketch-Book.* The uncollected "Job III, 19"[61] is from "Thanatopsis," and Bryant's "Bright visions! I mixed with the world, and ye faded" would seem to be echoed in "The Willows." I raise no question as to Whittier's "right" to do such things, but in view of the rabid accusations which Poe and others have brought against Longfellow for his alleged borrowings, it seems surprising that he should have escaped so lightly.[62]

It was well that Whittier should put his historical and legendary poems together, for historical accuracy was never his long suit. I think this is true even if we leave out such controversial cases as "Barbara Frietchie" and "The King's Missive"[63] and those which come under such headings as poetical license or misinformation.[64] Thus, Whittier would seem to have slandered Moll Pitcher in the long early poem he wrote about her.[65] In "The Pennsylvania Pilgrim" he calls Tobias Schumberg "Schurmberg," and in "Cassandra Southwick" he gives his heroine her mother's Christian name; her own was "Provided."[66] Barrett Wendell quotes the introductory note to "Skipper Ireson's Ride," in which Whittier admits not having "done full justice to the memory of poor Floyd Iresome," and then "proceeds to reprint his ballad."[67] This does show a rather cavalier attitude toward historical accuracy, but perhaps it also shows that Whittier honored the claims of the imagination more than he himself always realized. We have already seen that he did not get his own ancestry quite right, and Whitman Bennett remarks of the *Legends of New England* that

> It is amusing to note that he is not absolutely accurate as to his facts, even when he names the two Indians who first appeared at Plymouth in the spring of 1621, being just half right and half wrong, for all through life he had the habit of never being quite exact, twisting the facts of legends or events he commemorated. In his preface, he says

that he shall have accomplished his purpose if the book inspires further investigation and recording of New England antiquities, which have been sadly neglected. And here again he is not quite right, for [Samuel G.] Drake and [Charles W.] Upham had already begun their researches and publications.

In spite of all this, the past was very important to Whittier. He makes "The Norseman" say, "My thoughts are with the Past alone!" and "The Knight of St. John" adds:

My soul is in the past, and life
To-day is but a dream!

Whittier's own thoughts were seldom with the past "alone" however. What he does, characteristically, is to blend past and present, near and far, sometimes piling literary allusions one on top of another in the process:

With such a look Herodias read
The features of the bleeding head,
So looked the mad Moor on his dead,
Or the young Cenci as she stood
O'erdabbled with a father's blood!

"Skipper Ireson's Ride" is crammed with such allusions, and some of them are very recondite.[68] There is much of this kind of thing even in the anti-slavery poems, for example "The Relic," "The World's Convention," "The Branded Hand," and "Mithridates at Chios." In "The Hive at Gettysburg" Samson's riddle blends with the Civil War. Surely only a phenomenally unobservant reader could ever have supposed that Whittier did not care much for literature or that his mind was not steeped in it! Even in describing his own experience he can draw on legendry:

We have had a dim and dreary spring—a gray haze in the sky—a dim, beam-shorn sun—a wind from the northeast, cold as if sifted through all the ices of frozen Labrador, as terrible almost as that chill wind which the old Moslem fable says will blow over the earth in the last days.

At the same time he will draw upon the novels he has been reading:

I am forbidden to use my poor head at present—so I have to get along as I can without it. St. Leon, as thee knows, walked about as usual after his head was cut off.

Put it in type or on the fire, I am content, like Eugene Aram, "prepared for either fortune."

But none of this means that he idealized the past. He did not idealize even Bible times:

"O friend! we need nor rock nor sand,
Nor storied stream of Morning-Land;
The heavens are glassed in Merrimac,—
What more could Jordan render back?

"We lack but open eye and ear
To find the Orient's marvels here;
The still small voice in autumn's hush,
Yon maple wood the burning bush."[69]

What he always realized is that it is very important not to permit yourself to become imprisoned in your own time. Sometimes he blends Christianity and paganism, as when he tells Celia Thaxter that it is her "kismet" to write about the Isles of Shoals. Sometimes, like the Pennsylvania Pilgrim, he merely wants to get the best of two worlds together:

For well he loved his boyhood's brother band;
His Memory, while he trod the New World's strand,
A double-ganger walked the Fatherland!

If, when on frosty Christmas eves the light
Shone on his quiet hearth, he missed the sight
Of Yule-log, Tree, and Christ-child all in white;

And closed his eyes, and listened to the sweet
Old wait-songs sounding down his native street,
And watched again the dancers' mingling feet;

Yet not the less, when once the vision passed,
He held the plain and sober maxims fast
Of the dear Friends with whom his lot was cast.

Sometimes, too, as in "The Dole of Jarl Thorkell," he makes the old materials teach Christian—and Quaker—principles:

The gods are what you make them,
  As earth shall Asgard prove;
And hate will come of hating,
  And love will come of love.

And sometimes, as in "The Brewing of Soma," his musing over pagan materials may even give occasion for one of the great lyrical utterances of the Christian world:

And yet the past comes round again,
  And new doth old fulfil;
In sensual transports wild as vain
We brew in many a Christian fane
  The heathen Soma still!

Dear Lord and Father of mankind,
  Forgive our foolish ways!
Reclothe us in our rightful mind,
In purer lives Thy service find,
  In deeper reverence, praise.

IV

Whittier never pretended to be a good judge of either his own poetry or that of others. In his journalistic writings he praised some perfectly terrible verses, but this is no matter. All reviewers do it; even Poe did it at times. Whittier had little faith in critical standards or systems and little taste for "close reading." For him reading a poem was an act of communion between the soul of the reader and the soul of the poet, and in criticism as in religion he championed the right of private judgment.

As Gay Wilson Allen has noted,[70] there is hardly a word about prosody in all Whittier's critical writing. In his own work the octosyllabic four-stress iambic line dominates, but Allen also comments on his use of iambic pentameter, seven-stress verse, and anapaests. Allen finds Whittier's rhythms simple and does not think his ear good enough to permit him to be influenced by the poetical passages in the Old Testament, which the King James Bible prints as prose. Despite what has been said elsewhere of his color blindness, John B. Pickard finds that his color imagery was predominantly green, gold, and red, and that red, which is usually applied to images of war and destruction, is the only color which admits variations. Gold indicates "abundance and fullness, as sunsets, flowers, fields, and crops." [71]

It is probably not necessary to state that Whittier is not often considered a master of prosody. Most frequently he is attacked for his bad rhymes. Certainly this, in "Moll Pitcher," comes under the heading of rhymes which are so bad that they are good:

> Alas—the quiet sepulchre
> Than such a state were welcomer.

Yet Whittier has not lacked distinguished defenders, and practically all sensitive critics are agreed that much too much has been made of his bad rhymes. Kathryn Anderson McEuen points out,[72] among many other things, that many of his rhymes could be justified by reference to New England dialectal practice.[73] Whittier himself anticipated this view when he wrote Fields:

> See what thy good nature in sending me a proof has come to. I yield the rhyme of *martyr* and *water* to please thee; but reluctantly, for it is no time now to give up our Yankee rights of pronunciation. I should be hung for my bad rhymes anywhere south of Mason and Dixon's line. My "speech bewrayeth me."

But perhaps Carroll Wilson found a more rewarding approach when he wrote in his review of the Quynns book, *Barbara Frietschie:* [74] "Let the modern poetasters study the way Whittier shifts (I suspect quite unconsciously) his metrical feet in "Barbara Frietchie" for emphasis and variety, and they will learn how great *simple* poems are constructed."

Whittier often spoke disparagingly of his work:

> I am not a builder in the sense of Milton's phrase of one who could "build the lofty rhyme." My vehicles have been of the humbler sort—merely the farm wagon and buckboard of verse, and not likely to run so long as Dr. Holmes's "One Hoss Shay." . . . I shall not dare to warrant any of my work for a long drive.

In 1883 he wrote Underwood: "It is safe to say that there are now in the United States ten thousand boys and girls who can write better verses than mine at their age."

His most extended commentary upon himself as a poet is in the "Proem" of 1847 which stands at the beginning of his collected verse. He begins by paying homage to the great poets of England's past:

> I love the old melodious lays
> Which softly melt the ages through,
> The songs of Spenser's golden days,
> Arcadian Sidney's silvery phrase,
> Sprinkling our noon of time with freshest morning dew.

Such poetry, however, is beyond his capacity, and he tries to reason out why and at the same time to define his limitations:

> The rigor of a frozen clime,
> The harshness of an untaught ear,
> The jarring words of one whose rhyme
> Beat often Labor's hurried time,
> Or Duty's march through storm and strife are here.
>
> Of mystic beauty, dreamy grace,
> No rounded art the lack supplies;
> Unskilled the subtle lines to trace,
> Or softer shades of Nature's face,
> I view her common forms with unanointed eyes.

In these suggestions there is some justice, but when he goes on to deny himself power of penetration and interpretation, he is as wide of the mark as William Morris was when thinking of himself as "the idle singer of an empty day":

Nor mine the seer-like power to show
The secrets of the heart and mind;
To drop the plummet-line below
Our common world of joy and woe,
A more intense despair or brighter hope to find.

He ends by accepting his lot and consecrating such gifts as he possesses to poetry and to what lies beyond poetry:

O Freedom! if to me belong
Nor mighty Milton's gift divine,
Nor Marvell's wit and graceful song,
Still with a love as deep and strong
As theirs, I lay, like them, my best gifts on Thy shrine!

Sometimes Whittier achieved a fair evaluation of his own work, as when, sending "At Last" to the *Atlantic*, he wrote Aldrich: "As the expression of my deepest religious feeling it may not be without interest, and it may help some inquiring spirit. Apart from this, I think I have succeeded in giving it a form not unworthy of the theme." On the other hand, "Skipper Ireson's Ride" pleased him more in "the spirit" than "the execution." His judgment of his masterpiece *Snow-Bound* [75] was very uncertain; he wrote Lucy Larcom that he had had misgivings about it even while it was in press. It seems to have been his opinion that "The Pennsylvania Pilgrim" was superior to *Snow-Bound* (which is a comprehensible judgment, though not a just one), but at one time he apparently preferred even so mediocre a work as *The Tent on the Beach,* though fortunately he did not adhere to this view. Once, at least, he thought "The Pageant" a "more artistic" "snow picture" than *Snow-Bound*, and sometimes he seems to have rated the ballads more highly. But the most interesting point is the way in which Whittier both acknowledged his limitations and accepted them, as every man must do who does not wish to run mad. We have already heard this note sounded at the end of "Proem," but it sounds more clearly elsewhere.[76] "I have just sent a poem ["Rabbi Ishmael"] to the *Atlantic* which perhaps nobody will like. But I do and that is enough, as I wrote it to free my mind." And what are we to make of his 1883 letter to Underwood?

I am grateful for thy generous estimate of my writings . . . but I fear the critics will not agree with thee. Why not anticipate them, and own up to the faults and limitations which everybody sees, and none more clearly than myself? Touch upon my false rhymes, and Yankeeisms: confess that I sometimes "crack the voice of Melody, and break the legs of Time." Pitch into Mogg Megone. That "big Injun" strutting around in Walter Scott's plaid, has no friends and deserves none. Own that I sometimes choose unpoetical themes. Endorse Lowell's *Fable for Critics* that I mistake occasionally, simple excitement for inspiration. In this way we can take the wind out of the sails of our ill-natured cavillers. I am not one of the master singers and don't wish to pose as one. By the grace of God I am only what I am, and don't wish to pass for more.

There is genuine modesty here and, toward Lowell, an admirable lack of resentment of criticism. But can we honestly deny that there is also a touch of policy? and even, at the end, of self-satisfaction?

Whatever technical shortcomings Whittier's poems may have had, their defects were not due to carelessness. He tinkered with them endlessly, and when others sent poems to him for examination, he tinkered with these too. He often altered his own poems even after they had gone to the publisher. It is true that he did not, like some writers, revise his early work in later years; all he asked for this was that it should be forgotten. When Albert Le Roy Bartlett, writing the history of Haverhill Academy, asked him whether he could furnish him a copy of the dedicatory ode he had written for the opening exercises, he replied, "No, and I hope you'll not be able to find it either." [77] He was very much annoyed, too, when Underwood tried to dig up early poems in preparation for his study of 1883, complaining to Pickard that such methods would rob the book of "all dignity and decency," and threatening that if Underwood did not come to his senses, he would put a stop to his enterprise altogether. He once told Celia Thaxter that half his poems were too long, "and yet I can't see well what to omit," and even in the introduction to the 1887 edition he declared that, though he was not unmindful of the "occasional prosaic lines and verbal infelicities contained in them," he had "at this late day . . . neither strength nor patience to undertake their correction."

But while a poem was still fresh, and he still carried it in his mind and believed in it, he could not bear to let it go. Sometimes he even begged Fields not to let him see another proof, for fear he might not be able to let well enough alone. But he was also capable of suggesting that the first printing of *Songs of Labor* be kept small, "as I fear that there are some few verbal errors, which I would like to set right." Whittier knew that he was a nuisance to his publisher in this connection. "I am ashamed of my habit of troubling thee with such matters," he writes Fields. "I presume on thy patience, which exceeds Job's. What if Satan had made the old patriarch a publisher at the mercy of importunate authors male and female?" Between periodical publication and book publication he expanded the main section of "Among the Hills" from forty-two stanzas to eighty-six, but it cannot be claimed that he always had such brilliant success as in "Our Master," where "O Love of God, forever full" first became "O boon of Love, forever full," not arriving until the third try at the inevitable "Immortal Love, forever full." He was once foolish enough to change "Pulse o' the midnight, beating slow," to the much more commonplace "Like the night's pulse, beating slow." Apparently he was much more eye-minded than ear-minded in making his revisions. Sending *The Tent on the Beach* to Fields, he says, "I shall make it better if I can get it in type." In later years an Amesbury printer, Fred Brown, used to set up his poems for him before he submitted them to his publisher.

Not all the changes made at the suggestion of others were bad, however. He always deferred to his sister's advice while she was alive—"when it is agreeable to my wishes," as he says slyly—and after she was gone, he missed her "fine taste and judgment." Once, in 1877, he was emended, brilliantly, he thought, by no less a personage than James G. Blaine. But in general he depended upon his editors, especially James T. Fields. From him he invited suggestions; once he even sent him a poem with alternate endings between which Fields was to choose. He received suggestions from Lowell, too, when he was editing the *Atlantic*, but both Howells and Aldrich were too much in awe of their venerable contributor to express anything but gratitude. In all cases, however, Whittier reserved his right to reject suggestions and exercised it freely. It can hardly be claimed that he was much help to Horace E. Scudder when the "Riverside Edition" was in preparation. In his eyes, chronological order was "of small consequence," and when Scudder asked for the dates of composition of thirty poems, he furnished twenty, out of which fourteen were wrong! He told Scudder that "The Fish I Didn't Catch" appeared in *The Little Pilgrim* in 1843, whereas it was really written for *Our Young Folks* in 1865, and once, in reply to a question whether he could date a certain poem, he replied, "I cannot. It must be 1671 or 1672"! [78]

It hurt Whittier to be overpraised, for the same reason that it hurt him to be criticized: he did not like to be made to appear ridiculous. This is why, like Willa Cather at a later date, he wished to suppress his early work. Once he wrote a letter to W. L. Dempster, asking him to reply to a criticism which had appeared in the press. "It is only when they are blamed or praised," he wrote Fields, "that we fully realize how much we love these bantlings of ours." Once he unintentionally made himself absurd by vigorously applauding an unrecognized quotation from one of his poems in a public address. He was always grateful to E. P. Whipple as the first important critic to praise him warmly: "although I was partly conscious of what in me lay, thy assurance gave me courage to go on with my work." [79] And Julius Atwood says that he once expressed pleasure that his early political ambitions had not been realized—"for now I should be only a miserable politician"—which is hardly the statement of a man who feels that he has been unsuccessful in his life's work. "I am old enough to be done with work," he wrote Elizabeth Stuart Phelps touchingly in 1880, "only that I feel that my best words have not been said after all, and that what has been said is not its full expression." And the same year, in a letter to Paul Hamilton Hayne, he accepted his vocation, with all its glory and pain: "The poetical temperament has its trials and keen susceptibility to the hard, harsh, and unlovely things of life; but, my dear friend, we have also a capacity for enjoyment which others do not know. . . ."

CHAPTER FOUR

THE ALMOST PERFECT PACIFIST

I

The Christianity of Jesus Christ was a pacifist religion and up to the time of Constantine the Church knew it. Since then Christians have tried to forget it, but George Fox, who, in seventeenth-century England, founded the Society of Friends, did not forget it. He and his followers not only refused military service but tried to find a way of life that should "take away the occasion of wars." Since Quakerism is not an authoritarian religion, and since its whole sanction rests upon the Inner Light which is the God-illumination within every man, no Quaker is constrained to be a pacifist, and in every generation there have been those within the fold who have broken away from Fox's teaching. But the anti-war testimony of the Society as a whole has never been seriously undermined. Even in the face of the frightful pressures toward conformity which exist in a modern industrialized society in wartime, it still stands firm.

It should not be surprising, therefore, to find the Quaker Whittier taking a strong anti-war stand, and this is what he always intended to do. He says it in "In the Evil Days":

Not mine Sedition's trumpet-blast
  And threatening word;
I read the lesson of the Past,
That firm endurance wins at last
  More than the sword.

He says it in "Burial of Barber":

Well to suffer is divine;
Pass the watchword down the line,
  Pass the countersign: "Endure."
Not to him who rashly dares,
But to him who nobly bears,
  Is the victor's garland sure.

And he says it yet again in "The Quaker Alumni":

No honors of war to our worthies belong;
Their plain stem of life never flowered into song;
But the fountains they opened still gush by the way,
And the world for their healing is better to-day.

Though he once told Howells that he sympathized with Tolstoy's non-resistance principles, Whittier was never, by any proper definition, a non-resistant, for he was a lifelong crusader against social evil, but he did differentiate clearly between those weapons which were lawful for a Christian's handling and those that were not.

In God's own might
We gird us for the coming fight,
And, strong in him, whose cause is ours
In conflict with unholy powers,
We grasp the weapons He has given,—
The Light, the Truth, and Love of Heaven.[1]

He excoriated the motto "My country right or wrong," and felt that even the Crusaders fought not for Christ but for earthly pride. He excluded war poems from his anthology *Songs of Three Centuries*, though he compromised on "The Battle-Hymn of the Republic." He called Ethan Allen "a rash, profane, and intemperate man," outstanding only for animal courage. One of his early editorials questioned the need for West Point. He discussed military drill in some detail in "The Training" and military men as candidates for public office in "The Little Tin Soldier." At an Anti-Slavery Society convention in 1838 he took the extreme pacifist position by introducing a resolution (which failed to carry by a narrow majority) urging anti-slavery workers not to resist personal violence. He praised the bloodless Swiss revolution of 1308 and lauded Daniel O'Connell for his pacific ideals and methods in Ireland and for his declaration that "the best revolution which was ever effected could not be worth one drop of human blood." In both "The Exiles" and "Barclay of Ury" a Quaker is made to refuse being defended by violence. In "Skipper Ireson's Ride" violence gives Whittier one of his best subjects, but though he took full advantage of the color and excitement it afforded, violence itself is not glorified. Nor is its collapse and abandonment at the end of the poem merely negative; it proceeds from true humanity and a real appreciation of the spiritual meanings of the situation.

Yet there have always been those who felt that Whittier's temperament did not match his convictions. Two men of genius are among those who have taken this position. Hawthorne described him as "a fiery Quaker youth to whom the Muse has perversely assigned a battle-trumpet," while Whitman spoke of his "outcropping love of heroism and war, for all his Quakerdom, his verses at times like the measur'd step of Cromwell's old veterans." And since Whittier himself says that "without intending any disparagement of my peaceable ancestry for many generations, I have still strong suspicions that somewhat of the old Norman blood, something of the firm Berserker spirit, has been bequeathed to me," he must in some measure have agreed with them.

For that matter, he had, in a small way, his military forebears too, and alongside his peace poems there are others which can stir the blood with martial ardor. Not much stress should be placed upon such early efforts as "The Song of the Vermonters, 1779," which he published anonymously and later repudiated,[2] and "Judith at the Tent of Holofernes," which contains no word implying reprobation for the heroine's bloody and savage deed, but what are we to say about the martial imagery and spirit shown in such poems as "St. John" (1841), "The Pine Tree" (1846), "To Ronge" (1846), "Derne" (1850), and "The Pipes at Lucknow" (1858)? What is to be said of "The Prisoner for Debt" (1849), in which the unfortunate man seems to derive an additional claim from the fact that he has been a soldier? And, above all, of the Civil War ballad, "Barbara Frietchie," which Winston Churchill recited in its entirety while he and Franklin Delano Roosevelt rode through Frederick?

Whittier wrote a poem for the centenary of the Battle of Lexington but managed very skillfully not to make it an overt glorification of war.

> They went where duty seemed to call,
> They scarcely asked the reason why;
> They only knew they could but die,
> And death was not the worst of all.

But he refused to produce another poem when the Bunker Hill anniversary arrived: "I stretched my Quakerism to the full strength of its drab in writing about the Lexington folks who were shot and did not shoot back. I cannot say anything about those who *did* shoot to some purpose on Bunker Hill."[3] And when he was asked to celebrate the hundredth anniversary of the Battle of Bennington he replied: "As a member of the Friends' Society I could not write a poem of the kind consistently with my peace principles, without putting in a disclaimer which would spoil it for such an occasion."

In spite of his peace principles, however, he seems never to have had any doubts about the justice of the Revolutionary cause. In the *Essex Gazette* of 1830 he speaks of the Union as "a bond cemented by the blood which was poured out like water in the tremendous sacrifice of the Revolution" and praises Yankee and Southerner alike for their services. He glorified Washington in "The Sycamores" and winced when he heard him called a slave holder. In "The Landmarks," which was written to help save the Old South Church from demolition, he praises the contribution to the Revolution which had been made there. His early (1827) poem on "The Execution of Louis XVI" even glorifies that monarch for French services in the war. Whittier had a very warm feeling for the colonial period in general, and in spite of the persecution of Quakers by the men of the Massachusetts Bay Colony, he felt an allegiance to Puritans which even jumped the ocean. Though he rejected Carlyle's glorification of Cromwell, he quotes Marvell's ode to him admiringly, and he seems consistently to assume that in the English Civil Wars, the Roundheads were fighting God's battle. In one passage he even calls King Charles II "effeminate," which is one accusation I should think that lusty monarch might have been spared.

But the Revolutionary War was not a war situation Whittier had to face. The Mexican War was, and he had no problem here, for the Mexican War was a war for slavery, and he would have been against it even if he had not been opposed to war as such.

> Our armies are pushing their way into the heart of Mexico. The land before them is consecrated to personal freedom; behind them they leave slavery;—the clank of chains mingles with the music of their march: the *plaza* of every conquered Mexican village becomes a market-place for human flesh;—whip-driven slave gangs take the place of free laborers, whose blood, shed in defence of home and liberty, moistens the corn and cotton fields of Tamaulipas. All wars are wicked—but in the name of humanity, what shall we say of wars for Slavery? [4]

Under the pseudonym José de Santillo Whittier even wrote a battle hymn for the Mexicans, and Garrison printed it in *The Liberator*.

II

The real test of Whittier's pacifism came with the Civil War. For this, as he saw it, was a war to end slavery, and the abolition of slavery had been the whole end and aim of his reforming activities. He had written campaign songs for the Kansas emigrants.

Like Harriet Beecher Stowe, he had even believed crazy nonsense about Southerners using skulls for drinking bowls.[5] Now, if the North won the war, there was a good chance that a few years might see the end of all this anguish, but if the South won, the "peculiar institution" would be entrenched for as long as anybody could foresee.

Whittier had always tried to draw a distinction between acquiescence in wrong and resistance by immoral means.

Give us grace to keep
Our faith and patience; wherefore should we leap
On the one hand into fratricidal fight,
Or, on the other, yield eternal right,
Frame lies of law, and good and ill confound.[6]

In a way he had foreseen Armageddon for a long time, making his clearest prophecy in "What of the Day?" He had never encouraged slave insurrection, but in *Justice and Expediency* he had warned that unless the situation were altered, it would come. In 1848 he had even cried recklessly, "Let it come!"

Probably he was not clear just what "it" was, for there were times when, like all men who feel strongly, he could cry out for action without specifying just what action he had in mind.

Speak out in acts. The time for words
  Has passed, and deeds suffice alone;
In vain against the clang of swords
  The wailing pipe is blown!
Act, act in God's name, while ye may! [7]

And once at least he was appalled and frightened by the response which his own words evoked. On May 26, 1854, when Anthony Burns was captured in Boston under the Fugitive Slave Law, Whittier wrote Henry Bowditch:

That man must not be sent out of Boston as a slave. Anything but that! The whole people must be called out, the country must precipitate itself upon the city—an avalanche of freemen! Where are your circulars and your expresses? In the name of God, let the people be summoned!

Send out the fiery cross without more delay! Tell us what you want and what we can do! Thousands are waiting for the word from you.

But on May 29 he added:

I am sorry to see such a spirit of violence manifested, as it is useless and wrong in itself. I wish the demonstration of feeling to be deep and serious, but earnestly pray that there may be no resort to force. Cannot the man be bought? . . . I regret the use of my letter at a meeting of our colored friends. Surely no one who knows me could suppose that I wish to have any violent measures adopted. Pray see to it that no such impression was left in the minds of our colored friends. Oh, let them beware of violence! Let them not injure a holy cause by wrong action. God reigns, and if we are true to his laws we shall do more for liberty than by the use of the devil's weapons, of brute force.[8]

He was learning that our words are like our children: when we have sent them forth from us, we can no longer control what they do. Perhaps he was even learning that when we sow the dragon's teeth we reap the whirlwind. By John Brown's time he had it learned. Lydia M. Child asked him to write a poem for the meeting held in Tremont Temple the day the old fanatic was hanged. Not only did he fail to comply but on the very day of the meeting he published in the *Essex Transcript* an editorial called "The Lesson of the Day," [9] in which, though warning the South that John Brown's raid was the kind of thing slavery cannot fail to invite, he carefully dissociated himself from it. It is true that when "Brown of Ossawatomie" came out in *The Independent* in December, it was taken in some quarters as implying approval of Brown, but the extreme abolitionists disliked the poem.[10]

In the dedicatory address to William Bradford at the beginning of "Amy Wentworth," Whittier movingly describes the dilemma in which freedom-loving Quakers found themselves at the beginning of the Civil War.

As they who watch by sick-beds find relief
Unwittingly from the great stress of grief
And anxious care, in fantasies outwrought

From the hearth's embers flickering low, or caught
From whispering wind, or tread of passing feet,
Or vagrant memory calling up some sweet
Snatch of old song or romance, whence or why
They scarcely know or ask,—so, thou and I,
Nursed in the faith that Truth alone is strong
In the endurance which outwearies Wrong,
With meek persistence baffling brutal force,
And trusting God against the universe,—
We, doomed to watch a strife we may not share
With other weapons than the patriot's prayer,
Yet owning, with full hearts and moistened eyes,
The awful beauty of self-sacrifice,
And wrung by keenest sympathy for all
Who give their loved ones for the living wall
'Twixt love and treason,—in this evil day
May haply find, through automatic play
Of pen and pencil, solace to our pain,
And hearten others with the strength we gain.

He did not desire that Quakers should merely seek exemption from the horrors of war.

The levelled gun, the battle-brand,
　　We may not take;
But, calmly loyal, we can stand
And suffer with our suffering kind
　　For conscience' sake.

And we may tread the sick-bed floors
　　Where strong men pine,
And, down the groaning corridors,
Pour freely from our liberal stores
　　The oil and wine.[11]

In prose he spelled it out more clearly in a circular letter "to the Members of the Society of Friends," sent almost at the very beginning of the war:

We have no right to ask or expect an exemption from the chastisement which the Divine Providence is inflicting upon the nation. Steadily and faithfully maintaining our testimony against war, we owe it to the cause of truth, to show that exalted heroism and generous self-sacrifice are not incompatible with our pacific principles. Our mission is, at this time, to mitigate the sufferings of our countrymen, to visit and aid the sick and the wounded, to relieve the necessities of the widow and the orphan, and to practice economy for the sake of charity. Let the Quaker bonnet be seen by the side of the black hood of the Catholic Sister of Charity in the hospital ward. Let the same heroic devotion to duty which our brethren in Great Britain manifested in the Irish famine and pestilence be reproduced on this side of the water, in mitigating the horrors of war and its attendant calamities. What hinders us from holding up the hands of Dorothea Dix in her holy work of mercy at Washington? Our society is rich, and of those to whom much is given much will be required in this hour of proving and trial.

Gail Hamilton was not far wrong when she made Whittier a pair of slippers each bearing "an American eagle, with vigilant eyes, in belligerent attitude, ready for either defense or attack, with claws full of thunderbolts," but worked in Quaker drab! His Civil War poems are certainly not militaristic, but they could not be called strictly pacifistic either. "Laus Deo" thanks God not merely for having brought the war to an end but for having given victory to the North, and there are two poems for Thomas Starr King, the San Francisco clergyman and friend of Bret Harte who is credited with an important share in saving California for the Union. I have no doubt that King was a great and good man according to his lights, but I wonder if Whittier squirmed as I do when he read the letter in which King declared, "I rejoice to think that, if we conquer, the South is to be blessed more than the North. We are loving our enemies with our cannon, if they are battering down the bulwarks of the slavery Bastille. . . ."

Charles F. Whittier, the poet's nephew, served in the war and was afterwards an active member of the G.A.R., and Whittier himself wrote Sumner inquiring about an appointment for a friend as naval chaplain. "It is a queer inquiry for a Quaker to make, is it not?" He was as deeply moved by Robert Gould Shaw and his Negro regiment as William Vaughn Moody was to be in later years when he wrote his great "Ode in Time of Hesitation," and quite as much by Higginson, who served in a similar capacity:

> He will be a marked man, and especially exposed. But if he has a work to do under the Divine Providence, his head will be covered in the day of battle. How strange to think of him, so fresh, so beautiful in his glorious manhood, with his refinement, culture, and grace–leading that wild African regiment to avenge the wrongs of two centuries of slavery! How this one act of his is making his name historic!

And in 1864 he wrote to Bowditch, who had lost a son:

> I have looked over with the deepest interest this noble portrait gallery, this Valhalla of the patriot martyrs of our great day of trial, the young, the beautiful, the brave! I have read the touching, tender, but brave testimony of bereaved wives, mothers, and fathers. It seems to me that this collection is a most fitting memorial of thy own beloved one who so cheerfully laid down his young life on the altar of country and freedom.

I know that one may admire martyrs even when not approving of all their acts, and certainly one may pity those who suffer even if one believes that they are doing wrong, but it does seem to me that "Valhalla," with all its bloody associations, is a bit out of character for one who followed the orthodox Quaker custom in even refusing to use the conventional names for the days of the week and the months of the year because they were "heathen."

Whittier refused to accept a pike which was sent him as a memento of John Brown–"it is not a Christian weapon: it looks too much like murder"–but Robert Rantoul says he had "a murderous-looking musket, which had probably seen service in Kansas, standing behind his study door," and that when he was asked if it were a fowling piece, he replied, "Not exclusively," and smiled "a rather unregenerate smile." In 1866, however, he was badly embarrassed when the Amoskeag veterans from New Hampshire and a Massachusetts company with military bands paraded before his house and gave cheers and a grand military salute.

> Was ever a Quaker in such a predicament? I did, I fear, somewhat compromise myself by lifting, almost involuntarily, my hand to my

hat—but I resisted this temptation, and only pulled my hat lower down over my brow, by way of testimony.

He also declined to become an honorary civilian member of the Loyal Legion, a society of Union officers who had served in the Civil War.[12]

While the conflict raged, his emotional reactions had obviously varied considerably. He was oppressed by its horror—"The shadow of this terrible war rests heavily upon me"—and he was excited by its heroism and opportunity—"But what glorious times we live in! My heart is full of thankfulness. It is great to live now—to see and hear what will fill the horizon of history in all coming time, and sound on in all earth's voices forever." It was a comfort to know that at last there was "a *united North*," with "the old fires of Liberty . . . rekindled" and "a sublime spirit of self-sacrifice pervading all classes." But for himself that meant only trying to hold fast to "one central fixed thought—the Divine *goodness*" and the hope that God would bring good out of evil. Moreover, he thought of that good as consisting almost exclusively in the abolition of slavery; about Lincoln's paramount object, the preservation of the Union, he says very little.

Julius Atwood reports having once told Whittier that slavery could not have been destroyed nor the Union saved without war, to which he replied: "Yes. Thee remembers that in the old days, even Christ could not drive out some of the evil spirits without rending the body." Yet in 1875 he told Lydia Maria Child that the abolitionists had had no triumph. "The emancipation that came by military necessity and enforced by bayonets was not the emancipation for which we worked and prayed." But when it was over he admitted that a great achievement had been wrought by dreadful means.

No time is this for hands long over-worn
To task their strength: and (unto Him be praise
Who giveth quietness!) the stress and strain
Of years that did the work of centuries
Have ceased, and we can draw our breath once more
Freely and full.[13]

III

The pacifist issue did not wholly cease to trouble Whittier with the Civil War. Questions of violence and non-violence were more than once involved in Reconstruction problems. At one time he was anxious that Union men in the South should be protected against the Ku Klux Klan. He had a warm if inexplicable admiration for General Sherman and defended his conduct in Louisiana in 1875. He wrote poems in honor of Garibaldi's activities in Italy and exchanged autographs and "graven images" with him. In 1870 he sympathized with Prussia and inquired of Sumner whether America could do nothing to end the war. His fellow Quaker John Bright took him sternly to task for his admiration for General Gordon,

> a man whose reputation is founded solely on his engagement in war in distant countries, with which he had no necessary connection, and from which he had received no injury and no provocation.... In religion he was a strange fanatic, bordering on the insane, drawing his inspiration from the horrible stories of the Old Testament wars rather than from the New Testament and the Gospel narratives.... No Chinaman and no Sudanese had done him wrong, and yet he imagined that he was justified in engaging in the savagery of war, some thousands of miles from his own country, and in the slaughter of untold numbers of his fellow men.

Whittier's reply was rather lame. He agreed with Bright as to the iniquity of British policies, but he added, "I cannot withdraw my admiration for the man, while I disapprove of his warlike methods." Gordon "was a better man than David or Joshua," which, since Whittier himself, as a child, had pointed out to his elders that David would not be accepted by the Society of Friends, was not saying very much. "And he believed in a *living* God, who reveals himself now as in the old time."

If it is surprising to see how Whittier could take fire from the struggle in the Sudan as late as 1884, it is even more interesting that the conflict should appeal to his imagination as much as to his moral sense. One would almost think him a painter when he says:

What a place for an artist the Soudan would be—if an artist were sure of keeping his head on his shoulders! Those fierce wild hordes, in all variety of costumes and color, with their shields of hippopotamus hide, their long spears, and battle-axes, with El Mahdi at their head in his woven steel armor, the strange desert scenery and relentless sun, would be rare subjects for his pencil.

When he was asked to write something about Gordon, Whittier suggested that Tennyson was the one to do it, and it was his message, indirectly conveyed to the laureate, that inspired the epitaph in the Abbey. Dissatisfied with Tennyson's lines, Whittier then proceeded to write a poem of his own about Gordon but did not publish it; possibly John Bright's criticism had touched him more deeply than he realized or would have been willing to admit.

Was Whittier then a consistent pacifist in the Civil War crisis and elsewhere? I think he was as consistent as a man with his conflicting interests could have been expected to be. Like Falstaff's page, he had an angel about him, and though in this case the devil did not make the higher bid, he was able to get in a few licks now and then, as Whittier would have been the last man to deny. Probably the only way any human being in wartime could avoid all share in the guilt which attaches to war would be to leave his country altogether. Short of this, the best any man can do is to draw a line beyond which he will not suffer his cooperation to extend. Though his line sometimes wavered a little, Whittier did this more successfully than most.

CHAPTER FIVE

THE LIGHT THAT IS LIGHT INDEED

I

Whittier was a Christian and a Quaker, and his religion was the mainspring of his life. It is fitting, therefore, that the last chapter of this book should be devoted to his religion. But he was a poet, and he grew up in the shadow of the Romantic Movement, which came very close at times to making nature-worship a rival to Christianity. It may be well to begin then with his attitude toward nature.

There is no lack of fair prospect around Haverhill—George Washington thought it "the pleasantest village I have come through"—and Whittier enjoyed it to the full. There was more than a punning appropriateness in his use, on one occasion, of a green leaf as a calling card, and one cannot wonder over his inability to believe that Emerson himself loved nature any better than he did, for all that he had written so much more about it. "A farmer's son, I love a farmer's life which seems to me the noblest and the best." He often laments the destruction of natural beauty by advancing industrialism."[1] Nor was nature's spell in any sense weakened for him by the passing of time.

The years no charm from nature take;
As sweet her voices call,
As beautiful her mornings break,
As fair her evenings fall.[2]

And, again:

But still with every added year,
More beautiful thy works appear! [3]

If anything, natural beauty grew dearer to him with the thought that the time was approaching when he must leave it. All in all, Carpenter could hardly have been more wrong than when he wrote that "nature meant comparatively little to . . . [Whittier], as to most New Englanders." [4]

Spring he loved with a Chaucer-like love, and it had the same effect upon him that it had on Chaucer:

It is as if the pine-trees called me
From ceilëd room and silent books,
To see the dance of woodland shadows,
And hear the song of April brooks! [5]

"I am thankful that I have lived to see another spring," he wrote Mrs. Fields in 1888; "to watch the slow, beautiful resurrection of Nature." And his very last spring on earth he wrote Mrs. Kilham: "Nature does not disappoint me. Each season seems lovelier than when I was younger. This world of ours seems now almost too fair and sweet to leave in this glorious flower-time." For all that, it would be hard to believe that he cared less for autumn. "What a glorious October have we had! I lived a whole year in that golden week of 'Indian summer.'" And fifteen years later he could still write James T. Fields: "I hope thee will get a glimpse of Nature in her autumn glory. It is worth living the whole year for, and that is saying a good deal in New England where one is compelled half the year like Job's friends to 'fill his belly with the East Wind.'" But even winter, hard as it was on his physical constitution, was generous in feeding the springs of his art, and John Burroughs, who seldom found "a false note in any of Whittier's descriptions of rural sights and sounds," called *Snow-Bound* "the most faithful picture of our Northern winter that has yet been put into poetry," [6] and Whittier himself tells Gail Hamilton, "I have never tired of the white glory of the world about us—the low sun streaming through the west pines—the rose and purple horizon hills—the full moonlight photographing the beautiful and delicate tracery of elms and beeches!"

There is one undated letter fragment to an unidentified correspondent in which, having visited the Isles of Shoals, Whittier says that he prefers the mountains but admits that the sea has its charms. Certainly he revelled in the Shoals, where he was able to wander about at will, and where he could sit for hours without speaking to anybody, should he so choose. He says that "of all sweet sounds, that of water is to me the sweetest," and in *Snow-Bound* he tells of the "liquid lip" of "the buried brooklet," which

> Had been to us companionship,
> And, in our lonely life, had grown
> To have an almost human tone.

When he went to the White Mountains, he always took a southeast room if possible, and boasted of never missing a sunrise. This was his reward for being a poor sleeper, and the taste endured to the end. The morning before he died he was still sufficiently himself to forbid the nurse to draw the curtains in his chamber. But he could praise night as well as day, and his love of order did not prevent him from relishing the "picturesque inequality of nature," which "eschews regular outlines." [7]

For trees and flowers he had a special affection. Norman Foerster has found about forty different flowers in his poetry and thirty varieties of trees, his favorites being the elm, maple, birch, and pine, with the last-named leading all the rest. "The characteristics of the pine that he returned to again and again are its tenuous music when the wind touches its strings; its sturdy, steady growth, rarely tainted by decay; and its evergreen quality." [8] He was fond of quoting "the advice of the old Laird of Dombiedike to his son Jock: 'When ye have nothing better to do, ye can be aye stickin' in a tree; it'll be growin' when ye are sleepin.' "[9] He loved the aster, gentian, harebell, and goldenrod, and, as J. B. Pickard has observed, his most effective nature references have a distinctly Essex County provenance; it is only when these fail him or inspiration flags that he draws on stock phrases and figures.[10]

Animals, too, belong to nature, though since we can in a measure communicate with them, they seem closer to us than trees and flowers. As a countryman, Whittier had animals around him all his life, but though he wrote a piece on "Our Dumb Relations" and commended John Woolman for his kindness toward animals, they play a small part in his writings, and I cannot believe they were very important to him. I do not find that he ever hunted, but there is no sign of moral revulsion against hunting or eating meat either. It is certain that he was an incorrigible tease, and I find it difficult to reconcile this with real consideration for the brute creation. Elizabeth Hume says that at the White Mountains Whittier teased a Newfoundland and a bull terrier and "delighted to get them growling at each other, which was rather hard work as they were such good friends," and in *Snow-Bound* the schoolmaster even teases "the mitten-blinded cat"! [11] Whittier's "almost Irish hatred of snakes," as he calls it, goes back to the days when the barefoot boy was in danger of stepping on them in the meadow, and is shown most clearly not in direct expressions of dislike but in such passages as this in his poem about Anthony Burns and the slave-catchers in Boston:

I felt a sense of bitter loss,—
  Shame, tearless grief, and stifling wrath,
  And loathing fear, as if my path
A serpent stretched across.

It is quite clear that, like Emily Dickinson, he experienced that

tighter breathing
And Zero at the Bone

which all who fear reptiles know so well. Once, having given a friend a bunch of water-lilies, he remarked, "Thee'd hardly think that the same Hand that made those made snakes." The dualist Zoroaster assigned snakes, along with other malevolent aspects of creation, to the evil power Ahriman. If Whittier had been familiar with the "Personalist" philosophy, perhaps he might have regarded such creatures as by-products or failures in the evolutionary process of creation and thus absolved God of direct responsibility for having designed or intended them.

The few pets who call for special mention are of a rather unusual kind. There is one charming passage on squirrels in a letter to Caroline Johnson:

> A Committee of grey squirrels waited on us this morning on the east piazza. The chairman, whose gray hairs gave him a venerable appearance, stated that their stock of provisions was exhausted, and suggested that a fresh supply of nuts would be acceptable. Pray attend to the matter at once, and bring the necessary supply with thee this evening.

Whittier's own particular pet squirrel at Amesbury was a privileged character, for he not only ransacked his master's pocket for nuts but sometimes jumped on his desk and upset his papers. Whittier once had a turkey cock named General Gordon and a dog called Charles Dickens, and there was also a bantam rooster who liked riding on his shoulder or buttoned up in the front of his coat and who would perch on his niece Lizzie's door in the morning and crow when Whittier wanted her to get up for breakfast.

But the real individualist among Whittier's pets was the parrot Charlie, whose vocabulary sometimes harked back to the days before he became a Quaker and who liked to nip at the legs of guests or address passers-by from the top of the house, and who met his fate when he tumbled down the flue and was rescued only after considerable delay and effort. Covered with soot, he was able to whisper weakly, "Poor Charlie wants water," but he never really recovered. "I have met with a real loss," Whittier wrote Lucy Larcom. "Poor Charlie is dead. He has 'gone where the good parrots go.' He has been ailing and silent for some time:

and he finally died. Do not laugh at me—but I am sorry enough to cry if it would do any good."

Generally speaking, Whittier sees nature as being in harmony with nobility of thought and character and as inspiring holy thoughts.[13] Nature is also a source of peace and healing, as in "My Namesake":

On all his sad or restless moods
  The patient peace of Nature stole;
The quiet of the fields and woods
  Sank deep into his soul.

In "Hampton Beach" he is more specific:

While through my being seems to flow
The breath of a new life, the healing of the seas!

There are even poems like "Saint Martin's Summer" in which nature replaces revelation:

God's angels come not as of old
  The Syrish shepherds knew them;
In reddening dawns, in sunset gold,
  And warm noon lights I view them.

Nor need there is, in times like this
  When heaven to earth draws nearer,
Of wing or song as witnesses
  To make their presence clearer.

In "The Lakeside" too, he sees the Indian as having been vouchsafed a revelation of God through nature—

To him of light and shade the laws
  No forest skeptic taught;
Their living and eternal Cause
  His truer instinct taught—

and he thanks his Father that the same insight has been given him.

Did Whittier, then, take up a Wordsworthian attitude toward nature? There are times when one is tempted to think so. Nature seems to answer all the needs of the Barefoot Boy, who "eschews" both "books and tasks" and receives from her

Sleep that wakes the laughing day,
Health that mocks the doctor's rules,
Knowledge never learned of schools,
Of the wild bee's morning chase,
Of the wild-flower's time and place,
Flight of fowl and habitude
Of the tenants of the wood;
How the tortoise bears his shell,
How the woodchuck digs his cell,
And the ground-mole sinks his well;
How the robin feeds her young,
How the oriole's nest is hung;
Where the whitest lilies blow,
Where the freshest berries grow,
Where the ground-nut trails its vine,
Where the wood-grape's clusters shine;
Of the black wasp's cunning way,
Mason of his walls of clay,
And the architectural plans
Of gray hornet artisans!

Closely allied to the Barefoot Boy is the "child of the forest" in "The Bridal of Pennacook":

Unknown to her the rigid rule,
  The dull restraint, the chiding frown,
The weary torture of the school,
  The taming of wild nature down.
Her only lore, the legends told
  Around the hunter's fire at night;
Stars rose and set, and seasons rolled,
Flowers bloomed and snow-flakes fell, unquestioned
    in her sight.

Nor do these passages stand alone. In "Child-Songs" it is to "childhood's sweet appeal" that "the heart of genius turns,"

And more than all the sages teach
From lisping voices learns.

Certainly the Wordsworth of "Expostulation and Reply" and "The Tables Turned," which Irving Babbitt saw as "about the most complete denial of culture in Arnold's sense to be found in literature," [14] could not ask anybody to go further than Whittier seems to go in his poem "To–, with a Copy of Woolman's Journal," which he presented to one of the maidens "with the fair brown tresses" who always enthralled him:

Youthful years and maiden beauty,
  Joy with them should still abide,–
Instinct take the place of Duty,
  Love, not Reason, guide.

Nor is it only children to whom all this applies. The uncle in *Snow-Bound*, who was "innocent of books" but "rich in lore of fields and brooks," is only the Barefoot Boy grown older.

But this is far from being the whole story with Whittier, or even, taken by itself, a fair account. Even if he had not been a Christian, he could hardly have stopped here, for the harsher aspects of nature would still have given him pause.

The earthquake and the storm are God's,
  And good and evil, overflow.

Whether they are God's or not, they are certainly nature's, and William E. Barton used to say that sooner or later the consistent pantheist must find himself worshipping a cyclone. As a boy, Whittier sometimes read God's vengeance into baleful phenomena, much as Tom Sawyer did. Moreover, when nature was not baleful, she might be completely indifferent to man and his interests, and this was hardly more nourishing to faith.[15] As for primitivism, the prose introduction to "The Chapel of the Hermits" might have been written by a whole-hearted admirer of Rousseau, but the poem itself finds that

He loathed the false, yet lived not true
To half the glorious truths he knew;
The doubt, the discord, and the sin,
He mourned without, he felt within.[16]

For that matter, even the poem addressed to the "Maiden! with the fair brown tresses" is far from primitivistic if taken as a whole, and the feet of the Barefoot Boy are

> Happy if they sink not in
> Quick and treacherous sands of sin.

I have already objected to this last passage as an example of the dragged-in moralizing that mars the end of so many of Whittier's poems, but it still shows his conviction that salvation is not to be found in nature. Viewed in its relationship to its Creator, nature may well be a precious means of grace, but taken in isolation, it can hardly fail to act as a delusion and a snare. That, as Whittier saw it, was the mistake Tom Paine made. "He loved the works of God for their exceeding beauty—not for their manifestation of an overruling intelligence."

Lucy Larcom, then, probably exaggerated when she wrote of Whittier and his sister, "I love to sit with them in the still Quaker worship, and they love the free air and all the beautiful things as much as they do all the good and spiritual." Harry Hayden Clark has pointed out [17] that the first thirty-three lines of "Among the Hills" suggest "the sensuous magic of John Keats." In the violent anti-slavery poem, "A Sabbath Scene," nature is preferred to the Bible, as interpreted by the pro-slavery clergy, but it must not be forgotten that from Whittier's point of view this is not only a plain misinterpretation but anything but a disinterested one. The early uncollected poem, "The Convent" (1827) [18] must likewise be dismissed from consideration as a piece of anti-Catholic propaganda. The very next year Whittier ridiculed the nature-cult in "Rural Excursions" and "Midnight Thoughts," and in "The Worship of Nature," which dates from the same year as "The Convent" itself, nature is not deity but worshipper.

Occasionally Whittier expresses his great joy in nature, and, at the same time, indicates his fear that he may be indulging himself unduly: "The weather now is delightfully warm and bright, and the soft green of the meadows is climbing our hills. It is a luxury to live. One feels at such times terribly rooted to this world; old

Mother Earth seems sufficient for us." But though he is very fond of finding analogies between natural and supernatural, and between natural processes and magic, his real wariness about nature appears in such poems as "The Meeting," where the bareness of Quaker worship and the deliberate exclusion of all imagery and, so far as possible, of everything that might attract the eye is rationally defended, though naturally not all readers will accept his conclusion:

> Dream not, O friend, because I seek
> This quiet shelter twice a week,
> I better deem its pine-laid floor
> Than breezy hill or sea-sung shore;
> But nature is not solitude:
> She crowds us with her thronging wood;
> Her many hands reach out to us,
> Her many tongues are garrulous;
> Perpetual riddles of surprise
> She offers to our ears and eyes;
> She will not leave our senses still,
> But drags them captive at her will:
> And, making earth too great for heaven,
> She hides the Giver in the gift.

Martha Hale Shackford finds here a "very positive affirmation that the Quaker poet's senses were so imperious that they distracted from communion with the Divine," and Norman Foerster adds that the poem reveals Whittier as "the first important American writer to point out the perils of the 'nature cult,' the seduction of the spirit by the senses." I am always suspicious of the label "first"; otherwise both statements are correct. Whittier would not have approved of the western American church from which a vast glass expanse behind the altar gives a magnificent view of distant mountain and forest.

> We felt that man was more than his abode,—
>   The inward life than Nature's raiment more;
> And the warm sky, the sundown-tinted hill,
>   The forest and the lake, seemed dwarfed and dim

Before the saintly soul, whose human will
  Meekly in the Eternal footsteps trod,
Making her homely toil and household ways
An earthly echo of the song of praise
  Swelling from angel lips and harps of seraphim.[19]

This passage ends, to be sure, with a religious affirmation, but even if this were not present, the humanistic emphasis would survive, without danger of pantheism.

If Whittier sometimes had trouble, then, in making up his mind about nature, the reason is not far to seek. The Christian world as a whole has always had the same trouble. Nature is God's creation, bears His signature, and in a sense reveals Him, but nature also lies under the Primal Curse and in many of its aspects wars against Grace. The curse meant less to Whittier than it did to the Calvinist, and because he was a poet and a lover of beauty, the appeal to the senses was keener for him than it is for many men. Paradox appears even here, then, but if paradox means contradiction, it may also mean balance. And if the "raiment" presented dangers and problems, the "inner life" did not, for to a Quaker this is where God most intimately and inerrantly reveals Himself.

II

"I am a Quaker," said Whittier, "because my family before me—those whom I loved—were Quakers." But he was no sectarian, and he admitted that Friends' ways would not satisfy all temperaments. He was patient with Elizabeth Lloyd when she left the Society, and in *Margaret Smith's Journal* he allowed his heroine to state her decision against Friends quite without rancor:

> My Uncle Rawson need not fear my joining with them: for, although I judge them to be a worthy and pious people, I like not their manner of worship, and their great gravity and soberness so little accord with my natural temper and spirits.

For Whittier himself, however, no other religious affiliation was conceivable. In "The Pennsylvania Pilgrim," "The Meeting,"

"First-Day Thoughts," and elsewhere, he tried to describe what Quaker worship means.

"So sometimes comes to soul and sense
The feeling which is evidence
That very near about us lies
The realm of spiritual mysteries.
The sphere of the supernal powers
Impinges on this world of ours.
The low and dark horizon shifts;
The breath of a diviner air
Blows down the answer of a prayer:
That all our sorrow, pain, and doubt
A great compassion clasps about,
And law and goodness, love and force,
Are wedded fast beyond divorce." [20]

When Lucy Larcom joined Trinity Church, he said, "Well, if I was going to join any church myself, I would join Phillips Brooks's church." But he added, "I am mighty glad I haven't got to join any church."

The point has already been made elsewhere that Whittier was an old-fashioned Quaker with no sympathy for the evangelical tendencies that came into the Society with Joseph Gurney and others. He wanted no music in meeting, and he did not care much for speaking either. What he wanted was "to get into the silence," which, in view of his own statement that meditation was very difficult for him,[21] may seem somewhat surprising. He criticized Friends for their slowness to take a stand, their "narrowness and coldness and inactivity, the overestimate of external observances, the neglect of our own proper work while acting as a conscience-keeper for others." He complained of "uncouthness of apparel" and of "nasal *tone* and conventicle cant." He lamented their neglect of education and scholarship and thought their "plain speaking" sometimes deteriorated into rude speaking. He did not allow Bunyan's dislike of the "vile and abominable things fomented by the Quakers" to prejudice him against Bunyan, and though he was indignant over Macaulay's charges against William Penn, he realized that no reply could serve unless based on a scholarship equal to Macaulay's own. "The truth is what we want. If the character of William Penn will not abide the test of investigation, let it fall." [22] Though he tends to play down Quaker extremism and fanaticism in colonial days, he does not wholly deny it, and the picture of Margaret Brewster in the poem "In the 'Old South' " is considerably less favorable than the one in *Margaret Smith's Journal.*

Whittier's Quakerism was bred in the bone; he could not tear himself up by the roots, and he could no more have avoided being a Quaker than Gandhi could have prevented himself from being a Hindu or Martin Luther King, a Negro. But he never made a fetter of his Quakerism; within the bounds imposed upon him by his nature and his background, he was free. When he was in the legislature he would not take an oath or wear crape on his arm for a fellow member who had died; he refused to attend Angelina Grimké's wedding (though he sent greetings) because she was marrying "out of society"; he thought it too ostentatious to permit a silver cake-basket to be used in his house though it had been sent to him as a gift, and he clung to the Quaker "thee" even in his intercourse with non-Friends. But these were matters of sentiment rather than principle; as he once expressed it to Mary Claflin with reference to the last point named: "It has been the manner of speech of my people for two hundred years; it was my mother's language, and it is good enough for me; I shall not change my grammar." But where principle was concerned, he followed his own Inner Light, regardless of whether or not it coincided with that of his fellow Quakers, and this is just what, as a good Friend, he ought to have done. Some Quakers disapproved even of *Uncle Tom's Cabin* because it was a work of fiction, but this did not keep Whittier either from writing *Margaret Smith's Journal* or devouring other writers' novels by the bushel-basketful. At the Whittier centenary in 1907 a Quaker writer observed:

Glad as we are now to recognize his place among us, we should not forget that, especially during his more strenuous years, he was rarely regarded by our forefathers with complacency. He was radical and uncompromising in his religious as well as in his political attitude, and he expressed himself in ways which gave occasion for much heart-burning to the elders of his Church. The only orthodoxy to which he could subscribe was that of the Master who lived the life of love in the presence of God.

Though Quakerism has no formal creed, Whittier's own categorical statement of his religious beliefs is sufficient to establish his fundamental Christian orthodoxy:

God is One; just, holy, merciful, eternal, and almighty Creator, Father of all things; Christ, the same eternal One, manifested in our Humanity, and in Time; and the Holy Spirit, the same Christ, manifested within us, the Divine Teacher, the Living Word, the Light that lighteth every man that cometh into the world.

Though he often found the Hicksite or Unitarian Friends more in sympathy with his anti-slavery ideas than his more orthodox brethren there is no justification for the attempt which has sometimes been made to represent him as Unitarian in his own religious views. He honored William Ellery Channing deeply but the prefatory note to his poetic tribute carefully disclaims sympathy with his "peculiar religious opinions." He sympathized with the anti-Calvinist bias of the Unitarians, and he defended them against those who sought to exclude them from the Christian fellowship, but that was all.[23]

Chauncey J. Hawkins lists the following terms applied by Whittier to Christ: Christ of God; The Holy One; Suffering Son of God; The Lowly and Just; Humanity Clothed in the Brightness of God; Loved of the Father; Christ the Rock of Ages; Elder Brother; The World's Overcomer; Immortal Love; Light Divine; and Healer. Though he would have been—and was—horrified by the jaunty intimacy with Christ which some Evangelicals assume, his religion was Christocentric if any man's ever was.

"So, to the calmly gathered thought
The innermost of truth is taught,
The mystery dimly understood,

That love of God is love of good,
And, chiefly, its divinest trace
In Him of Nazareth's holy face." [24]

And, at greater length, in one of his most famous devotional passages:

But warm, sweet, tender, even yet
  A present help is He;
And faith has still its Olivet,
  And love its Galilee.

The healing of His seamless dress
  Is by our beds of pain;
We touch Him in life's throng and press,
  And we are whole again.

Through Him the first fond prayers are said
  Our lips of childhood frame,
The last low whispers of our dead
  Are burdened with His name.[25]

He had always believed (as Browning teaches in "Saul") that the creature cannot surpass the Creator, that God reveals Himself supremely in human life, and that the best in humanity is a key to the character of God, and it has always been the heart of Christian belief that in Christ God made the supreme revelation of Himself in terms which human beings could understand. After reading Gail Hamilton's book, *What Think Ye of Christ?* Whittier wrote the author:

My own mind had, from the same evidence which thee adduce, become convinced of the *Divinity* of Christ; but I cannot look upon him as other than a man like ourselves, through whom the Divine was made miraculously manifest. Jesus of Nazareth was a man, the *Christ* was a God—a new revelation of the Eternal in Time. Thy book seems to me written with wonderful clearness and ability, and will command the respect and attention of the best thinkers.

For all his love for Jesus, Whittier did not *confine* the Christ-manifestation to him, though it is clear that he found there its supreme expression. He liked Alexander V. G. Allen's book, *The Continuity of Christian Thought* (1884) for "its resuscitation of the doctrine of the Divine Immanence as taught by the Greek Church in the early Christian centuries." Harking back to Justin and Clement of Alexandria, he believed in an Eternal Christ, immanent in every race and clime, the manifestation of a God who has never left Himself without witnesses, the Light that lighteth every man coming into the world, and he reminds us that William Penn thought Socrates as good a Christian as Richard Baxter. Consequently he had no sympathy with religious exclusivism in any form, and nothing could have been more foreign to his spirit than to attempt to set bounds to the Father's redemptive love.

All souls that struggle and aspire,
All hearts of prayer by Thee are lit;
And, dim or clear, Thy tongues of fire
On dusky tribes and twilight centuries sit.[26]

Theories of the Atonement did not greatly concern Whittier, for he had never believed that God was estranged from men. "Man turns from God, not God from him," and the barrier that must be surmounted if harmony is to be re-established is in the heart of man; there is nothing in the nature of God that needs to be propitiated.

. . . to be saved is only this,—
Salvation from our selfishness,
From more than elemental fire,
The soul's unsanctified desire,
From sin itself, and not the pain
That warns us of its chafing chain.[27]

Obviously, such salvation cannot be achieved by believing something in the sense of yielding intellectual assent to it, and neither can it be lost by intellectual error. The most orthodox believer may be damned if he lacks charity, and the most blatant heretic may find union with Christ in the spirit of love. In prose and verse alike, Whittier says many harsh things of creeds, speaking of those who rest "in bondage to the letter still" and even of the salvation achieved "in spite of all the lies of creeds."

> From the death of the old the new proceeds,
> And the life of truth from the rot of creeds.[28]

And again:

> Hatred of cant and doubt of human creeds
> May well be felt; the unpardonable sin
> Is to deny the word of God within! [29]

But, as Rufus Jones points out, none of this indicates any "weakness of faith" or "blurring of truth" in the poet's mind. "It only meant that he looked upon religious truth, as all mystics do, primarily as personal experience and not as dogma, and as therefore being too rich, complex, and many-sided to be forced into inelastic phrases." Actually, he did not have much interest in theology, formal theology at any rate; he shows this very clearly in his essay on Richard Baxter. He loved those persons whose lives showed their kinship with the spirit of love and whose faith expressed itself in works of charity and love. As he himself puts it:

> Of course I object to creeds which virtually compel people to profess to believe them, when they really do not. In speaking of religious matters I have ventured only to speak of my own experience and conscientious belief.... Some of the worst forms of blasphemy are embodied in creeds which good men try to persuade themselves that they believe in.

Whittier believed in prayer as a necessity of our human nature: "we cannot live without it: and that we do pray is itself evidence that Our Father is near us." But it seemed to him presumptuous for any man to believe that he had such control over the Divine Will as to be sure that he would get everything he prayed for, and he once modestly expressed doubt that his own prayers accomplished much.

He was in line with the traditional Quaker position in regarding the Bible as "*a* rule, not *the* rule of faith and practice." Of "The Pennsylvania Pilgrim" he records that

> Within himself he found the law of right,
> He walked by faith and not the letter's light,
> And read his Bible by the Inward Light.

Not so interpreted, it became a stumbling-block and was used to justify monstrous established evils like war and slavery. "We can do without Bible or church," he says: "we cannot do without God." It is not surprising, then, that he scornfully rejected the prooftext method upon which Fundamentalists have always relied nor that such of his religious poems as he devoted to Biblical paraphrase should be bad while those which rest upon his own first-hand religious experience are good. If the Bible sanctions evil, then the Bible itself must be rejected; the only alternative would be to deny God's witness in the worshipper's own heart, close the book of revelation, and make a vital religious life thereafter impossible.

> If the light given *immediately* by the Holy Spirit is *dim* [so Whittier once wrote Lyman Abbott], what must that be which comes to us through the medium of human writers in an obsolete tongue? Is the bible more and better than the Spirit which inspired it? Shall the stream deny the fountain?

Whittier himself was steeped in the Bible, but his Bible references, though numerous, are not pietistic. Indeed, he draws upon the Bible for inspiration and illustration much as he draws upon other books. But when he seems to denigrate it, it is only because he will not allow even the Bible to replace God.

> He went to it [writes Rufus Jones], he lived upon it, he loved it, because it found him and searched his heart and spoke to his condition and revealed life to him and made him confident that in all ages God, who was speaking here, spoke His thoughts, and made known His will in the shekinah within men's souls.

Because Whittier's religious assurance rested finally upon the witness within himself and not upon any material witness in the world outside, he escaped the whole dismal (and terribly misnamed) "conflict between religion and science" which was such a live issue in his time. "We must never be afraid of truth; truth can never contradict itself." He was aware that something was going on both in natural science and in the application of scholarly or scientific principles to the study of the Bible. He could call Mrs. Humphry Ward's novel, *Robert Elsmere*, which deals with a clergyman's departure from Christian orthodoxy through the Higher Criticism, "unsettling" and tell Celia Thaxter that "to think of one's venerable ancestor, like Coleridge's devil clad in

breeches of blue
With a hole behind where his tail came through!

isn't agreeable at all." But he was never seriously troubled.

These and other controversial matters are bravely faced and clearly considered in "Our Master," but the lyricism of the poem so outweighs its controversial quality that the latter is often missed.

We may not climb the heavenly steeps
  To bring the Lord Christ down:
In vain we search the lowest deeps,
  For Him no depths can drown.

Nor holy bread, nor blood of grape,
  The lineaments restore
Of Him we know in outward shape
  And in the flesh no more.

Here is the Quaker rejection of the sacraments, and specifically of the Eucharist, as an outward observance, along with the doctrine of transubstantiation or any other doctrine which may replace it, and, by implication, of the whole sacramental conception of religion. The days of Christ's flesh are past and cannot be restored. Now He can only be known spiritually, and to identify Him with anything material is to degrade Him.

He cometh not a king to reign;
  The world's long hope is dim;
The weary centuries watch in vain
  The clouds of heaven for Him.

The Jews are still waiting for the Messiah to come; Christians are waiting for Christ to come again. Both will be disappointed. Whittier here voices an out-and-out rejection, again on the ground of unspirituality, of millenarian belief or the doctrine of the Second Advent, about which many people were seriously disturbed in his time, partly because of the activities of the notorious William Miller and his "Millerite" followers, who not only preached the Second Advent, but actually set dates for it.[30]

The letter fails, the systems fall,
  And every symbol wanes;
The Spirit over-brooding all
  Eternal Love remains.

And not for signs in heaven above
  Or earth below they look,
Who know with John his smile of love,
  With Peter his rebuke.

The "signs" are the circumstances which seem to indicate the imminence of the Second Advent; the "systems" are creeds and ecclesiastical organizations; the "symbols" are whatever means the churches may have used as a means of expressing religious truth. But what can the "letter" be except the Bible itself, toward which the Higher Criticism was forcing believers to take up a fresh attitude?

In joy of inward peace, or sense
  Of sorrow over sin,
He is His own best evidence,
  His witness is within.

No fable old, nor mythic lore,
  Nor dream of bards and seers,
No dead fact stranded on the shore
  Of the oblivious years:—

(nothing, in other words, that depends upon historical evidence, or is recorded in the Bible or any other book)

But warm, sweet, tender, even yet
  A present help is He;
And faith has still its Olivet,
  And love its Galilee.

Here is the heart of the Quaker—as of all mystical conceptions—of religion, not as belief but as experience. The final reliance is not upon what any book records or any church teaches, but upon what the believer has felt within himself. Sources external to himself have not given him his faith, and therefore they cannot take it away from him. To quote from Rufus Jones again, but now in a wholly different connection:

The most the mystic can say in the last resort is that something in the very structure of the soul seems to be linked up with that higher world with which he feels himself in contact. He is committed to the faith that we can trust this highest verdict of the soul as surely as one can trust the testimony of mathematics or of beauty. It feels to him like the surest and safest cosmic investment. But to the non-beholders he can only cry in the wilderness: "I have seen and here are my tokens." [31]

Whittier is quite in harmony with all this when he writes in "Miriam":

Why mourn above some hopeless flaw
In the stone tables of the law,
When scripture every day afresh
Is traced on tablets of the flesh?

He spells it out in prose also:

...Christianity is not simply historical and traditional, but present and permanent, with its roots in the infinite past and its branches in the infinite future, the eternal spring and growth of Divine love; not the dying echo of words uttered centuries ago, never to be repeated, but God's good tidings spoken afresh in every soul,—the perennial fountain and unstinted outflow of wisdom and goodness, forever old and forever new.

They fail to read clearly the signs of the times who do not see that the hour is coming when, under the searching eye of philosophy and the terrible analysis of science, the letter and the outward evidence will not altogether avail us; when the surest dependence must be upon the Light of Christ within, disclosing the law and the prophets in our own souls, and confirming the truth of outward Scripture by inward experience....

And in 1884 he wrote President Thomas Chase, of Haverford College:

It was Thomas Story, a minister of the Society of Friends, and member of Penn's Council of State, who, while on a religious visit to England, wrote to James Logan that he had read on the stratified rocks of Scarborough, as from the finger of God, proofs of the immeasurable age of our planet, and that the "days" of the letter of Scripture could only mean vast spaces of time.

May Haverford emulate the example of these brave but reverent men, who, in investigating nature, never lost sight of the Divine Ideal, and who, to use the words of Fénelon, "Silenced themselves to hear in the stillness of their souls the inexpressible voice of Christ." Holding fast the mighty truth of the Divine Immanence, the Inward Light and Word, a Quaker college can have no occasion to renew the disastrous quarrel of religion and science. Against the sublime faith which shall yet dominate the world, skepticism has no power. No possible investigation of natural facts; no searching criticism of letter and tradition can disturb it, for it has its witness in all human hearts.

III

Religion is a life-matter, but it involves the consideration of life's antithesis—death. A conventionally pious acceptance of immortality is found in many of Whittier's early poems, preserved in

Pray and elsewhere, as in the effusion of 1827, where a mother is exhorted not to mourn for the death of her child.

Who, in the dawn of life hath fled,
  Where sorrows cannot dim
That purity and innocence
  Which mark'd his transient stay,
Since life hath nought to recompense
  The woes that throng its way.

On a much higher level, the same attitude is expressed in the noble lyricism of *Snow-Bound:*

Yet Love will dream, and Faith will trust,
(Since He who knows our need is just,)
That somehow, somewhere, meet we must.
Alas for him who never sees
The stars shine through his cypress-trees!
Who, hopeless, lays his dead away,
Nor looks to see the breaking day
Across the mournful marbles play!
Who hath not learned, in hours of faith,
  The truth to flesh and sense unknown,
That Life is ever lord of Death,
  And Love can never lose its own!

Taken as a whole, however, Whittier's attitude toward immortality was considerably less bland than such ideas might suggest. Faith in immortality was very important to him, and I should say that he was a convinced believer, but there was nothing smug about his belief, and sometimes it dwindled into a hope. On the one hand, he was capable of the sharp retort he made to the rude and blatant atheist who vociferated that he knew there was no immortality because he was sure he had no soul. "Friend," said Whittier, "I quite agree with thee. I am ready to admit that thee has no soul. But speak for thyself, friend, speak for thyself!" He was always sure that immortality must be felt, not argued. But, as he himself said, his hope was "always associated with dread, like the shining of a star through mist," and the "mystery of Death never ceased to be dark and fearful." He knew there were no reasonable alternatives to the traditional Christian belief. Certainly the Hindu idea of Nirvana would not do.

Not mine the sad and freezing dream
  Of souls that, with their earthly mould,
  Cast off the loves and joys of old,
Unbodied like the pale moonbeam,
  As pure, as passionless, and cold;
Nor mind the hope of India's son,
  Of slumbering in oblivion's rest.
Life's myriads blending into one,
  In blank annhilation blest;
Dust-atoms of the infinite,
Sparks scattered from the central light,
And winning back through mortal pain
Their old unconsciousness again.[32]

On the other hand, the idea of heaven entertained by many Christians appealed to him no more than it did to the Mark Twain who created Captain Stormfield. As he asked Elizabeth Lloyd,

Did thee ever think what a dull place Heaven must be if the popular notion of it is correct? A state of sheer spiritual laziness–nothing to do because everything is *done*–nobody to help–nobody to pity–nobody to pray for–no employment but to sing hymns!

And to Elizabeth Stuart Phelps he added that if she were condemned to that kind of heaven she would soon be leaving it to go to the other place, where she could help somebody. In his old age, Whittier said, "As I grow older, a future life seems to me more certain, though I think less and less of definite details. When Lydia Child died, and Dickens too, he wondered aloud what had become of them, where they might be, and what they were doing. It was not that the idea of survival itself caused his difficulties. "I can conceive of no end to myself. I expect to live on, but how?" And he added, rather pathetically, "I have a constitutional dread of change and newness." [33]

Nor was it only in connection with the thought of the life to come that doubt troubled him. Though it is correct to regard him as primarily a poet of religious faith and certitude, a quietist, it must not be assumed that this was his exclusive interest. He even assumed a certain amount of determinism in religious as in other matters. Perhaps it was only his charity that led him to try to attribute Puritan intolerance to the harsh New England climate, but he was certainly serious when he wrote,

"Is it choice whereby the Parsee
Kneels before his mother's fire?
In his black tent did the Tartar
Choose his wandering sire?"[34]

Theoretically he knew also that an evolving and aspiring being like man must be willing to accept and allow a place for the agonies of imperfection: "The Divine Ideal must always, I think, be *before* us, never completely overtaken, for that would be absorption in it, and the consequent loss of our individuality." But in practice he found all this rather uncomfortable.

"The unsolved mystery presses heavily upon me," he says. He did not claim to "*know* anything!" and he had "no great expectation of a mathematical demonstration of the spiritual life. I believe it, and trust." Howard Mumford Jones finds him haunted by time, transience, the thought of everything passing away. And I think he would have accepted the truth of John Buchan's observation:

Every man has a creed, but in his soul he knows that his creed has another side, possibly not less logical, which it does not suit him to produce. Our most honest convictions are not the children of pure reason, but of temperament, environment, necessity, and interest. Most of us take sides in life and forget the one we reject.[35]

The terrible mystery of suffering impressed him also. Sometimes he tried to persuade himself that human shortcomings were responsible for most of it, but he was not always sure of that. "How much of sin and want and pain there is in the world!" He was also oppressed (as in "Revelation") by what is now called "cosmic horror." And, as seems to be the rule with very good men, his own sense of personal unworthiness was very keen.

I have been thinking over my life [he wrote Harriet Pitman in 1880], and the survey has not been encouraging. Alas! if I have been a servant at all, I have been an unprofitable one. And yet I have loved goodness and longed to be good, but it has been so hard to bring my imaginative, poetic temperament into subjection. I stand ashamed and almost despairing before holy and pure ideals. As I read the New Testament I feel how weak, irresolute and frail I am and how little I can rely on anything save Our Lord's mercy, and infinite compassion, which I reverently and thoughtfully own have followed me through life, and the assurance of which is my sole ground of hope for myself and for those I love and pray for.

Certainly he was never in any danger of believing himself to be in a state of grace. "I do not believe it possible . . . to be sinless," he said, and he was eighty when he said it. Waggoner compares him to Hawthorne in feeling "the brotherhood of guilt in 'secret sin.' "

Other things being equal, persons with a strong interest in immortality seem more inclined than others to believe in psychic forces and in what is called, loosely and generally, the occult. Whittier grew up against a background rich in New England folklore and superstition, much of it transplanted from old England, some perhaps native to the soil, and in his family, as in most families, people had had experiences which seemed inexplicable from a rationalistic basis. There is room here for only the most impressive of these, that of his Aunt Mercy.

In her youth . . . she was betrothed to a worthy young man. Late one evening, as she sat musing by the fire in the old kitchen, after the rest of the family had retired, she felt impelled to go to the window, and, looking out, she recognized her lover on horseback approaching the house. As she had reason to suppose that he was then in New York, she was surprised at his unexpected return, and his call at so late an hour. Passing the porch window as she hastened to open the door, she saw her lover ride by it, and turn as if to dismount at the step. The next instant the door was open, but no trace of man or horse was to be seen. Bewildered and terrified, she called her sister, who listened to her story, and tried to soothe her and efface the painful impression. "Thee had better go to bed, Mercy; thee has been asleep and dreaming by the fire," she said. But Mercy was quite sure she had not been asleep, and what she had seen was as real as any waking experience of her life. In recalling the circumstances of her vision, one by one, she at length took notice that she had heard no sound of hoofs! It may be imagined what was the effect of all this upon the sensitive girl, and she was not unprepared, after a weary waiting of many days, to learn through a letter from New York, written by a strange hand, that her lover had died on the very day, and at the hour, of her vision.[36]

As all readers of *The Supernaturalism of New England*[37] and of many of his poems know, psychic phenomena appealed to Whittier, both because he was a man of imagination and because his convictions were anti-materialistic.

Better is it, in a life like ours, to be even a howling dervish or a dancing Shaker, confronting imaginary demons with Thalaba's talisman of faith, than to lose the consciousness of our own spiritual nature, and look upon ourselves as mere brute masses of animal organization,—barnacles on a dead universe; looking into the dull grave with no hope beyond it; earth gazing into earth, and saying to corruption, "Thou art my father," and to the worm, "Thou art my sister."

Yet I should not call Whittier a superstitious man. Though there were times when nostalgia and his sympathy with the ways of old New England caused him to sigh momentarily even over the passing of the more unsavory aspects of occult belief,[38] on the whole he was very successful in holding the balance even. He bluntly calls the Essex County witchcraft epidemic "the dreadful delusion," and he must please even materialists when he writes that "a new coat of paint, in almost all cases, proves an effective exorcism" for whatever inhabits a haunted house. Since he always rejected supernaturalism when it was allied with cruelty, his consistent skepticism on the witchcraft issue is not surprising. He did not pretend to be able to explain everything that occurred at the witch trials, but he suggested that the solution be sought "in the indefinable power of mind over mind—magnetic forces of attraction and repellence—the mental enslavement of the weak and honest by the strong and evil will." J. B. Pickard has pointed out the resemblance between his story "The Weird Gathering" (*Legends of New England*) and Hawthorne's much finer tale of "Young Goodman Brown." It is interesting to remember that Hawthorne disliked *The Supernaturalism of New England* on the ground that Whittier "stoops to the theme with the austere dignity of a schoolmaster at his amusements; a condescension that may seem exaggerated, when we consider that the subject will probably retain a human interest, long after his more earnest efforts shall have lost their importance, in the progress of society." He added that "a narrator should have faith for the time being. If he cannot believe a ghost-story while he is telling it, he had better leave the task to somebody else." [39] Considering the matter, as he did, from the aesthetic point of view, Hawthorne was right, but for Whittier it was basically a moral question. Remembering what superstition in its more horrible aspects had done to his own dreams in childhood, he would not "even for the sake of poetry and romance . . . confirm in any mind a pernicious credulity, or *seek* to absolve myself from that stern duty which the true man owes to his generation, to expose error, whenever and wherever he finds it."

Later, when the spiritualistic movement got under way, the situation was somewhat altered, for phenomena do occur in the séance room, and one cannot explain all of them by simply shutting one's eyes and saying that such things cannot be. Whittier had many friends who were greatly interested in spiritualism—Mrs. Child, Mrs. Stowe, Mrs. Thaxter, and William Lloyd Garrison—but he himself was extremely wary. He participated in séances but without very satisfactory results.

> I have had as good a chance to see a ghost [Mrs. Fields reports him as saying] as anybody ever had, but not the slightest sign ever came to me. I do not doubt what others tell me, but I sometimes wonder over my own incapacity. I should like to see some dear ghost walk in and sit down by me when I am here alone.

This suggests Thomas Hardy's saying that he would be willing to give ten years of his life to be able to see a ghost. But when

Robert Dale Owen asked Whittier what he would do if he did encounter some of the phenomena which others had described, he replied, "I should run."

He found no difficulty in believing "that the spirits of the dead are the viewless watchers of the living—attending and beneficent spirits and retaining the love and sympathy of their humanity," but this was a matter of faith, and not of knowledge attested and authenticated by the five senses. Perhaps in his heart he knew that that was the way he wanted to keep it; perhaps spiritualism seemed too materialistic to him, as it did to Hawthorne. He longed "to get something from the dear ones beyond," but he also felt that he must "wait God's time." As things are now—or as they were in his time—he feared that spiritualism induced credulity in the inquirer and corruption in the medium. Yet when he thought Oliver Wendell Holmes "a little material" in his attitude toward these things, he told him he ought to read the reports of the Society for Psychical Research, and Holmes said he would. Whittier himself went on reading them until he died.

He thought it a little late in the day to regard mesmerism as "wholly charlatanry and imposture," and he was not willing "to reject at once everything which cannot be explained in consistency with a strictly material philosophy. Our whole life is circled about with mystery.... There is a credulity of doubt which is more to be deprecated than that of belief." He indicates some tendency to believe in what is now known as extra-sensory perception or ESP, and he considers the views of Swedenborg both in his essay on the subject and in "My Summer with Dr. Singletary." But he seems to have had no tolerance whatever for phrenology and physiognomy.

In some of Whittier's poems, like "The Cry of a Lost Soul," "Divine Compassion," and "The Two Angels," he may appear to be committing himself to belief in universal salvation, for here God's love brings hope even in hell. Actually, however, he was never a universalist; he simply rejected the idea held by most Christians that probation ends with bodily death. "The Answer" makes all this very clear.

"Though God be good and free be heaven,
No force divine can love compel;
And though the song of sins forgiven
May sound through lowest hell,

"The sweet persuasion of His voice
Respects thy sanctity of will.
He giveth day; thou hast thy choice
To walk in darkness still.

"No word of doom may shut thee out,
No wind of wrath may downward whirl,
No swords of fire keep watch about
The open gates of pearl.

"Forever round the Mercy-seat
The guiding lights of love shall burn;
But what if, habit-bound, thy feet
Shall lack the will to turn?

"What if thine eye refuse to see,
Thine ear of Heaven's free welcome fail,
And thou a willing captive be,
Thyself thy own dark jail?"[40]

In other words, God wills that all men should be saved and sets no arbitrary limits to His love. But the final decision is the man's own: though God "elects" him to salvation, his election is not valid until he himself has accepted it. And even those who, in evangelical parlance, are "saved" when they die, will be obliged to continue to exercise choice in the life to come.

I do not think that God's love for his creatures ever ceases, or that his probation closes with the grave. This view seems to me the necessary consequence of our retaining our personality in the other life. God will not in the resurrection make us mere automata. We *must* have the exercise of free-will, the power of choice, or we cease to be ourselves.

IV

Whittier sympathized with all forms of religious faith and practice—or at least with the spirit behind them—and in a sense assumed the identity of all. For this reason he did not hesitate to use "pagan" materials even in distinctly religious poems.

> He dared not mock the Dervish whirl,
> The Brahmin's rite, the Lama's spell;
> God knew the heart; Devotion's pearl
> Might sanctify the shell.[41]

He did not want Quakers to "beg the world's pardon for having been born," nor, on the other hand, to

> pray over the Pharisee's prayer,
> Nor claim that our wisdom is Benjamin's share.

But I think it must be admitted that he did assume the culmination in Quakerism of tendencies elsewhere only foreshadowed:

> The Word which the reason of Plato discerned;
> The truth, as whose symbol the Mithra-fire burned;
> The soul of the world which the Stoic but guessed,
> In the Light Universal the Quaker confessed!

In 1881 Whittier was very enthusiastic about Protap Chunder Mozoomdar, a delegate from the Oriental society of Brahmo-Somaj, who preached in various Boston churches and in Appleton Chapel at Harvard, but it is clear that this man at no point challenged any of his own beliefs; in fact, Whittier says specifically, "He regards Christ as his divine Master. Though perhaps not a Trinitarian, he is nearer a *Friend* than anything else."[43] I have observed elsewhere[44] that though Whittier uses Oriental materials freely, he always tends to evaluate them in terms of Christian ideals and use them for Christian exhortation. Even in reading his poems about the American Indian, I think one cannot but feel that while he has a strong fellow-feeling for Indians as children of the Great Father, he also assumes that they are still in the primary class.

He was also well aware that many Christians entertained religious beliefs very different from his own. Specifically he was called upon to give careful consideration to the views of Catholic and Calvinist.

Of the two, the Catholics concerned him less, for he was in much less close contact with them. In a sense, we may say that he sympathized with them more, for it was not Catholics but Puritans who had persecuted Quakers, and it was also Puritans who adhered to what he considered the hideous doctrines of foreordination and election.

But Catholicism, too, had several scores against it for Whittier. Ritual held no religious significance for him, and authoritarianism in all forms seemed to him positively anti-religious.[45]

Like all Christians, Whittier nourished his soul on Catholic literature—St. Augustine, Thomas à Kempis, and others—and when he thought Catholics discriminated against, he could always be counted on to take their part. As early as 1829 he favored Catholic emancipation in England. He opposed the anti-Catholic Know-Nothing Movement in this country, and when an anti-Catholic mob burned a convent in Charlestown in 1834, he did his valiant, though fruitless, best to persuade the legislature of Massachusetts to reimburse the Ursuline order for their loss. In 1853 he opposed an attempt to force a Catholic child to read the Protestant Bible in West Amesbury. "That would be little short of persecution—and would be a good cause of complaint in the part of our Catholic fellow citizens." [46]

What he opposed were the ultramontane tendencies in the Catholic Church, which he hated as allying her with religious and political tyranny. When republicanism raised its head in Europe, her influence was on the side of the ancient oppressors, and in this country he found her on the side of the slave traders. "Ireland," he said, "is cursed with Popery. The Protestant section of the island never starves and never begs." He himself spoke of "To Pius IX" and "The Dream of Pio Nona" as anti-Catholic poems, but, he added, "as a Quaker loving peace, and a republican I could say no less, and have nothing to retract." When the

Papacy lost its temporal power, he saw spiritual gain in the deprivation. But he always insisted that there was no theological animus in anything he wrote. "I only hate bigotry, intolerance and persecution, and the sin against the Holy Ghost in opposing every movement of the age for freedom and humanity. It is the Church as a vast political power that I dislike." Over against his anti-Catholic poems stood "The Female Martyr," "Marguerite," "The Men of Old," "Tritemius," and "Mary Garvin," which he considered friendly to Catholicism. Both lists could easily be extended. He was pleased and honored when the Cathedral of St. Boniface in Winnipeg celebrated his eighty-fourth birthday with a "joy-peal" from the tower, ushering in the day. By this time he was eager for an ecumenical movement which should unite all Christians "with no other creed or pledge than a simple recognition of Christ as our leader." "Quakerism has no church of its own," he said—"it belongs to the Church Universal and Invisible."

But if the Catholic Church was unprogressive, this fault was not peculiar to her, nor did Whittier ever suppose that it was. He is comparatively severe in his criticism of Martin Luther and other Reformation leaders on this very score, and we have seen elsewhere how he felt about Protestant apologists for slavery. I have said something in these pages about his attitude toward Puritanism in America, and both Louis C. Shaedler and Cecil B. Williams have said much more elsewhere.[47] Lucy Larcom once asked him, "How can you, a Quaker, enter into the Puritan spirit as you do?" The reason obviously was that he was a child of New England as well as a son of George Fox, and for him "the Pilgrim banner" led "the vanguard of the race." He grumbled at the New England climate, wished the Pilgrim Fathers had drifted around the Horn and landed at Santa Barbara, and once even considered a westward move himself, but in his heart he knew that this was out of the question.

> Then ask not why to these bleak hills
>   I cling, as clings the tufted moss,
> To bear the winter's lingering chills,
>   The mocking spring's perpetual loss.

I dream of lands where summer smiles,
And soft winds blow from spicy isles,
But scarce would Ceylon's breath of flowers be sweet,
Could I not feel thy soil, New England, at my feet! [48]

In less material matters his attitude toward New England was much the same. "There have been dark deeds done in New-England worthy only of the darkest ages of crime and bigotry," and he felt it his duty to point them out, but he is well within his rights when he declares:

I have in many instances alluded to the superstition and bigotry of our ancestors—the rare and bold race who laid the foundation of this republic; but no one can accuse me of having done injustice to their memories. A son of New England, and proud of my birthplace, I would not willingly cast dishonor upon its founders.

He made this statement in his first book, and it never ceased to be true. He loved New England

because it is the home of liberty and equal rights; because the name of slave is not known in her borders; and because no degraded creatures of God are writhing under the oppression of her sons. We rejoice in New England as the native home of intellect—where minds are nurtured into power which may fitly compare with the eternal mountains of her territory or the giant oaks which overshadow them, unbroken by the hurricanes of centuries. We love our birthplace for the manifestations of her moral power—for her free institutions and her quiet religion. These are the monuments of her true glory, for they are unstained with blood, and unmoistened with the tears of the trodden down and oppressed. We boast of no others.

Yet that "quiet religion" included for many of its adherents an acceptance of the whole Calvinistic system, according to which, as the result of Adam's fall, mankind was totally depraved and worthy of damnation. Through Christ's sacrifice and His own mercy, God had elected to save some, but salvation was a free gift—there would have been no injustice had all been lost—and it could therefore be made no reproach against Him that He should have chosen to elect at His own pleasure without regard to the individual merit or lack of it in those who enjoyed the benefit of His bounty. In a race totally corrupt and depraved, what question of merit worthy of salvation could possibly arise?

This point of view was as repugnant to George Fox—and to Whittier—as it was to Milton. None of these denied the sinfulness of mankind, but none would admit that corruption was total and irredeemable.

As a child Whittier refused to study the catechism in school because, in his view and in that of his family, it "contained errors." But his fullest statement of his dissent from the Calvinistic point of view was made in "The Eternal Goodness."

O friends! with whom my feet have trod
  The quiet isles of prayer,
Glad witness to your zeal for God
  And love of man I bear.

I trace your lines of argument;
  Your logic linked and strong
I weigh as one who dreads dissent,
  And fears a doubt as wrong.

But still my human hands are weak
  To hold your iron creeds:
Against the words ye bid me speak
  My heart within me pleads.

The "friends" are fellow Christians who are not Friends, that is, not members of the poet's own religious group—this much is clear from the beginning. He admires their loyalty and devotion but he cannot share their creed. When we come to the "logic" and the "iron creeds" in the second and third stanzas, it becomes clear that Whittier is talking about the Calvinists, who prided themselves upon their logic, which Oliver Wendell Holmes so happily satirized in "The Deacon's Masterpiece." When its time came, the one-hoss shay of Holmes's poem, equally strong (and therefore equally weak) in all its parts, collapsed completely, and there was nothing left. For Whittier, as for Holmes, the shay had already collapsed.

Who fathoms the Eternal Thought?
  Who talks of scheme and plan?
The Lord is God! He needeth not
  The poor device of man.

I walk with bare, hushed feet the ground
  Ye tread with boldness shod;
I dare not fix with mete and bound
  The love and power of God.

Ye praise His justice; even such
  His pitying love I deem:
Ye seek a king: I fain would touch
  The robe that hath no seam.

Ye see the curse which overbroods
  A world of pain and loss;
I hear our Lord's beatitudes
  And prayer upon the cross.

More than your schoolmen teach, within
  Myself, alas! I know:
Too dark ye cannot paint the sin,
  Too small the merit show.

I bow my forehead to the dust,
  I veil mine eyes for shame,
And urge, in trembling self-distrust,
  A prayer without a claim.

I see the wrong that round me lies,
  I feel the guilt within;
I hear, with groan and travail-cries,
  The world confess its sin.

Yet in the maddening maze of things,
  And tossed by storm and flood,
To one fixed trust my spirit clings;
  I know that God is good!

Not mine to look where cherubim
  And seraphs may not see,
But nothing can be good in Him
  Which evil is in me.

Whittier feels man's sinfulness as strongly as any Calvinist, but he feels God's mercy much more strongly. Simply because he does not pretend to understand all mysteries, he does not dare to assume full knowledge of the Mind of God or to set up boundaries beyond which His mercy cannot extend. God is free; He will not be fenced in by the petty logic of man. But there is one thing about which the poet is even more sure than he is about his own sinfulness, and that is that God must be much kinder, better, more merciful than he is. Whittier would not roast a poor sinner forever in the flames of hell for transgressions committed in this earthly life as the result of having inherited a corrupted nature, and therefore he dares not commit the monstrous blasphemy and impiety of assuming that God would do so.

In spite of all his disagreements with members of other religious groups, Whittier's fundamental toleration is clear. He regarded Voltaire, Gibbon, and Hume as having performed valuable service in breaking down old superstitions, insisted that Tom Paine's freethinking was no excuse for failing to acknowledge his great services, and regarded Robert Ingersoll as more unfortunate than wicked. He would not pluck away a defense from the faith of another even if it were a faith he could not share.

> So the man be a man, let him worship at will,
> In Jerusalem's court, or on Gerizim's hill.[49]

But because he believed in religious freedom he also realized that freedom to believe necessarily involves the right to disbelieve:

> I have never joined in the popular clamor against those who are so unfortunate as to doubt or disbelieve the divine origin of the Gospel: I have on all occasions, and at some cost, vindicated their rights of speech and fair hearing; and have, at the risk of misapprehension and obloquy, rebuked the intolerance of and bitter spirit of some of their assailants, who had undertaken to be God's avengers in the matter.[50]

John Greenleaf Whittier was not a great poet. He was not even the best among American poets, having neither the charm and skill of Longfellow nor Whitman's vitality. "He is not rich, nor sonorous, nor a splendid artist," wrote Edmund Gosse; "he is even rather rarely exquisite, but he has an individuality of his own that is of durable importance." If one could have only one word to indicate the nature of that individuality, I think one would choose the word "integrity," and at this point the man and the poet were one. If he sometimes did easy things quite badly in his verses, he also sometimes did difficult things—even impossible things—surprisingly well. Edmund Clarence Stedman was not absurd when he wrote,

"Hermann and Dorothea," "Enoch Arden," even "Evangeline," memorable for beauty of another kind, leave the impression that each of their authors said, as Virgil must have said, "And now I will compose an idyll." Whittier found his idyll already pictured for him by the camera of his own heart.

When he is at his best, Whittier has the rightness of the inevitable about him, and nobody else before Robert Frost was ever able to capture both the face and the soul of New England in verse quite as he did it. Somebody has said that if there were no God, it would be necessary to invent Him. America being what it is, and New England being what it is, it is hard to see how we could have managed to get along without Whittier.

APPENDIX A

Two Problems of Interpretation: Whittier and Mr. and Mrs. James T. Fields

Most of the problems which a biographer must face in interpreting ambiguous evidence concern himself alone. His reader is interested in his conclusions and not in the mental processes he has had to go through in reaching them. Occasionally, however, a question arises which is sufficiently interesting to make the reader enjoy being taken, for a change, behind the scenes.

Two such questions have come up during the writing of this volume. Oddly enough, both involve James T. Fields and his wife.

In her *Whittier: Notes of His Life and of His Friendships*, published in 1893, Mrs. Fields wrote:

> In speaking of Rossetti and of his ballad of "Sister Helen," he [Whittier] confessed to being strangely attracted to this poem, because he could remember seeing his mother, "who was as good a woman as ever lived," and his aunt, performing the same strange act of melting a waxen figure of a clergyman of their time.
>
> The solemnity of the affair made a deep impression on his mind, as a child, for the death of the clergyman in question was confidently expected. His "heresies" had led him to experience this cabalistic treatment.

In other words, Mrs. Fields recorded, without giving any sign of realizing the seriousness of the charge, that Whittier's mother and aunt were witches, or, at least, that on this one occasion they practised witchcraft!

That black magic was practised in New England, as, for that matter, it is still practised in America and elsewhere today, I make no doubt. For New England we may consult Whittier's own study of *The Supernaturalism of New England* and many other books clear on down to Richard M. Dorson's *Jonathan Draws the Low Bow*[1] and beyond. Undoubtedly, many innocent persons were falsely accused of witchcraft in New England as elsewhere, but we must not allow our sympathy for them to cause us to imagine that no one has ever been guilty. I am not of course saying that I *believe* that witches caused thunderstorms by pulling off their stockings and doing all the other crazy things they were accused of doing, but I *am* sure that a good many of them tried their best. This, however, is a very different thing from believing that Whittier's mother and aunt were witches, that they allowed a child to watch their nefarious practices, and that he took it so lightly that, many years afterwards, he could tell Mrs. Fields about it, without any (recorded) sign of moral revulsion. She does say that "the solemnity of the affair made a deep impression on his mind," but not one word is said as to its wickedness, and he is supposed to have gone on believing that his mother was "as good a woman as ever lived."

Human nature is an unbelievably complicated thing, and I am not prepared to say that this incident *could not have happened*. But all the probabilities are against it, and I feel strongly that it should not be accepted on Mrs. Fields's say-so alone. Nothing that we *know* about Whittier's mother causes us to doubt that she *was* as good a woman as ever lived. Moreover, she was a Quaker. I do not wish to suggest that Quakers are necessarily better than other people, but I never heard of a Quaker witch, and even aside from all questions of right and wrong, I find it difficult to believe that Mrs. Whittier could have permitted the faith and practice of witchcraft to co-exist in her life and mind with the other ideas which as a Quaker she must have held. Moreover, the victim in this alleged operation was a clergyman of the neighborhood who was being punished for his "heresies." Why should two Quaker women, who never went to "steeplehouses," and who were living long past the day when clergymen persecuted Quakers, be so upset over the "heresies" of a clergyman who had nothing to do with their family or their own religious lives that they should set out to murder him by supernatural means?

What, then, is the explanation of the story? Mrs. Fields certainly did not mean to lie. It is, of course, *possible* that the child Whittier witnessed some innocent operation which he misinterpreted or misremembered so that afterwards he related it to Mrs. Fields in the manner indicated. But it does not seem very likely. His youthful hunger for marvels would be an argument in favor of this interpretation, but the attitude he held toward his mother militates against it. It is much more likely that Whittier passed on to Mrs. Fields something which, sometime when they were talking about New England superstitions (which, judging by Whittier's interest in the subject, one would suppose they must often have done), his mother related to him as a thing she had, perhaps in her own youth, witnessed in the neighborhood, or which she had been told had occurred. And this Mrs. Fields might easily have misremembered as a thing in which Whittier's mother had herself participated.[2]

The second problem concerns a letter which Whittier wrote Lucy Larcom on February 7, 1866, according to the date on the manuscript in the Morgan Library, though Professor Tryon (*Parnassus Corner*) argues cogently that this must be as error for 1868:

> Tell *Annie Fields* that I was sorry to miss of a visit at her house when I was in Boston. Gail Hamilton advised me not to think of going to Charles Street. The lack of domestic peace and harmony there—Mrs. F's brusque rough way and Mr. F's exacting and tyrannical behavior would, she said, make my visit anything but agreeable!

Mordell, who prints this passage (*Quaker Militant*, p. 303) not uncharacteristically takes it as manifesting Whittier's ability to come "perilously near the verge of duplicity," since he continued to praise James and Annie Fields to their faces. So it does, and worse, if it is to be taken at face value. But can it be?

Whatever variations of opinion may exist as to the character and personality of Annie Fields, to describe her as "brusque" or "rough" seems utterly fantastic. And that Fields himself should have become so "exacting" and "tyrannical" in his home as to disturb the comfort of so honored a guest as Whittier—and that guest one of his own most prized authors—none of this makes sense. "My dear Annie Fields," wrote Whittier on February 8, 1867, "thy little note did me good, although I did not need its assurances of thy generous hospitality."

Fields was the publisher who "made" Whittier one of the standard American poets. It was to this man's faith in his poetry and his skillful marketing thereof that all the comfort and prosperity of Whittier's later years was due. "With God all things are possible, and He might have made a better man and more generous publisher—but, He never did." In 1877 Whittier wrote Lucy Larcom herself of Fields that "he is a genuine kind-hearted man and Annie is of the best," and when the publisher died in 1881, Whittier described him to Elizabeth Stuart Phelps as "my friend of nearly 40 years," with "never a shadow . . . for a moment on the sunshine of that friendship." He had no reservations about Fields's character either. "He loved much, pitied much, but never hated. He was Christlike in kindness and sympathy and doing good." There does not seem to be any harshness or tyranny here. As for Mrs. Fields, she was the friend

whose generous love has made
My last days best

and

her in whom
All graces and sweet charities unite,
The old Greek beauty set in holier light.

On March 25, 1866, Whittier writes Lucy Larcom of "that flower of Christian womanhood, our dear good Annie Meadows" (a playful variant on "Fields"), and on May 10 he asks Celia Thaxter: "Does thee see Mrs. Fields often? It always does me good to meet her she is so thoroughly good and charming." When, after her husband's death, Mrs. Fields gave herself to good works, the poet was greatly impressed by her self-sacrifice:

I think of thee in this town toiling at thy holy work, literally giving thy dear life for the poor and suffering who may never know or thank their benefactor, and I have an inexpressible desire to manifest in some way my love and sympathy. Thee have been so much to me—not only an inspiration and ideal but a blessed human friend.

Only a year before his death he is still asking her: "And how shall I speak of all thou hast been to me?"

Gail Hamilton's part in the "brusque rough" letter needs less interpretation. If it was written in 1868 it comes out of the heart of the period when she was engaged in the bitter controversy with Fields over royalty payments which culminated in her publication of *A Battle of the Books* in 1870.[3] The problem here is different in character from the previously considered reference to witchcraft, for this time there can be no question that Whittier wrote the words under consideration: the only question is, what did he mean by them? Gail Hamilton was, as we have seen, a close friend, and I once wondered whether Whittier might have been so much under her influence at this time as to believe everything she told him, even to the extent of allowing her to poison his mind against Mr. and Mrs. Fields or, as Mordell suggests, to cause him to behave hypocritically toward them. In the light of the evidence already presented, however, this hypothesis is quite untenable, and there is this further letter to Mrs. Fields herself, December 1, 1884:

I have not seen Hawthorne's book and do not care to. I hope thee will not let it trouble thee. I tried to stop G.H.'s foolish and as it seemed to me unjust course, and when I heard her book was ready for publication I urged her to suppress it, and even offered to pay one half of the expense of the suppression. It fell dead from the press, and I don't know of anybody who read it. I don't see how thee can blame thyself for poor Mrs. Hawthorne's misapprehensions, or feel any misgivings for the enjoyment of an exceptionally sheltered and beautiful life, the great happiness of which was so generously shared with others. We were all thankful for its warmth and brightness.

It might of course be argued that what Whittier felt in 1884 was not necessarily what he had felt in 1868 (or 1866), but from the retrospective references in this letter, it seems clear that he at no time accepted Gail Hamilton's views about Fields, that he regarded her as having misled Mrs. Hawthorne, and that he did his best to prevent the publication of *A Battle of the Books.* But we are not dependent upon retrospective references alone. For in 1870 Whittier had written Fields himself:

I've looked over Gail's book slightly. I cannot help thinking you might have managed her more shrewdly. You should have remembered... that women are "kittle cattle to show behind." If thee was an old bachelor like myself I should pity thee under such clapper-clawin, but haven't thee one of the dearest and best of women to heal the scratches?

He advised against replying: " 'The battle of the books' would only 'make sport for the Philistines.' It will die in nine days."

"Hawthorne's book" was obviously the official biography, *Nathaniel Hawthorne and His Wife,* by their son, Julian Hawthorne. Neither James nor Annie Fields is mentioned in it, though it was published by what had been Fields's house, then called James R. Osgood and Company. I would add that since *A Battle of the Books* went through three editions, it can hardly have fallen "dead from the press."

The "brusque rough" letter, then, remains something of a problem, but it seems to me that it was a joke which Miss Larcom understood because she and Whittier had already talked about the matter, and which appears cryptic to us only because we have not had that experience. I believe, further, that if there is any barb in this letter, it is directed against Gail Hamilton, and not against Mr. and Mrs. Fields. Notice the underlining of "*Annie Fields*" and the exclamation point after "agreeable," which latter, by the way, is omitted, no doubt inadvertently, from both the Mordell and the Tryon texts. Does not Whittier mean to imply that the sentiments he has recorded and attributed to Gail Hamilton are unreasonable and absurd, and that both he and his correspondent view them in that light? If not, what is he exclaiming about? Obviously, for some reason, perhaps the pressure of business, Whittier had failed to visit Mrs. Fields during his recent stay in Boston. But he would hardly have sent his regrets for this failure through Lucy Larcom afterwards if the reason he gave his correspondent was the real reason. Mr. Mordell "wonders" if Mrs. Fields "ever suspected that the poet spoke of her 'brusque, rough way.' " But how do we know that Lucy Larcom, conveying Whittier's message, did not show her the letter which they both understood, as we do not, and that they shared the wry amusement which is the best anyone can derive from such a reference?

To this Mr. Mordell and those like-minded might no doubt reply that I have tried to clear Whittier of the charge of having acted hypocritically toward Mr. and Mrs. Fields only to convict him of similar behavior toward Gail Hamilton. But if he was as frank with Gail herself concerning his disapproval of her course as his 1884 letter to Mrs. Fields seems to prove he was, even this could hardly be said to follow. I may add that Mr. Roland H. Woodwell believes that the underlining and the exclamation point in Whittier's letter to Lucy Larcom indicate that he was not merely laughing *at* Gail Hamilton but *with* her, or, in other words, that the harmony between the Fieldses was accepted as axiomatic to such an extent that when Gail warned Whittier not to go there, she was consciously being absurd, and that this was clear to Whittier, to Lucy Larcom, and to Gail Hamilton herself. But *could* Gail Hamilton, being as angry as she was with Fields at this time, have been that playful about him? I do not know; I let the question stand. Whether the reader prefers Mr. Woodwell's interpretation or the one that I have set forth here, it is still clear, I think, that Whittier was *not* taken in, and that he never believed Mrs. Fields to be brusque and rough or her husband tyrannical and exacting. And this is really all that I have tried to show.

APPENDIX B

Whittier On War

Whittier's ability to face a war situation and to rebuke his country in truly prophetic strain when she did wrong deserves fuller illustration than it can be accorded in the text. Fortunately such illustration lies ready to hand in two magnificent editorials published in *The National Era* May 20 and June 3, 1847, respectively, which have, unhappily, lost none of their bite during the century and a quarter that has passed since they appeared. They have nowhere been reprinted, though they have been quoted by James Welford Holmes in his unpublished Ph.D. dissertation, "Whittier's Prose on Reforms Other than Abolition," University of Pittsburgh, 1945. The innocent titles add notably to the ironic effect, and the fact that the first begins as it does conveniently illustrates Whittier's saneness and lack of fanaticism. He was a very prim and proper person, but he kept sins as well as virtues in proper proportion, never confusing peccadilloes with crimes against humanity.

DANCING AND SABBATH BREAKING

Now, as in the days of our savior, there are those who may be said to "strain at a gnat, and swallow a camel"—men who are sorely afflicted with the running of the mails on the first day of the week, and are very solemn and emphatic in their condemnation of dancing, who can nevertheless look with complacency upon the sin and horror of slavery, and upon the unutterable horrors of war.

Now, as to dancing in general, we shall undertake no defence of it, although we are scarcely prepared to subscribe to the stern sentiment of Luther, that "as many steps as one takes in a dance, he takes towards hell." We leave the matter to be settled between the Presbyterian General Assembly and the Shakers. But there is a dance going on at this time in Mexico, to which we particularly invite the attention of respectable doctors of divinity who are weeping between the porch and the temple over the saltatory sins of the people. Did these reverend gentlemen ever hear of Holbein's *Dance of Death?* That dance, with the Arch Fiend for piper, is now going on. It is an out-of-door dance, on a magnificent scale, with the whole universe for spectators. The plains and mountain slopes of Mexico are

the ball-room,
With the cannon's lightning lit;
O'erspread with gay, green carpets,
Which the dancing steeps in wet.

Then, as to the desecration of the Sabbath day. The zeal which claps in prison the poor "Comeouter" for esteeming all days alike, and which runs a tilt at steam cars, and lays a *taboo* upon Sunday mail bags, may or may not be according to knowledge. We venture no opinion in respect to it, but would simply suggest, with the deference befitting to one of the laity, that its attention might be very profitably turned to some recent transactions of our Christian army and navy, engaged in opening the way for the introduction of the Gospel into Mexico. If our Almanac does not deceive us, our navy spent a Sabbath at Tabasco some months ago, and performed "services" of an impressive but somewhat equivocal kind, sending messengers of peace and good will among the poor, benighted Catholics, in the shape of red hot balls and shells. More recently General Scott, has "kept the Sabbath" on the heights of Cerro Gordo, storming batteries, blowing whole squadrons into eternity, impaling men on bayonets, and tearing off their limbs with cannon shot. We should like to know what General Assemblies and Conferences think of this way of spending holy time. The occasions referred to were doubtless solemn enough to satisfy the Puritan tythingman—as much so, in short, as dying groans and ghastly corpses could make them. But apart from this, we cannot see that storming of forts, and slaughter of women and children on their own hearths, or while kneeling in their places of worship is a more appropriate Sunday business than the running of the United States mail or the delving of a Seventh-Day Baptist in his potato field. We respectfully refer the whole matter to the Tennessee Methodists, who have made Captain Walker of the Texas Rangers, and the leading heroes of Monterey, life members of their Missionary Society; and to the Western Home Missionary Society of Baltimore, of which General Taylor has just been made a life member; and to the Old and New School Presbyterian Assemblies subject, as a matter of course, to the formal action of the Evangelical Alliance.

PIETY AND JUSTICE

No one can well doubt that in matters civil, military, and religious, this is a great country, and that General Scott is representing it very appropriately in Vera Cruz. After raining down fire on Vera Cruz for four days and nights, burying a thousand women and children under the ruins of their dwellings, blowing up crowded hospitals, dropping ninety-pound shells through the roofs of churches, and sprinkling altars with the blood of the kneeling worshippers, the very next we hear of the victorious General, he is found in a Catholic cathedral, which he had just shattered and defaced by his horrible projectiles, amidst the friends and relatives of the slaughtered victims, devoutly, and, as the letter-writers who describe the scene tell us, "very solemnly holding a long wax candle," as doing penance for the desecration of the church and the massacre of the female devotees—making, in short, like Louis XV on his deathbed, "the *amende honorable* to God!" Verily, if the Catholics of Mexico, after such a signal manifestation as this of the piety of their country's invaders, harden their hearts against them, and refuse to recognize them as their true friends and benefactors, there is no longer any virtue in Paixhans guns, and wax candles, Bowie knives and Bibles, patent revolvers and certificates of life membership in missionary societies!

In accents startlingly anticipative of Mr. Dooley, Whittier then goes on to describe a recent incident which proves "that the hero of Vera Cruz is as just as he is pious." This concerns the case of a Negro hanger-on of the army who had been hanged for looting.

And very pleasant and satisfiactory it must have been to that shrewd hoydenish dame known as American Justice, who, we are given to understand, is now campaigning in Mexico in the capacity of camp follower, with one eye partially clear of her bandage, for the laudable purpose of due discrimination as to color. Having hung out the "slovenly unhandsome corpse" to the sun and wind, we can imagine the redoubtable General turning with no slight degree of complacency to the assembled multitude: "There, you poor miserable misguided Mexicans, saw you ever the like of that? There is law and order for you—there's a sacrifice. There you have the astounding moral spectacle of a *black* Yankee hung like a dog for insulting Mexican ladies. Now let me hear no more of your pitiful complaints of the conduct of our chivalrous volunteers at Matamoras, Monterey, and Saltito. There's your negro, gentlemen and ladies; you can't deny the evidence of your own eyes; it's a "fixed fact," as my friend Colonel (I beg his pardon, General) Cushing would say, that he hangs there as dead as Julius Caesar, in expiation of all offences of the kind you complain of, past, present, and to come. If my soldiers had not pawned their Bibles for Whiskey I could show you, what as Catholics you are doubtless ignorant of, that that negro answers practically the same purpose to the American army that the scape-goat which General Moses sent into the chapparals did to the Jews, when they were engaged like ourselves in conquering a peace with the heathen round about. Now, ain't you ashamed of yourselves for your folly in opposing me? Ain't you thankful that you have fallen into the hands of a chieftain who holds a candle to the Virgin, and hangs black Yankees, to expiate the sins of the white ones?"

Seriously, our readers must pardon us for our manner of dealing with this subject. What with ringing bells of Protestant meeting-houses and chanting *Te Deums* in Catholic ones; equipping volunteers with Bibles and Bowie knives; hounding on the way with the yell of "No Popery" at home, and holding candles before the image of the Virgin in Mexico; winking at wholesale rape and murder perpetrated by whites, and hanging a black loafer for following their example; praying for peace on earth, and making professional fighters life members of missionary societies—this whole Mexican War matter at times assumes the appearance of a hideous joke—a grim farce, the plot of which must have been borrowed from beneath.

NOTES

The Notes and the Bibliography in this book are intended to be used together. Bibliographical items given in the Notes are not generally repeated in the Bibliography.

The following abbreviations have been used in both Notes and Bibliography:

ABC	American Book Company
AF	*The American Friend*
AL	*American Literature*
BFHA	*Bulletin of the Friends' Historical Association*
C	Thomas Y. Crowell & Co.
D	Doubleday & Co. (and their predecessors)
EIHC	*Essex Institute Historical Collections*
ESQ	*Emerson Society Quarterly*
FIJ	*Friends' Intelligencer and Journal*
FQE	*Friends' Quarterly Examiner*
H	Harper & Brothers
HB	Harcourt, Brace & Co. (under all firm names employed)
HM	Houghton Mifflin Company (under all firm names employed)
HUP	Harvard University Press
IJHP	*Iowa Journal of History and Politics*
JGW	John Greenleaf Whittier
JRUL	*Journal of the Rutgers University Library*
LB	Little, Brown and Company
M	The Macmillan Company
NEM	*New England Magazine*
NEQ	*New England Quarterly*
OUP	Oxford University Press
PQ	*Philological Quarterly*
S	Charles Scribner's Sons
W	Whittier

BIOGRAPHY

1 The British writer W. J. Linton, in the *Life of Whittier* published in Scott's "Great Writers" series, 1893, says, "Yet I have a letter from him [Whittier] in his own handwriting, bearing date of '13, 9mo, 1875,' in which, answering my inquiry, he writes: 'My birthday was the very last of the year 1807.'"

2 Elizabeth French, transcriber, "English Ancestry of the Whittier and Rolfe Families," *New England Historical and Genealogical Register*, LXVI (1912), 244-57; Pollard, *JGW, Friend of Man*, Appendix A, pp. 583-8.

3 See Roland H. Woodwell, "The Hussey Ancestry of the Poet W," *EIHC*, LXX (1934), 56-68. For an entertaining account of Stephen Bachiler's career, see S. T. Pickard, *JGW*, I, 10-13.

4 See Whittier's poem, "A Name." Among his intimates, Whittier seems generally to have been called "Greenleaf," not "John."

5 The special problems involved in this task, which were great, are well described in a fascinating article by Eleanor M. Tilton, "Making Whittier Definitive," *NEQ*, XII (1939), 281-314.

CHAPTER ONE: A SIDE TO FACE THE WORLD WITH

1 This does not mean that Longfellow lacked the courage to stand up and be counted. He, too, mourned Webster as "Fallen, fallen, fallen from his high estate." Though the *Poems on Slavery* were written "in a kindly—not a vindictive spirit," they sufficiently pleased Whittier himself so that he urged their author to run for Congress on an anti-slavery platform, and Longfellow allowed the New England Anti-Slavery Association to reprint and circulate them in the South, precisely where they could hurt his reputation most. When, in 1858, Edward Everett remarked that he had signed a certain petition, Longfellow could barely refrain "from asking him if he 'signed it without reading it,' or 'under the effects of an anodyne,' as he said at the South he had done the Sumner testimonial, the coward!" And when a Florida judge argued that "Do unto others" merely meant that you must treat your slaves as you would wish to be treated if you were a slave, the poet did not restrain himself at all: "If you were a slave, the thing you would wish for most of all would be your freedom. So your Scripture argument for Slavery is knocked into a cocked hat." It is true, nevertheless, that Longfellow was temperamentally unquali-

fied to give himself to a systematic course of anti-slavery agitation, and if the freedom of the slaves depended upon such agitation, then they would never have been freed if all men had been like Longfellow. But this disqualification in itself testifies to Longfellow's pacific temperament. Perhaps the truth of the matter is that W was a pacifist by conviction and Longfellow by temperament.

2 For a letter of 1885, showing how carefully W studied his pictures and how anxious he was that they should not misrepresent him, see *BFHA*, XLVI (1951), 35-6. Albert Mordell, *Quaker Militant*, p. 300, takes this kind of thing as manifesting W's vanity, but it is a mistake to suppose that those who primp and edit their looks most elaborately are necessarily the most self-satisfied of mortals. Some of the worst egotists are to be found among those who force their contemporaries to accept them as they are, in all their native crudity and ugliness.

3 *Silhouettes of My Contemporaries* (D, 1921).

4 Richard Burton, *JGW*, says W also lost all his teeth in old age, but I have found no confirmation of this. Though he frequently apologizes for the illegibility of his letters, his handwriting shows no real deterioration, such as might be expected from failing sight, until just before the end.

5 Not to alarm his family, W bound up his face in a handkerchief and hurried to the doctor to have the wound dressed. The unintentional assailant, Philip Butler, afterwards the artist who painted the picture of the Haverhill homestead still to be seen at the birthplace, was greatly moved by W's kindness to him.

6 "To one who had not heard from many patients the tale of their sufferings exactly like that of W, and who had not observed in them the same results of self-scrutiny, exhaustion, and sensitiveness, the fact of his daily concern and emphasis of pain, might itself seem morbid. But the sympathetic oculist will make no such mistake. There is no disease more terrible in its intensity of pain [than presbyopia], more likely to crush out vitality and morale than this agonizing affliction. Had W not been essentially of the heroic type, a Friend who by ancestry, faith, and nurture had not [*sic*] been predestined to quiet valor and endurance, the pain he suffered would not have left him his heart of healthy and sunny manliness." George M. Gould, *Biographic Clinics*, Vol. II (P. Blakiston's Son & Co., 1904). Dr. Gould may have been right, but the layman's faith in his diagnosis must, I think, be

weakened by the astonishing number of literary persons whom he finds to have been similarly afflicted.

7 "The Garrison of Cape Ann." Cf. Longfellow's "The Beleaguered City."

8 This seems very close to Christian Science. Though he nowhere refers to it in print nor in any letter that I have seen, W received a visit from Mrs. Eddy, whom he is said to have found a "bright and interesting woman." She sent him an autographed copy of *Science and Health*, but since it was found in the attic after his death, he does not seem to have prized it very highly. W does not appear to have had much sympathy with the nineteenth-century passion for hydropathy either. A rainy autumn day reminded him of "that rayless atmosphere of Dante's Third Circle, where the infernal Preissnitz administers his hydropathic treatment."

9 Like Robert Burns, W certainly overstrained himself in farm work as a boy, in addition to which he nearly froze to death in winter. Early New Englanders dressed in homespun, which supplied very inadequate protection against the rigorous climate. Their homes were inadequately heated by wood-burning fireplaces and their meeting-houses not at all. Much as young W loved Quaker meeting, he was never sorry when circumstances decreed that he should miss the eight-mile winter drive from Haverhill to the meeting-house in Amesbury. The wildest conjecture as to the cause of his physical condition is of course that of Mordell, who attributes it to sexual suppression. Perhaps the best reply was that of the blunt contemporary reviewer who invited him to consider instead the possible influence of the old New England habit of pie for breakfast and baked beans for supper.

10 "W," *AL*, IX (1937), 335-42. Even the angel at the end of *Snow-Bound* has "wings of ashen gray." "Patterns of light and shade in summer woods," "autumn eves when the spectrum begins to disappear," "the sea when shadows fell dark upon its face"—this was W's material. Powell further found W's imagery largely visual, with no auditory image in the whole of "Summer by the Lakeside" and only two color adjectives in nearly 100 lines.

11 It is possible that he may also have torn the title page from B. L. Mirick's *History of Haverhill* because he was annoyed over Mirick's not having given him proper credit, but in this case the evidence is not conclusive. See Currier, *Bibliography*, p. 19. The most substantial argument in favor of the view that Whittier had a substan-

tial share in this book is in Theodore Roosevelt Garrison's unpublished dissertation, "JGW, Pioneer Regionalist and Folklorist." Garrison not only finds two distinct styles in the book but believes that W later paraphrased portions of it in "The Boy Captives" and "The Border War of 1708."

12 S. T. Pickard, *JGW*, I, 327-8. For other slavery poems containing vituperation, see "At Washington," "Official Piety," "Lines on the Portrait of a Celebrated Publisher," "The Panorama," "The Mantle of St. John de Matha," "A Sabbath Scene," and "Moloch in State Street." See Carpenter, *JGW*, pp. 221-2, for the view that W later regretted his attack on Webster. All that can be stated with certainty is that he once asked Elizabeth Stuart Phelps whether she thought he had been too severe. In "The Lost Occasion" (1880), he takes the position that if Webster had lived into Civil War times, he would have been a strong champion of the Union cause. For an analysis of "Ichabod," see J. B. Pickard, *JGW*, pp. 106-7. If Lewis Leary's interpretation of the poem in his *JGW*, pp. 107-8, is correct, W was also hitting below the belt by including oblique reference to Webster's alleged drinking, but this cannot be proved. It was not his habit to introduce irrelevant considerations into anti-slavery controversy.

13 Reprinted in Cady and Clark, *W on Writers and Writing*, pp. 54-66.

14 Published in S. T. Pickard, *JGW*, I, 106-9.

15 See Mary Thacher Higginson, ed., *Letters and Journals of Thomas Wentworth Higginson, 1846-1906* (HM, 1921), pp. 8-11.

16 W's introduction to Oliver Johnson's *William Lloyd Garrison and His Times* (HM, 1881), in which he looked back over his association with Garrison, was very generous.

17 *Works*, V. Cf. in the same sketch, the sympathetic portrayal of the renegade clergyman. "The Opium Eater," too, seems an odd subject for W, and though it was doubtless derived mainly from his interest in De Quincey, his attitude is strangely tolerant.

18 Pollard is wrong, however, when he states that Whittier is known to have taken a drink only in 1849, when he used brandy as a remedy for seasickness between Hartford and New York. He had the exaggerated nineteenth-century notions concerning the medicinal value of alcohol, and the "small phial of brandy" seems to have been part of his travel equipment. When he inadventently left it behind in 1881, he wrote Phebe Woodman about it, adding that the loss was

"of no consequence" since, should anything of the kind be needed, the "good cider" available would serve the same purpose. In 1830 in Hartford, he had "gin sling and brandy and laudanum" for medicinal purposes. In 1867 he wrote Mrs. Fields of having used "the heroic remedy of quinine and whiskey" for neuralgia, adding that "if Neale Dow," the renowned temperance advocate, "had an hour's taste of my ache, he would waive his scruples and do likewise," and more than twenty-five years later, he wrote her of having used "milk toddy" with rum for sleeplessness, but without much success.

Probably in 1884, Whittier wrote Fields himself asking for "some nice grapes,—a few only—and a bottle of pure Sherry wine, [if] the last is to be had in Boston." Since most of this letter is concerned with Elizabeth's illness, the wine may well have been intended for her. Though I have no doubt that Whittier's teetotalism was far more consistent than that of Harriet Beecher Stowe, for example, it cannot be called absolute. In 1868 he declined to come to the Fieldses for a birthday party to Longfellow, "but although a cold-water man by habit and principle, I may by virtue of the doctor's prescription be able to drain at my own fire-side my glass of Brown Sherry, to the Health, happiness and long life of Longfellow." But it was in October 1891 that he really seemed to be "going it" for him, for a New York banker had sent him "a bottle of wonderful old whiskey" (how did he know it was "wonderful"?), Mrs. Fields had sent "a bottle of the famous Tokaya wine, like liquid sunshine," and the ladies of the neighborhood were keeping him "abundantly supplied" with wine jelly. The next year he received some "rare old Andalusian" for his birthday. "I am not accustomed to tarry long at the wine," he tells Frank P. Stearns—"in this case I shall remember Paul's advice to Timothy."

In addition to these references, there is a very puzzling letter, written to Jonathan Law from New York, January 5, 1831. W reports having declined an invitation to a convivial evening from Halleck, Edwin Forrest, and others. "I have no idea of soaking my brains in champagne or Madeira, when I have so much use for them," presumably in connection with the life of Clay that was in preparation. But he goes on: "Once let this ugly affair be off my hands, and I will drink with the hardest skull among them," and this passage is completely out of character with all that we know of him or with anything that he says elsewhere. In another letter to Law, January 15, 1831, there is another amazing statement: "Tell Mary that she must have some snuff in her box by the time I get home." Possibly these are jokes, perpetrated by W or another. I quote from the copies of these letters in the Whittier-Pickard papers at Harvard; the location of the originals, if they exist, is unknown to me.

19 *Autobiography, Memories and Experiences* (HM, 1904).

20 "Tauler."

21 See, in the present volume, pp. 108-9. The long poem "The Panorama" describes that popular form of nineteenth-century entertainment, and there is a sympathetic reference to dancing (see also Appendix B) in *The Stranger in Lowell:* "With a little effort of fancy, one could readily transform the huge mills, thus illuminated, into palaces lighted up for festival occasions, and the figures of the workers, passing to and fro before the windows, into forms of beauty and fashion, moving in graceful dances." W himself watched the Virginia reel at the White Mountains. In a letter to Mary Emerson Smith he speaks of waltzing.

22 There is also a better-known reference to Barnum in the famous letter to Fields (S. T. Pickard, *JGW*, II, 512) in which W expressed his amused dismay at the unexpected success of *The Tent on the Beach:* "This will never do. The swindle is awful. Barnum is a saint to us."

23 *Biography and the Human Heart* (HM, 1932), p. 124.

24 Did Emmons hunt for pictures? Was Jonathan
Edwards peeping
Into the chambers of imagery with maids for
*Tammuz weeping?

* Eze. 8:14

Ah well! tho times are sadly changed, and I myself
am feeling
The wicked world my Quaker coat from off my
shoulders peeling,
God grant that in the strange new sea of change
wherein we swim,
We still may keep the good old plan of simple
faith in Him!

25 "I would be happy to meet the wonderful violinist at thy house. If I am able—just now I am suffering too much with my head and eyes to listen even with any satisfaction to the harp of Orpheus—I will try to arrange it. I am greatly obliged to him for thinking of me and volunteering to play for me." Letter to Whipple, Nov. 25, 1880, quoted by Lilian Whiting, *Boston Days* (LB, 1902), p. 414.

26 See Bliss Perry, in *The Early Years of the Saturday Club* (HM, 1918), p. 188: "He had fought the 'Cotton Whigs' of State Street too bitterly to stretch his legs under respectable Boston mahogany and feel quite at ease in Zion."

27 It is interesting that Mark Twain, who made the *faux pas* of his life at the Whittier Birthday Dinner, where Boston failed to appreciate his skit about the three mining-camp "bums" who impersonated Longfellow, Emerson, and Holmes and conversed in terms of quotations from their poetry, should have apologized afterwards to all three of these, but was too much impressed by "the well-nigh sacred place" which the guest of honor held "in his people's estimation" to venture to write to him. "I do not reverence Mr. Emerson less, but somehow I could approach him easier."

28 "The Voices."

29 See "The Last Walk in Autumn," XII, XIII.

30 See "The Pageant."

31 But he made no idol of truth-telling either, as witness this paragraph in Mrs. Fields's diary: "Whittier said one day, when we were talking of the *Life of Charlotte Brontë* by Mrs. Gaskell, and I was saying how sad it was she should have made the old man, her father, suffer unto death, as she did, by telling the tale of his bad son's life, and 'still worse,' I said, 'she came out in the Athenaeum and declared that her story was false, when she knew it was true, hoping to comfort the old man,'—'I don't know,' said Whittier; 'I am inclined to think that was the best part of it, if her lie would have done the old man any good!'" M. A. de Wolfe Howe, ed., *Memories of a Hostess* (Atlantic Monthly Press, 1922), p. 131.

32 See Joseph Shearing's novel, *Airing in a Closed Carriage* (H, 1943) and Edgar Lustgarten's factual account in his *Verdict in Dispute* (S, 1950).

33 *Memorial to JGW by the Citizens of Amesbury*, p. 48.

34 See, especially, *Quaker Militant*, pp. 243-5, 294.

35 The most amusing sexual reference in W occurs, I think, in his poem about Adam and Eve, "A Lay of Old Time":

> She, blushing in her fig-leaf suit
> For the chaste garb of old....

But surely the most sophisticated touch of feminine psychology, and an amusing piece of double entendre besides (I know no parallel to it in any of his other portraits of women), occurs in "The Witch of Wenham," after the daughter of the falsely accused woman has been carried off to safety by her lover:

> The maiden laughed, as youth will laugh
> At all its fears gone by;
> "He does not know," she whispered low,
> "A little witch am I."

With this compare the last stanza of "Mabel Martin," Part IV. Mr. Woodwell tells me that these passages have been considered false notes historically, since in those days nobody joked about witchcraft, and I am sure he is right. But they are not therefore less revealing of Whittier's own attitude.

36 *Eighty Years and More* (European Publishing Company, 1898).

37 Leary, *JGW*, pp. 112, 129, acutely observes in W's humor certain anticipations of Huckleberry Finn.

38 *Literary Friends and Acquaintance* (H, 1900), p. 135.

39 Children were something of a special case. Though his relations with Phebe Woodman, his cousin's adopted daughter, and with Margaret Lothrop, daughter of Daniel Lothrop and his wife Margaret Sidney, author of *Five Little Peppers and How They Grew*, were very affectionate (see Margaret Sidney, "W and the Children," *Wide-Awake*, XXXVI [1893], 11-28), he could not romp with children as Dickens and Mark Twain did. Still he agreed with Dickens that it was unimaginative to dismiss children's problems as trifling simply because they did not appear serious from the adult point of view. It has been recorded that he once startled a child who was staring at his sister Elizabeth's large nose by asking, "Well, and how does thee like Quaker noses?" but Caroline Carter told Mr. Woodwell that she was the child and that it was Elizabeth herself who asked the question. Martha Hale Shackford admits that W was "not fertile in finding topics for conversation" with children but praises him because "he refrained from making the stereotyped inquiries into school life and such affairs, never feeling it necessary that something should be said at all hazards. With some tangible object before him, a photograph, or a book, he gained a sort of protection, and, thus fortified, loved to point out interesting features, taking in this mode of entertainment what seemed to be an absorbing pleasure." When Martha embarrassed her

elders and attracted attention to herself by propounding the riddle "What is it that is put on the table and cut but not eaten?" (the answer was "Cards"), W laughed heartily and gave no sign of having been offended. In his introduction to *Child-Life in Prose,* he finds that "the happiest people in the world are those who still retain something of the child's creative faculty of imagination, which makes atmosphere and color, sun and shadow, and boundless horizons out of what seems to prosaic wisdom most inadequate material...." There is, however, a disappointing passage at the close of "Charms and Fairy Faith" (*Works,* V), where he seems to take the view that the day of the child's fairy tale has gone by. "The wonderland of childhood must henceforth be sought within the domains of truth."

CHAPTER TWO: POWER AND LOVE

1 "An Autograph." W may have had something of a spiritual awakening at the Newport Quarterly Meeting of 1840, when Richard Mott apparently communicated to him a conviction that the Lord had laid His hand on him. If not a "conversion," in the Calvinistic sense, this may well have approximated, in a quiet Quaker way, what a prophet might describe as a "call."

2 "A Retrospect," in S. T. Pickard, *Whittier-Land,* p. 35.

3 George F. Hoar, *Autobiography of Seventy Years* (S, 1903). Cf. C. Marshall Taylor, "JGW, The Quaker Politician," in Howard H. Brinton, ed., *Byways in Quaker History* (Pendle Hill, 1944).

4 W never abandoned this point of view. In 1889 he contributed to Abby Johnson Woodman's *Picturesque Alaska* (HM), an introduction in which he shows his sense of "the value and importance of the acquisition of Alaska" and of the "material benefits which must accrue to the country, from its vast resources of mines, lumber, and fisheries" as well as "the grandeur and picturesqueness of its scenery...." Whitman Bennett remarks that W's campaign song for Henry Clay, Cincinnati *Advertiser,* May 30, 1830, was "the first W ballad to sweep the country."

5 For W's intercourse with Cushing from an extreme pro-Cushing point of view, see Claude M. Fuess, *The Life of Caleb Cushing* (HB, 1923). Fuess extravagantly compares W's methods to those of Tammany Hall and writes that "it was Whittier's avowed aim to extort from the Massachusetts Congressman every concession to anti-

slavery principles which could be secured by any kind of strategy short of criminal methods." Cushing's niece probably echoed her uncle's point of view when she told Mr. Woodwell that the slavery problem would have solved itself if the abolitionists had not stirred it up. For Sumner see J. Welford Holmes, "W and Sumner: A Political Friendship," *NEQ*, XXX (1957), 58-72.

6 In 1855, W even reached out into Iowa and helped secure the defeat of the pro-slavery senator, Augustus Caesar Dodge. See C. A. Hawley, *BFHA*, XXVIII (1939), 19-20.

7 Quoted by T. F. Currier, "W and the *New England Weekly Review*," *NEQ*, VI (1933), 589-97.

8 For W's shoemaking see Pollard, *JGW*, pp. 507-8, n. 23. If W seems a little coy about it, perhaps the reason is merely that he did not wish to give the impression that shoemaking had been his trade. Mr. Woodwell tells me that he was described as "a shoemaker" in the Harvard hymn book as late as 1926.

9 The figures are from Pollard and apparently derived from his inspection of the will at the Essex County Probate Court, Salem.

10 Appendix III of J. W. Holmes's dissertation, "Whittier's Prose on Reforms Other than Abolition," comprises a list of "W's Personal Acts of Charity and His Appeals for Victims of Disasters."

11 Through Sumner, W got his brother, Matthew Franklin Whittier (the humorist "Ethan Spike"), a place in the Boston Custom House in 1861 and intervened to keep him in office in 1865 and again in 1877. In 1865 he wrote Hannibal Hamlin: "He [MFW] is a true Republican and has done all in his power as a writer to promote the cause of loyalty and freedom. He is a poor man, and the small salary is his sole dependence." As to himself he added: "I have no claim to thy attention in his behalf, beyond the fact that I have given the best years of my life to the cause of freedom, without asking anything from the party or government for myself. I was Presidential Elector in 1860–and again in 1864." In 1880 W offered to take care of Matthew, making it possible for him to give up his clerkship, but he declined. Shortly thereafter his health broke, and he died in 1883. See Lloyd W. Griffith, "Matthew Franklin Whittier, 'Ethan Spike,'" *NEQ*, XIV (1941), 646-63.

12 Mordell accuses W of meanness toward Lucy Larcom, who edited *Child Life*, *Child-Life in Prose*, and *Songs of Three Centuries* with him. It does seem odd that he did not put her name on the title-

pages of these books along with his own (he acknowledged her services in his prefaces), but there is no evidence that the division of the rewards was unfair to Miss Larcom, whose whole literary career W had sponsored. In the 1880's, when she was in need, he set to work to raise an annuity for her and contributed to it. In 1892, Lucy Larcom wrote W's niece, Mrs. S. T. Pickard: "He used to want to pay my bills when we were at West Osipee, etc., but I declined, for I supposed he was almost as poor as myself.... I am very glad he left me the copyright of the books I compiled with him, and indeed it was only right, as I worked so hard on them. The *Songs of Three Centuries* nearly cost me my health; the publishers "rushed" it so.... But he never knew."

W was himself on the receiving end with the "weighty" British Friend, Joseph Sturge, with whom he traveled on anti-slavery business from April to August 1841, and through whose generosity the "Garden Room" was added to the house in Amesbury. Apparently Sturge made three offers of financial aid, only one of which was accepted. See S. T. Pickard, *Whittier-Land*, pp. 60-64.

13 It is interesting to compare W's attitude toward slavery with that of Harriet Beecher Stowe. Both were Christians and humanitarians, and they would have had little difficulty in achieving a meeting of minds. But Mrs. Stowe's attitude was much more emotional. *Uncle Tom's Cabin* was a *woman's* protest against slavery, and its essential point of departure was its author's conviction that the slave system made chastity impossible for Negro women and outraged their most sacred instincts as wives and mothers. See my *Harriet Beecher Stowe: The Known and the Unknown* (OUP, 1965), especially pp. 104-6, 180-84.

William M. Griswold, ed., *Passages from the Correspondence and Other Papers of Rufus W. Griswold* (W. M. Griswold, 1898) contains a letter allegedly written by W to Griswold in which the former writes: "Touching the free negroes of whose suffering thou writest, they must wait for relief until slavery be abolished. They should willingly defer their sensual gratification for the benefit of their brethren in bondage, and be content to live in wretchedness and die of starvation, for the good of the cause." This does not sound like W. The tone is entirely too fanatical, and fanaticism which allocates the suffering to other people is always the most unpalatable kind. "Sensual gratification" is also a false note. So far as I know this letter has not been seen except in the Griswold text, and in view of that worthy's proved falsification of Poe documents, I would not accept his unsupported testimony to the goodness of God or the wickedness of the devil. See my *Edgar Allan Poe: The Man Behind the Legend* (OUP, 1963).

14 Those in "My Double" (Pickard, *Whittier-Land*, pp. 124-6) are from the point of view of the Democrats being satirized; see, however, the letter to Elizabeth Whittier in Albree, *W Correspondence*, p. 36. "A Love Story," *American Manufacturer*, June 4, 1829, has a plot for all the world like that of a film comedy short of c. 1910: a young man elopes, as he supposes, with a girl he has long courted in vain, only to discover, at last, that his veiled companion is her colored maid Dinah.

15 For an interesting expression of another view, see Rebecca Harding Davis, *Bits of Gossip* (HM, 1904): "He did not consciously pose, but he never for a moment forgot his mission. He was thin, mild, and ascetic, looking like a Presbyterian country minister. He gave his views of slavery and the South with a gentle, unwearied obstinacy, exasperating to any one who knew that there was another side to the question."

16 Mary Haldane Coleman, "W on John Randolph of Roanoke," *NEQ*, VIII (1935), 551-4.

17 For W's attitude toward the South from a pro-Southern point of view, see Howard R. Floan, *The South in Northern Eyes, 1831 to 1861* (University of Texas Press, 1958). Floan's reiterated charges that W judged Southern slavery without having investigated it are sicklied o'er with the pale cast of apologetics, but it is clear that, like Mrs. Stowe, the poet was predisposed to believe whatever redounded to the discredit of the "peculiar institution."

18 See Osborn T. Smallwood, "The Historical Significance of W's Anti-Slavery Poems as Reflected by their Political and Social Background," *Journal of Negro History*, XXXV (1950), 150-73. Cf. Hyatt H. Waggoner: "W's anti-slavery poems are not irrelevant to us because legal slavery no longer exists, nor is their relevance simply a function of the fact that the fight for justice and freedom and brotherhood is never ended. The poems themselves supply the explanation of their continuing vitality: they are not propaganda verse so much as they are visions of the great society, the city of God on earth, and denunciations of all that hinders its arrival."

19 Cecil B. Williams, "W's Relation to Garrison and the *Lib-*

erator," *NEQ*, XXV (1952), 248-55: "It was only in the first heat of his anti-slavery activities that he was reasonably content with a minimum of literary expression." Does it not also seem likely that W's increased stress upon literary activity after 1843 may have been determined in part by the fact that, after a decade of labor, he saw few positive fruits of his labors or promise thereof? The very title *Lays of My Home* (1843) suggests a turning away from agitation.

20 This does not seem a very disinterested basis upon which to decide the matter.

21 The Haverhill Petition of 1842, requesting the dissolution of the Union, and presented by John Quincy Adams in the House of Representatives, where it was received with great indignation, has hitherto been regarded as having been written by W, at least in part, but this now seems at best doubtful. In any case, it indicates no truly anti-Union sentiment upon the part of any writer, for it was purely a tactical move in the war against slavery. There was no chance of its being acted upon; neither did its sponsors intend that it should be. See S. T. Pickard, *JGW*, I, 179-81.

22 Sarah Forbes Hughes, ed., *Letters and Recollections of John Murray Forbes* (HM, 1899).

23 W's essay, "Peculiar Institutions of Massachusetts," shows his interest in juvenile criminals and idiots; "Lord Ashley and the Thieves" shows that he had much greater interest in reclaiming offenders than in punishing them. When he attacked imprisonment for debt at the close of the twenties, 75,000 persons were still being incarcerated for this reason annually. See the poem "The Prisoner for Debt."

24 See W's introductory note to "The Truce of Piscataqua." The Richter novels involved are *The Light in the Forest* and *A Country of Strangers* (Knopf, 1953, 1966). It is amusing that the new (1966) Howard Johnson Motor Lodge at Haverhill should have a W Room and a Hannah Duston Room! Local patriotism produces strange couplings.

25 In 1945, J. W. Holmes was strangely shocked by this, thinking W should have been restrained by a sense of decorum and apparently surprised that Jackson did not retaliate. I wonder just what he thought the President could have done.

26 Reprinted in *Works*, VII. See also J. A. Russell, "The Aboriginal Element in W's Writings," *Granite Monthly*, LX (1928), 217-33.

27 "The Problem."

28 For further discussion of some of the points considered here, see John A. Pollard, "W on Labor Unions," *NEQ*, XII (1939), 99-102, and T. F. Currier, "W and the Amesbury-Salisbury Strike," *NEQ*, VIII (1935), 105-12. See also Pollard's more general consideration in *JGW*, Ch. XVII. The strongest statement of the point of view that W was reactionary in his attitude toward labor is in Mordell, *Quaker Militant*, Ch. XXIV.

29 See also "The Republican Party," in *Works*, VII.

30 "The Reward."

31 S. T. Pickard, "The Student Life of S. R. Crockett—His Correspondence with JGW," *Independent*, LI (1899), 2666-7.

32 Mordell's idea that W wrote the article on himself in *Appleton's Cyclopaedia of American Biography* (1887-89)—see *Quaker Militant*, pp. 304-5—is decisively rejected by T. F. Currier, Boston *Evening Transcript*, August 17, 1933. The sketch was written by James Russell Lowell, "and it is almost self-evident that W did not even see the proof for he surely would have corrected the egregious misstatement that in 1830 he succeeded Prentice as editor of the Haverhill *Gazette;* he probably would also have noticed the error of 1840 as the date of his removal to Amesbury." Mordell, p. 288, also gives an unsympathetic account of the publication of the "Haverhill" poem of 1890; for an account more friendly to W, see *Bibliography*, pp. 255 ff. Currier, p. 29, seems to have shown conclusively that W did not edit the *Poems Written During the Progress of the Abolition Question* (1837) with its very eulogistic introduction; cf. Whitman Bennett's discussion, *W, Bard of Freedom*, pp. 116-19. Bennett also thinks that the corrections and alterations in *Voices of Freedom* (1846) make it impossible to take "too literally" W's disclaimer of responsibility for its publication. In 1832 W certainly denied having written "Moll Pitcher" (see Bennett, pp. 329-34), but this was probably playful; he can hardly have expected to be believed.

33 Some of the members of his family created problems for W, but these were not women. It has sometimes been suggested that his brother, Matthew Franklin, was a problem, but I have never been able to isolate any specific charges against him. W himself speaks of Matthew as "one of the best fellows living," whose "life has been full of trial and suffering," and "an affectionate brother, unselfish and generous to a fault." The real black sheep of the family was Lewis Caldwell, Mary Whittier's son. W did his best to find employment for him

and was sometimes compelled to shelter him when he lost it, but when he left at the end of one visit the poet remarked grimly that if his nephew had stayed longer he would not have been able to endure it.

34 Joseph M. Ernest, Jr., "W and the 'Feminine Fifties,'" *AL*, XXVIII (1956), 184-96, makes W responsible for Hawthorne's "damned mob of scribbling women" by giving him a substantial share in the improved position of the American woman writer in the 'fifties.

35 See, however, T. F. Currier and Donald E. Emerson, "Two Notes on W's 'To ——, With a Copy of Woolman's *Journal*,'" *BFHA*, XXX (1941), 69-79, which suggests that W used this poem to two different girls, and the communications of both Currier and Enoch W. Pearson in the Exeter *News-Letter*, Exeter, N.H., June 19, 1941. This last fugitive item is included in the volume in the Widener Library, Harvard (AL 4162.003) in which a number of articles by Currier have been bound together.

36 "Memories."

37 Mordell is the writer who made W scholars Mary Emerson Smith-conscious (see his somewhat melodramatic account in *Quaker Militant*, Ch. V), but S. T. Pickard had already written about her in *Whittier-Land*. The authoritative account now is John B. Pickard, "JGW and Mary Emerson Smith," *AL*, XXXVIII (1967), 478-97.

38 See Mary Minerva Barrows, "The Love Story of W's Life," *NEM*, N.S. XXXII (1905), 173-9, which gives Evelina's memories in later life, including a very long letter. A very pietistic but affectionate letter to W from "Your affectionate sister Evelina" is given in *EIHC*, LXIX (1933), 88. Mary C. Crawford, *The Romance of New England Rooftrees* (L. C. Page, 1902) says W left $10,000 for an Amesbury Home for Aged Women and that, two years after his death, Evelina applied for admission but died before her application could be acted on. See also S. T. Pickard, *Whittier-Land*, pp. 67-72; Pollard, *JGW*, p. 593.

39 First published by William Lyon Phelps, "A Noteworthy Letter of W's," *Century*, LXIV (1902), 15-17, reprinted in Mordell, *Quaker Militant*, pp. 60-61.

40 "W and Lucy Hooper," *NEQ*, VII (1934), 316-25.

41 See Appendix A.

42 S. T. Pickard, "A Merry Woman's Letters to a Quiet Poet," *Ladies' Home Journal*, XVII, December 1899, pp. 7-8, January 1900, pp. 9-10.

43 See especially the poem "Raphael."

44 W's correspondence with Celia Thaxter is interesting as showing that he was not afraid to form a friendship with a woman who was known to be unhappily married. But in writing her he never fails to include greetings to her husband.

45 "Among the Hills."

46 "Amy Wentworth." For other poems in which this theme is treated see "The New Wife and the Old," "The Bridal of Pennacook," "Marguerite," "The Bay of Seven Islands," and, in a different way, "Maud Muller."

CHAPTER THREE: BEAUTY AS GRACE AND SNARE

1 Such of these books as are identifiable are named by Pollard, *JGW, Friend of Man*, pp. 589-91—Appendix B, "The Library of John Whittier."

2 Thomas Wentworth Higginson, *Contemporaries* (HM, 1899), p. 64.

3 "To My Old Schoolmaster."

4 *W's Use of the Bible* (Orono, Maine, University Press, 1930). Stevens finds 284 references to the Gospels, 67 to Genesis, 56 to Revelation, 54 to Psalms, 47 to Exodus, 32 to Acts, 29 to Isaiah, 28 to Corinthians, 19 each to Ezekiel and Kings, 14 to Judges, 13 to Job, 12 each to Samuel and Numbers, 11 to Daniel, and 10 each to Romans and Deuteronomy. There are no more than 9 references to any other book. Notley Sinclair Maddox, "W's 'Ichabod,' 33-6," *Explicator*, XVIII (1960), Item 38, is excellent on the whole complex of Scriptural references, with their devastating yet pitying, implications. W is here shown practising the very kind of poetic complexity which is in vogue today.

5 See Arthur Christy, "Orientalism in New England: W," *AL*, I (1930), 371-92.

6 "My Namesake."

7 *Works*, V, 226-30.

8 W's references to Dante are carefully studied and reasonable inferences concerning the extent of his reading are drawn from them by J. Chesley Mathews, "W's Knowledge of Dante," *Italica*, XXXIV (1957), 234-8.

9 "The Chapel of the Hermits."

10 W's use of German themes is studied by Iola Kay Eastburn, *W's Relation to German Life and Thought*, "Americana Germanica," Vol. XX (University of Pennsylvania, 1915). Miss Eastburn lists the books translated from the German in W's library and his poems inspired by German themes.

11 See Edward Wagenknecht, *Henry Wadsworth Longfellow, Portrait of an American Humanist* (OUP, 1966); consult index.

12 There is, however, one curious passage in an 1883 letter:

> After Bacon and Shakespeare Milton is the greatest name in English literature. His prose writings have been my peculiar delight. I have studied them more closely than his poetry. I should place him at the head of the list for breadth of thought and splendor of diction. Bunyan is perhaps the best writer of the homely Saxon school.

Insofar as it relates to Bacon, this seems to me W's most amazing literary judgment. I find no evidence of special fondness for Bacon elsewhere, though there are several references to him, and in "The Last Walk in Autumn" he is paired, oddly, with Pascal:

> I talk with Bacon, grave and wise,
> I read the world with Pascal's eyes.

13 See Pollard, *JGW, Friend of Man*, pp. 597-9–Appendix D, "Debt to Burke and Milton."

14 See Pray, p. 189.

15 In his Preface to *Songs of Three Centuries*, W pays tribute to Chaucer, King James I of Scotland, Dunbar, and Sackville, all of whom have been omitted from his anthology because of language difficulties. One of the *Stranger in Lowell* papers takes an epigraph from *Piers Plowman*. His essay on "Utopian Schemes and Political Theorists" (*Works*, VII) comments on More's *Utopia* and many other works.

16 Pray, pp. 165-6.

17 Here, as elsewhere, he does not always quote accurately; sometimes he seems to have quoted from memory. Thus Coleridge's

> Ah! from the soul itself must issue forth
> A light, a glory, a fair luminous cloud
> Enveloping the Earth–

becomes

> from the mind itself must issue forth
> A light, a glory, a fair luminous mist,
> Enveloping the earth.

For that matter, Whittier sometimes refers to his own publishers as "Houghton and Mifflin." "I never pretend to quote correctly," he told Celia Thaxter.

18 There is one reference to Mrs. Shelley, in an 1877 letter, in which W makes the common mistake of calling the monster "Frankenstein."

19 Cady and Clark, pp. 32-4.

20 *Free Press,* December 2, 1826; reprinted *EIHC,* XCI (1955), 137-8.

21 See "To 'Roy,'" Haverhill *Gazette,* August 11, 1827; reprinted in Pray, pp. 148-50.

22 See Alwin Thaler, "Tennyson and W," *PQ,* XXVIII (1949), 518-19; also his more general article, "W and the English Poets," *NEQ,* XXIV (1951), 53-68, which shows, among other things, that W later came to think more highly of Browning than he did when he expressed the opinions quoted in my text.

23 W told Mrs. Fields that after Tennyson, William Allingham was his favorite among modern British poets. His delight in these lines shows his relish of delicate fancy, even when it was quite unrelated to moral meaning:

> Up the airy mountain,
>   Down the rushy glen,
> We daren't go a-hunting
>   For fear of little men.
> Wee folk, good folk,
>   Trooping all together;
> Green jacket, red cap,
>   Gay cock's feather.

On the other hand, he valued Edwin Arnold's poem, "He Who Died at Azan," as a useful antidote to *The Rubáiyát of Omar Khayyám:* "I know of nothing ancient or modern which is so filled with a robust and satisfying faith as this little poem." In 1863 he thanked her American publishers for sending him the poems of Jean Ingelow: "I have read them with great satisfaction–glad that such a singer lives." He wrote a poem in 1828 on "Death of Ossian" (Pray, pp. 170-72); he also wrote verses in praise of the ill-starred L.E.L. (Pray, pp. 221-3) and of Ebenezer Elliott, of the *Corn-Law Rhymes.* At one time he admired Mrs. Hemans. Jack Stillinger, "W's Early Imitation of Thomas Campbell," *PQ,* XXXVIII (1959), 502-4, argues that "The Exile's

Departure," W's first published poem, was modeled not on Thomas Moore, as Carpenter believed, but on Campbell's "Exile of Erin."

24 These stanzas are quoted, not consecutively, from W's "Burns."

25 "The Sisters," which suggests the traditional Scottish ballad, "The Twa Sisters," is also of quality, and "The Brown Dwarf of Rügen," "King Volmer and Elsie," and "Kallundborg Church" all draw fruitfully on foreign sources. But John B. Pickard has anticipated me in pointing all this out; see his *JGW: An Introduction and Interpretation*, pp. 68-9, 76-8.

26 Printed in part in Pray, pp. 167-8, and Kennedy, *JGW, The Poet of Freedom*, pp. 50-51.

27 The most detailed consideration of the influence of Burns on W is in Theodore Roosevelt Garrison's dissertation, "JGW, Pioneer Regionalist and Folklorist," pp. 100 ff. Garrison also has much on Robert Dinsmoor, who, though writing in Scottish dialect, also encouraged W's local interests. He reminds us that Joshua Coffin had much knowledge of and interest in local history and argues a close resemblance between three items in *Legends of New England* and poems by John G. C. Brainard, whose literary remains W edited. On pp. 163-4 Garrison points out a strong resemblance between a passage in *Snow-Bound* and Brainard's "To the Connecticut River." Pray, pp. 52-3 also concerns the influence of Dinsmoor.

The only passage into which I could possibly read any suggestion of decline in W's regard for Burns during later years apparently dates from the 'eighties: "Moore is now forgotten but for his songs; Byron is going out of fashion; Burns lives,—perhaps partly because of the clannishness of the Scotch."

28 *National Era*, September 16, 1847, reprinted in Cady and Clark, pp. 125-8.

29 In "Portraits and Sketches," now included in *Works*, V.

30 *American Manufacturer*, Jan. 8, 1829, reprinted in Cady and Clark, p. 23.

31 Cady and Clark, p. 190. As an influence on W's own writing, Scott was less important than either Burns or Byron, but he did exist. W himself later described his Mogg Megone as a big Indian strutting about in a Walter Scott plaid.

32 H. Augusta Dodge, ed., *Gail Hamilton's Life in Letters* (Lee and Shepard, 1901).

33 In his dissertation on "W and the American Writers," Joseph E. Ernest, Jr. gives the details of Whittier's contacts with more than 500 persons. "Other studies indicate his significance as one of the great advocates of American abolitionism. This study reveals his significance also as one of the great promoters of American literature."

34 Whether W felt less strongly about Poe's derelictions than he did about those attributed to Whitman it would be hard to say. When he was asked to contribute to a Poe monument, he expressed no criticism of Poe, but neither did he send a check. "No one can doubt that Edgar Allan Poe was endowed with the divine gift of genius. . . . The scruples which I feel in the matter of monuments prevents me from any action in this particular case, beyond the expression of sympathy with the sentiment which underlies the effect you are making to keep green the memory of the author of some of the truest lyrics in the language."

35 Mrs. Sigourney's is the name deleted in S. T. Pickard's printing of W's letter to Lucy Hooper, *Life and Letters,* I, 213-14.

36 Emerson may well have had more influence upon W than he has been given credit for. W's conception of beauty was certainly close to that which Emerson expressed in "The Rhodora," and both John B. Pickard, *JGW,* pp. 49-50, and Wilfred Townley Scott, *Exiles and Fabrications* (D, 1961), p. 29, have stressed the point that *Snow-Bound* owes more to Emerson than the epigraph from "The Snow Storm," Scott even going so far as to say that Emerson may have been more important for it than Burns.

37 One of the most vivid personal glimpses we have of W is the account by Elizabeth Stuart Phelps, *Chapters from a Life* (HM, 1896) of the attempt he made to call at the Longfellow house just before the Cambridge poet's death and how shocked he was to find that his friend was too ill to receive him.

38 *Works,* VII, 365 ff. W himself treated the expulsion of the Acadians in the poem "Marguerite."

39 W once tried to tone down one of Taylor's poems; see his letter to Fields, Dec. 29, 1864, in James C. Austin, *Fields of* The Atlantic Monthly, p. 192. In a letter to Fields, Dec. 12, 1870, W holds himself unworthy to untie the "poetical shoestrings" of Emerson, Lowell, Longfellow, or Taylor.

40 See Joseph M. Ernest, Jr., "W and Whitman: Uncongenial Personalities," *BFHA,* XLII (1953), 85-9, and "Holmes to W on Whit-

man," *Walt Whitman Newsletter*, III (1957), 76-7; Albree, *W Correspondence*, pp. 239-44.

41 See Jay B. Hubbell, ed., *The Last Years of Henry Timrod, 1864-67* (Duke University Press, 1941). W also admired as poetry Randall's "My Maryland" and "Stonewall Jackson's Way," by John Williamson Palmer.

42 See Ferris Greenslet, *Life of Thomas Bailey Aldrich* (HM, 1908), p. 258.

43 Laura E. Richards and Maud Howe Elliott, *Julia Ward Howe, 1819-1910* (HM, 1915), I, 138-39. It is interesting to compare W's reaction to *Passion Flowers* with that of Longfellow, who also found "genius" and "beauty" in it but was distressed by its spirit of "revolt" and "discontent." See my *Henry Wadsworth Longfellow: Portrait of an American Humanist*, p. 83.

44 "Fanaticism," in *Works*, VII.

45 W refers to the novel in the introduction to "The Dead Ship of Harpswell" in *The Tent on the Beach*. He produced a lengthy "Greeting" to Mrs. Stowe on the occasion of her seventieth birthday festival.

46 See "Mrs. Judge Jenkins," in Harte's *Poems*. W himself once parodied "Maud Muller":

> Of all good things of tongue or verse
> The best are these–
> It might be worse!

Ernest quotes some unpublished lines of W's on the theme of Harte's "Plain Language from Truthful James," popularly called "The Heathen Chinee."

In 1871 Harte wrote W, expressing his regret at not being able to come to Amesbury while in the Boston area, "but when I come again, I hope to see you–to talk with you of [Thomas Starr] King, whom we both loved; who perhaps knew you better, but hardly admired you more than your friend, Bret Harte."

47 For good summaries of W's prentice work, and the influences discernible in it, see Carpenter, *JGW*, pp. 34-52; Pray, pp. 107-8; J. B. Pickard, *JGW*, pp. 18-21, and in much greater detail in his dissertation. Of course, the writing impulse was not wholly poetical. When W got to Haverhill Academy, his master at first found it almost impossible to believe that the composition he offered was his own work. W "once

said that his collected prose would occupy at least twelve octavo volumes."–Mordell.

48 "An Artist of the Beautiful."

49 "Songs of Labor–Dedication."

50 Quoted by E. D. Snyder, *Pennsylvania Magazine*, LXII (1938), 155.

51 That this is wholly wrong could be argued only by one who believes that the personality of the writer has nothing to do with his creation, and if this is true, then literature is a non-human art, with very little significance for human beings. Dr. Johnson said: "Sir, the biographical part of literature is what I love best."

52 Especially, of course, in

> Happy if they [the boy's feet] sink not in
> Quick and treacherous sands of sin.

Being human, the boy is presumably a sinner, but his sinfulness is not the subject of the poem, which deals with the innocent joys of boyhood and the inestimable privileges of growing up in the country; and the reflection has, therefore, no more legitimate place here, at the end of the poem, than any other element which had not been prepared for could have. Curiously enough, there is a close parallel to this unity-shattering irrelevance at the close of Poe's wholly non-didactic poem, "The Sleeper":

> Thrilling to think, poor child of sin!
> It was the dead who groaned within.

53 There are striking parallels in two of John Masefield's finest poems, *The Everlasting Mercy* and *The Widow in the Bye-Street.*

54 "W," *AL*, IX (1937), 335-42.

55 "What I Had to Give I Gave: Another Look at W," *EIHC*, XCV (1959), 32-40. Harry Hayden Clark was the pioneer in the serious study of W's aesthetic; see his notes in *Major American Poets* (ABC, 1936); see, further, E. H. Cady's introduction to *W on Writers and Writing,* which he edited in collaboration with Clark. The fullest study now is in John B. Pickard's dissertation, "The Artistry of JGW," which was done under Clark. The essence of Pickard's discussion has been published in "The Basis of W's Critical Creed: The Beauty of the Commonplace and the Truth of Style," *Rice Institute Pamphlet*, XLVII (1960), 34-50 and, in a different form, in his *JGW*, Ch. V.

56 See, further, the rhymed letter to Lucy Larcom in Daniel D. Addison, *Lucy Larcom: Life, Letters, and Diary* (HM, 1894), pp. 161-2.

57 On August 14, 1884, W wrote Dr. Hugo Erichson, who had evidently written him while gathering data about the habits of writers: "(1) I prefer day—and the morning in fact—for writing. (2) I make no outline or skeleton of my work. My verses have been made as the Irishman made his chimney by holding up one brick and putting another under. (3) I use no stimulants whatever for literary labor. (4) no particular habits of writing (5 & 6) For many years I have not been able to write or study more than half an hour at a time without suffering." (Quoted by permission of Northwestern University Library.)

58 "A Memorable Murder," now, perhaps, most conveniently to be found, in Joseph Henry Jackson, ed., *The Portable Murder Book* (Viking Press, 1945).

59 Nelson F. Adkins, "W's 'The Barefoot Boy.'" *NQ*, CLXV (1933), 78-9.

60 Blair, *Mark Twain and* Huck Finn (University of California Press, 1960); Turner, *The Making of* The Cloister and the Hearth (University of Chicago Press, 1938). A reviewer accused W of having plagiarized an article from *Blackwood's* in his introduction to Brainard; see Mordell, p. 36. T. R. Garrison has a detailed commentary on the supernatural and folklore elements in the *Legends*, with many comments on W's correspondence and lack of correspondence with the methods of modern folklorists. Considering the date at which he worked alone—there is no evidence that he had even heard of the Grimms—he does not emerge badly. Says Garrison: "W was a student of folklore before W. J. Thoms had even coined the word; and while Irving was combing England, Germany, and Spain for tales out of the romantic past, W was doing the same thing to his native Essex County, Massachusetts."

61 The last stanza of "The Lumbermen" may owe something to Longfellow's "Psalm of Life"; see Nelson F. Adkins, *NQ*, CLXIV (1933), 242. Cf. Oal S. Coad, "The Bride of the Sea," *AL*, IX (1937), 71-3, for Longfellow's borrowing from "The Ship-Builders" in "The Building of the Ship."

62 Pray, p. 133.

63 For the controversy with G. E. Ellis concerning "The King's

Missive," see *Proceedings of the Massachusetts Historical Society*, 1881, pp. 18, 357-62, 387-99. For "Barbara Frietchie" see Caroline H. Dall, *Barbara Fritchie: A Study* (Roberts Brothers, 1892) but especially Dorothy Mackay Quynn and William Rogers Quynn, *Barbara Frietschie* (Maryland Historical Society, 1942).

64 As, for example, in *The Narrative of James Williams, An American Slave* (1838), which W edited for the Anti-Slavery Society, and which went through six editions in eight months before being withdrawn because its authenticity had been questioned.

65 W's Moll Pitcher is not the Revolutionary War heroine but a once-famous psychic who lived in Nahant, Mass. Kennedy, *JGW, The Poet of Freedom*, pp. 278 ff., describes her as a benevolent and kindly woman, not the evil witch whom W portrays. (The last two chapters of this book point out many other examples of W's departure from historic fact.) However, Garrison (pp. 254-5), who derives from Upham, Drake, and Alonzo Lewis, *The History of Lynn* (1829) gives a much less favorable view of her.

66 See M. Jane Griswold, "American Quaker History in the Works of W, Hawthorne, and Longfellow," *Americana Illustrated*, XXXIV (1940), 220-63, which contains a detailed study of W's Quaker narratives.

67 *Stelligeri and Other Essays Concerning America* (S, 1893).

68 See J. B. Pickard, *JGW*, pp. 69-70.

69 "The Chapel of the Hermits."

70 In *American Prosody* (ABC, 1935), the standard book on the prosody of all the leading older American poets.

71 Pickard also finds that in *Margaret Smith's Journal*, W's prose sometimes lends itself to "a free verse arrangement, which is surprisingly close to Amy Lowell's imagistic type of verse." Thus:

> No sounds
> Save the heavy plash of muddy feet
> (on the pavements)
> the monotonous melancholy drip
> from trees and roofs
> the distressful gurgling of water-ducts,
> swallowing the dirty amalgam of the gutters.
> A dim, leaden-colored horizon
> of only a few yards in diameter
> shutting down about one.

And again:

> Poverty came upon the house...
> Like an armed man.
> Loose clapboards rattled in the wind,
> Rags fluttered from the broken windows,
> Within doors...tattered children and scanty fare.

It is not true, as has sometimes been said, that W wrote no sonnets. "Forgiveness," "Leggett's Monument," and "An Artist of the Beautiful" are sonnets, though certainly not according to Petrarch or quite according to Shakespeare either.

72 "W's Rhymes," *AS*, XX (1945), 51-7.

73 As in

> And Autumn's rainbow-tinted banner
> Hang lightly o'er the Susquehanna...

where it is impossible to tell whether W dropped the "r" at the end of the first verse or added it at the end of the second. Steven T. Byington, "W's Rhymes," *AS*, XXI (1946), 37-9, reinforced the McEuen argument but goes further: "Instead of saying that many major poets have used bad rhymes, it would be more correct to say that no first-class poet in the English language has tried to confine himself to exact rhyme; that so far as any English poets who have undertaken to use only exact rhymes can be found, they must be sought among the minor or even the obscure poets; that English poets use inexact rhymes as a means of getting more melodious effects than they could have got by never using any rhymes but exact ones."

74 *AL*, XV (1943), 309-11.

75 See J. B. Pickard's fine analysis of *Snow-Bound* in his *JGW*, pp. 90 ff. and cf. Winfield Townley Scott, "Something about *Snow-Bound*," *Exiles and Fabrications*.

76 It is interesting to find it as early as 1827 in the uncollected poem "I Would Not Lose That Romance Wild"; see S. T. Pickard, *Whittier-Land*, pp. 130-31, or Pray, pp. 152-3.

77 Bartlett, *Some Memories of Old Haverhill* (Privately printed, 1915).

78 See Eleanor M. Tilton's fascinating and extremely important article, "Making Whittier Definitive," *NEQ*, XII (1939), 281-314.

79 Quoted by Martha S. Porter, *Recollections of Louisa May*

Alcott, JGW, and Robert Browning, etc. (New England Magazine Corporation, 1893).

CHAPTER FOUR: THE ALMOST PERFECT PACIFIST

1 "Moral Warfare."

2 "I have never intentionally written anything in favor of war, but a great deal against it." See S. T. Pickard, *JGW*, I, 67-70.

3 In *The Independent*, LXIII (1907), 1490-91, S. T. Pickard published a Revolutionary War poem written for the *fiftieth* anniversary of Bunker Hill but withheld from publication, in which Whittier glorifies the patriots.

4 Maud Elma Kingsley, "A Quaker Poet in Puritan New England," *Poet-Lore*, XXI (1910), 330-36, is of course incorrect (see Appendix B) when she finds W strangely silent on the Mexican War. Her article is an extreme and exaggerated commentary on the combative element in W's temperament. Thomas Wentworth Higginson (*Letters and Journals*, p. 7) quotes W as having "taken up the vague notion of annexing all Mexico" and seeming to "lord it in a very loose way too; even said more war would be better than making peace and getting slave territory...." If W ever said this, it cannot have been more than rhetorical exaggeration and an expression of his disgust over the way things were going.

5 This is referred to in "Amy Wentworth" and even in *Snow-Bound.*

6 "A Word for the Hour."

7 "The Sentence of John L. Brown."

8 Vincent Y. Bowditch, *Life and Correspondence of Henry Ingersoll Bowditch* (HM, 1902).

9 Reprinted in Pollard, *JGW*, pp. 600-604.

10 Cecil D. Eby, Jr., "W's 'Brown of Ossawatomie,'" *NEQ*, XXXIII (1960), 452-61.

11 "Anniversary Poem." The stanzas quoted are not consecutive.

12 I can accept S. T. Pickard's story (*JGW*, II, 477) of W's teasing a Friend who had accepted a wartime contract for timber, and then, when he got his conscience all stirred up, concluding the conversation with, "My friend, if thee does furnish any of that timber thee spoke of, be sure it is all sound!" But I would have to have proof before I could accept Miss Sparhawk's story (she cites no authority)

that once when the people of Amesbury were slow to make their pledges to the Sanitary Commission, W rose in town meeting and said, "If this sum needed is not raised by this meeting, I shall write to Salmon Chase [the Secretary of the Treasury] to have the exemption money on the next draft of men put up to seven hundred dollars instead of three hundred, as it is now." I know of no instance in which W threw his weight about to the extent here suggested, and I feel sure that he would have regarded the application of such pressure as immoral.

13 "Among the Hills."

CHAPTER FIVE: THE LIGHT THAT IS LIGHT INDEED

1 See, for examples, the following poems: "The Fountain," "The Bridal of Pennacook," "Mary Garvin," "The Truce of Piscataqua," and "Birchbrook Mill."

2 "My Birthday."

3 "The Clear Vision."

4 That this was true of the old Puritans is one of the charges W himself brings against them; see "The Old Burying Ground" and the prose piece "Pawtucket Falls" (*Works*, V).

5 "The First Flowers." See also "Sweet Fern" for W's sensitiveness to smell.

6 *Pepacton*, "The Writings of John Burroughs," Autograph Edition, Vol. V (HM, 1904).

7 See the essay "The Beautiful," in *Works*, V.

8 *Nature in American Literature* (M, 1923).

9 W is quoting, from memory as usual, from Scott's *The Heart of Midlothian*. The correct form of the name is Dumbiedikes.

10 For poems about trees, see S. T. Pickard, *Whittier-Land*, p. 100.

11 Foerster, having found that bees were the only insects who got much attention in W's poetry, went on to observe that "he seemed to care little for the larger creatures about him, unless we except the squirrel and a number of birds. His birds are about thirty in number. ... But he had apparently no favorites ... and ... did not observe the ways of birds more attentively than most countrymen."

A little girl once came to W for a poem for her kitten's tombstone, and he immediately improvised:

Bathsheba! to whom none ever said scat
No worthier cat
Ever sat on a mat
Or caught a rat
Requiescat!

Later the same child's pony broke his leg, and she brought W a "poem" she herself had started and been unable to finish–

My pony kicked to the right, he kicked to the left,
The stable post he struck it,
He broke his leg short off–

and W added:

And then he kicked the bucket!

Neither of these effusions seems to me much more remarkable for tenderness than for poetic beauty. W once wrote Mrs. Fields that he was "looking over the proofs of my verses for the new edition, with a strong desire to drown some of them like so many untimely kittens," and having left home for a trip to Boston, he wrote back, "I forgot that miserable cat. He can get in and out of the cellar but he will want something to eat. Do fodder him occasionally."

There is, of course, a danger of being overimpressed by these things. Joel Bean has described how W fed the squirrels at Oak Knoll and records that the birds would come and hop about him when he went walking.

12 "The Rendition."

13 See in *Margaret Smith's Journal* the entry for October 20, 1678.

14 See "The Primitivism of Wordsworth," in his *On Being Creative and Other Essays* (HM, 1932).

15 See, for example, "The Voices."

16 This may not be quite fair to Rousseau, since in "The Eternal Goodness" W tells us that the same was true of himself:

More than your schoolmen teach, within
Myself, alas! I know:
Too dark ye cannot paint the sin,
Too small the merit show.

17 *Major American Poets* (ABC, 1936), p. 814. This magnificent anthology, which has been unfortunately allowed to go out of print,

is rich in insights not only into W but all the poets treated in it. More than one bibliographical essay on W notes that an "excellent" or "easily available" text of selections from W is that edited by Professor Clark and Norman Foerster for the "American Writers Series" in 1935. Unfortunately this book was prepared and announced but never published, which illustrates the danger of making a bibliography without bothering to look up your references.

18 Pray, pp. 137-9.

19 "Mountain Pictures."

20 "The Meeting."

21 He wrote Harriet Pitman, Jan. 24, 1885: "The lack of concentration of thought, which thee complain of, is the result of nervous debility. I have for years suffered from it: and it is only by a painful effort that I can hold my thought steadily before me. But, after all I think, it may be quite as well. To have *fixed* ideas is insanity: and it is safest to let the mind wander a little at its own sweet will. Some one has said that 'thinking is an idle waste of thought.' "

22 See *BFHA*, XXXVII (1948), 23-35.

23 See George W. Cutter, "W," *Unitarian*, VI (1891), 526-8, which reports a conversation with W, and Edward D. Snyder, "W and the Unitarians," *BFHA*, XLIX (1960), 111-16. Miss Sparhawk says W told her he had asked Emerson whether he did not believe that Christ was divine and that Emerson had said yes. "If thee does," said W, "thee ought to confess it in thy writings." See also Claflin, *Personal Recollections of JGW*, pp. 26-7.

24 "The Meeting."

25 "Our Master."

26 "The Shadow and the Light."

27 "The Meeting."

28 "The Preacher."

29 "The Word." See also "The Bridal of Pennacook," "The Chapel of the Hermits," "The Book," "Requirement," and the Prelude to "Among the Hills."

30 "The New Year" (1839) is the only poem of W's in which I can find even a suggestion that he ever believed in the Second Advent, and this reference is too vague to build upon. Generally he treats it as a species of madness: see the papers "Fanaticism," "The World's End," and "James Nayler." In the last named, seventeenth-century millenarians are considered. It should be remembered that millenarian

beliefs were a very important element in the eccentricity of Harriet Livermore, the "not unfeared, half-welcome guest" of *Snow-Bound;* see S. T. Pickard, *JGW*, I, 35-6, and *Whittier-Land*, p. 39.

31 *New Eyes for Invisibles* (M, 1943).

32 "Lucy Hooper."

33 Perhaps the best reasoned consideration of immortality in W's prose writings is at the end of Chapter V in "My Summer with Dr. Singletary." See also "Hamlet Among the Graves."

34 "My Namesake." W says surprisingly little about Jews. They might, I think, well resent such a statement as he made when he wrote of an English Friend's book in 1886 that "it retains and emphasizes all that is vital in Christianity, while freeing it from much that is Jewish or Heathen." Of course the New Testament was much more important to him than the Old, and of course his sensibilities were outraged by much that is barbaric in the Old Testament, but he did not therefore perceive no value in it. In "Our Age," a prose passage published in *The Outlook*, LXXIII (1903), 809, he says, "It is well for us that we have learned to listen to the persuasions of the Beatitudes; but there are crises in all lives which require the emphatic 'Thou shalt not' of the Decalogue." His most considered statement on Judaism was sent to *The Jewish Messenger* in 1889: "I don't know what it is to be a Jew, but I know what it is to be a Christian who has no quarrel with others about their creed, and can love, respect, and honor a Jew who honestly believes in the faith of his fathers, and who obeys the two great commandments 'Love to God and Love to Man.' "

W was impressed by the wisdom of Confucius but thought him no more spiritually minded than Benjamin Franklin. I think he comes closest to intolerance in his references to Mohammedanism in "Satire on Doughfaces," *Liberator*, Feb. 6, 1857, where he compares the slavery apologists to

> . . . some poor wretch, whose lips no longer bear
> The sacred burden of the mother's prayer,
> By fear impelled, or lust of greed enticed,
> Turns to the Crescent from the Cross of Christ.

There are twelve more lines of very abusive description of Muslim practices. The errors of the Muslims are arbitrarily dragged into a discussion of slavery; they would seem, therefore, to have been much on W's mind when he wrote this piece. There is a much later reference to Mohammed as the "Arch Imposter" in a piece of doggerel written for Lucy Larcom (see Addison, *Lucy Larcom*, p. 161), but this is much more playful in tone. On the other hand, W rebukes the narrowness of Christian missionaries to Islam in "The Star of Bethlehem."

35 Janet Adam Smith, *John Buchan: A Biography* (LB, 1965), p. 300.

36 S. T. Pickard, *JGW*, I, 33-4.

37 Portions of *The Supernaturalism of New England* have been preserved in three essays included in the collected works: "Charms and Fairy Faith," "Magicians and Witch Folk," and "The Agency of Evil." See also the 1833 paper, "New England Superstitions," reprinted in Cady and Clark, *W on Writers and Writing*, pp. 107-115. For the omens, etc. which centered around W's own death, see S. T. Pickard, *Whittier-Land*, pp. 94-5.

38 See, for example, "Extract from 'A New England Legend' " and "The Demon of the Study."

39 *Literary World*, I (1847), 247-8, reprinted in Randall Stewart, "Two Uncollected Reviews by Hawthorne," *NEQ*, IX (1936), 504-9.

40 These stanzas are not all consecutive.

41 "My Namesake."

42 "The Quaker Alumni."

43 See *BFHA*, XXV (1936), 38-9. See, also, Arthur Christy, "The Orientalism of W," *AL*, V (1933), 247-57.

44 See p. 95.

45 The denunciation of "the pomp of rituals" and all that goes with it in "Worship"—

> He [God] asks no taper lights, on high surrounding
> The priestly altar and the saintly grave,
> No dolorous chant nor organ music sounding,
> Nor incense clouding up the twilight nave—

is considerably less sweet than the lovely passage beginning,

> Oh, brother man! fold to thy heart thy brother:
> Where pity dwells the peace of God is there;

which is sung every week with unction in many churches which do not by any means go along with W in all the rejections he has recorded in the poem.

46 We get a suggestion of how tolerant W was, compared to many other good people, when we learn that Mrs. Child reproached

him for including an Italian poem in *Child Life* because it might make Catholicism attractive to his young readers!

47 Respectively in "W's Attitude toward Colonial Puritanism," *NEQ*, XXI (1948), 350-67, and his dissertation on *Margaret Smith's Journal*. The *Journal* contains W's most elaborate consideration of Puritanism, but his most succinct summary of his views is in his article on *Evangeline*, in *Works*, VII.

48 "The Last Walk in Autumn."

49 "The Quaker Alumni."

50 In *The Stranger in Lowell* he describes a visit to "A Mormon Conventicle." Himself clearly regarding Mormonism as a delusion, he accounts for its power, and the power of all such movements, on the ground that they reassert the ancient vitality of religious belief and of primitive Christianity in an age when the larger and more established denominations have grown sleek and comfortable.

APPENDIX A

1 HUP, 1946. See also William Seabrook, *Witchcraft, Its Power in the World Today* (HB, 1945).

2 This matter has previously been discussed, so far as my investigations have informed me, only by Edward D. Snyder, *BFHA*, XLIII (1954), 7: "This amazing story was picked up by Van Wyck Brooks and repeated in his *Flowering of New England*—to the regret of many who knew the W tradition well. As Rufus Jones told me out and out, it simply could not have been true of W's mother and aunt. My own guess is that W told Mrs. Fields that his mother or his aunt had heard that the waxen image ritual had been performed in New England."

3 For an excellent account of Gail Hamilton's quarrel with Fields, see W. S. Tryon, *Parnassus Corner: A Life of James T. Fields, Publisher to the Victorians* (HM, 1963). Not only did she pursue it to the bitter end of adjudication between Fields and herself before a tribunal which, though refraining from censuring either party, ordered the publishers to pay her $1,250, but carried on a propaganda campaign against Fields among his other authors. Her only important convert was Mrs. Hawthorne: see three articles by Randall Stewart: " 'Pestiferous Gail Hamilton,' James T. Fields, and the Hawthornes," *NEQ*, XVII (1944), 418-23; "Mrs. Hawthorne's Financial Difficulties: Selections from her Letters to James T. Fields, 1865-68," *More Books*, XXI

(1946), 45-53; "Mrs. Hawthorne's Quarrel with James T. Fields," same, pp. 254-63. Fields did not "cheat" either Hawthorne or Gail Hamilton; neither did he do anything illegal, but he did conduct his business in an extremely personal, unsystematic way which, in her case at least, was not calculated to redound to the disadvantage of the firm.

BIBLIOGRAPHY

Because so many of his poems were published serially and because so much of his prose remains uncollected in the anti-slavery papers he edited and elsewhere, W bibliography is an extremely complicated business. Fortunately Thomas Franklin Currier covered it wonderfully well in *A Bibliography of JGW* (HUP, 1937), which obviously cannot be duplicated here. See also *The Stephen H. Wakeman Collection of Books of Nineteenth Century American Writers...* (American Art Associates, 1924) and Jean C. S. Wilson and David A. Randall, eds., *Carroll A. Wilson: Thirteen Author Collections of the Nineteenth Century...* Vol. II (Privately printed for S, 1950). Three W sales catalogues are reproduced in *ESQ*, No. 34 (1964), where see also some valuable quotations from letters.

HM has published a number of editions of W's writings, but all have been printed from the same plates. I have used *The Works of JGW*, "Artists' Edition," 7 volumes (1892).

W excluded many early poems from his collected editions, for which see Frances Mary Pray, *A Study of W's Apprenticeship as a Poet...*, a Pennsylvania State College Ph.D. dissertation, which was printed by Musgrove Printing House, Bristol, N.H., in 1930. Other uncollected poems will be found in S. T. Pickard's *Whittier-Land...* (HM, 1904) and in many cheap, unauthorized, and now out-of-print collections, among which I have used the *Poems* published by Syndicate Trading Company, n.d.

Legends of New England (1831) is not included in the collected editions but may now be had, with an introduction by John B. Pickard, in an edition published by Scholars' Facsimiles & Reprints (1965).

The Stranger in Lowell (Waite, Peirce and Company, 1845) and *The Supernaturalism of New England* (Wiley and Putnam, 1847) are included in collected editions only in part. A modern edition of *Supernaturalism,* with an introduction by the present writer, will be published by the University of Oklahoma Press shortly after the publication of the volume in hand.

W edited several anthologies: *The North Star: The Poetry of Freedom,* by Her Friends (Merrihew and Thompson, 1840); *Child Life: A Collection of Poems* (HM, 1871); *Child Life in Prose* (HM, 1873); *Songs of Three Centuries* (HM, 1877). He contributed introductions to several books, including Thomas Clarkson, *The Portraiture of Quakerism* (1876), which introduction is reprinted in *BFHA,* XLIII (1954), 33-4; Oliver Johnson, *William Lloyd Garrison and His Times* (HM, 1881); Edwin P. Whipple, *American Literature and Other Papers* (HM, 1887).

Edwin H. Cady and Harry Hayden Clark made a very valuable collection from W's critical writings in *W on Writers and Writing* (Syracuse University Press, 1950). For various fugitive items see Nelson F. Adkins, "Two Uncollected Prose Sketches of W," *NEQ,* VI (1933), 364-71; Henry J. Cadbury, "W's Early Quaker Poems," *NEQ,* XVIII (1945), 251-6; Katherine Crosby, "W by his Fireside at Oak Knoll," Boston *Evening Transcript,* Feb. 7, 1925; Robert S. Forsythe, "An Uncollected Poem by W," *AL,* IV (1932), 194-5; Frank Foxcroft, "Mr. W and the 'Autocrat,' with Some Hitherto Unpublished Verses by Mr. W," *Congregationalist and Christian World,* XCII (1907), 871; John C. Hepler, "'Gordon'–A New W Poem," *NEQ,* XXXIV (1961), 93-5; Walter McIntosh Merrill, "Uncollected Early Poems of JGW," *EIHC,* IX (1955), 128-46; John M. Moran, Jr., "Eight Ungathered W Poems," *ESQ,* No. 38 (1965), 92-5 (seven of these are in the collected editions); "W and Mrs. Piatt," *JRUL,* VII (1944), 63.

What will be the definitive collection of W letters is now being prepared by John B. Pickard. Until it shall appear, the largest collections available will be those in Samuel T. Pickard's biography (see second paragraph below) and his *W as a Politician* (Charles E. Goodspeed, 1900); John Albree, ed., *W Correspondence from the Oak Knoll Collections, 1830-1892* (Essex Book and Print Club, 1911); T. F. Currier, ed., *Elizabeth Lloyd and the Whittiers* (HUP, 1939); Marie Denervaud, *W's Unknown Romance: Letters to Elizabeth Lloyd* (HM,

1922); Martha Hale Shackford, *W and the Cartlands: Letters and Comments* (Wakefield, Mass., The Montrose Press, 1950).

For additional letters see James C. Austin, *Fields of* The Atlantic Monthly: *Letters to an Editor, 1861-70* (Huntington Library, 1953); Charlotte Fiske Bates, "Glimpses of W's Faith and Character, through Extracts from Unpublished Letters," *McClure's Magazine*, II (1894), 125-9; Raymond M. Bennett, "An Unpublished W Letter," *JRUL*, IX (1945), 30-32; T. C., "W Introduces Elizabeth Lloyd Howell," *More Books*, XXII (1947), 29-30; Richard Cary, "W Regained," *NEQ*, XXXIV (1941), 370-75; Jean Downey, "W and [Rose Terry] Cooke: Unpublished Letters," *Quaker History*, LII (1963), 33-6; R. Craig Fabian, "Some Uncollected Letters of JGW to Gerrit Smith," *AL*, XXII (1950), 158-63; Donald C. Freeman, "JGW and his Birthplace," *EIHC*, LXXXVI (1950), 299-310; Max L. Griffin, "W and Hayne: A Record of Friendship," *AL*, XIX (1947), 41-58; Earl L. Griggs, "JGW and Thomas Clarkson," *AL*, VII (1963), 458-60; Charles A. Hawley, ed., "Correspondence between JGW and Iowa," *IJHP*, XXXV (1937), 115-41, and "JGW and his Middle Western Correspondents," *BFHA*, XXVIII (1939), 19-29; Elizabeth Hume, "Neighbor to a Poet," *EIHC*, LXXVI (1940), 345-54; Annie Russell Marble, "Some Friendships of W, with Letters Hitherto Unpublished," *Dial*, XLIII (1907), 409-10; S. T. Pickard, "Unpublished Correspondence between W and John Bright," *Independent*, LV (1899), 7-9; Kenneth Scott, "The Source of W's 'The Dead Ship of Harpswell,'" *American Neptune*, VI (1946), 223-7; Grace P. Shepard, "Letters of Lucy Larcom to the Whittiers," *NEQ*, III (1930), 501-18; Edward D. Snyder, ed., "JGW to William J. Allinson," *BFHA*, XXXVII (1948), 17-35, "W Manuscript Discovered 'to Order,'" *The Friend* (1936), 225-6, and "W's Letters to Ann Elizabeth Wendell," *BFHA*, XXIX (1940), 62-92; Edward D. Snyder and Anna B. Hewitt, eds., "Letters of JGW," *BFHA*, XXV (1936), 33-43; Richard Henry Stoddard, *Recollections Personal and Literary* (A. S. Barnes and Company, 1903); Lucy Gray Swett, *John Ruskin's Letters to Francesca, and Memoirs of the Alexanders* (Lothrop, Lee & Shepard, 1931); Rosamond Thaxter, ed., *Sandpiper: The Life and Letters of Celia Thaxter* (Marshall Jones Company, 1963); Arlin Turner, "W Calls on George W. Cable," *NEQ*, XXII (1949), 92-6; Lewis E. Weeks, Jr., "JGW to Harriet McEwen Kimball: Eight Letters," *EIHC*, XCV (1959), 41-51; Roland H. Woodwell, "W on Abolition: A Letter to Emerson," *EIHC*,

XCIII (1957), 254-9; "A W Autograph," *Colby Library Quarterly*, Series IV, No. 5, pp. 103-4; "W's Choice for Congress," *More Books*, XVIII (1943), 432-3; "W to John Bright," *NEQ*, VIII (1935), 554.

The authorized biography is Samuel T. Pickard, *Life and Letters of JGW*, two volumes (HM, 1894), reissued in a revised one-volume edition in 1907, and importantly supplemented by the same writer's *Whittier-Land ...* (HM, 1904). See also his "W's Literary Methods," *Independent*, XLIX (1897), 1258-9.

The first biography of W was W. Sloane Kennedy's unauthorized *JGW, His Life, Genius, and Writings* (Boston, S. Cassino, 1882). The revised edition of 1892 seems to have been issued under various imprints; mine carries that of Derby and Miller, New York. W intensely disliked this book. He co-operated, though under some protest, in the production of Francis H. Underwood, *JGW, A Biography* (HM, 1883). In 1892 Kennedy published a second book, *JGW, The Poet of Freedom*, in the "American Reformers" series (Funk and Wagnalls). Other early books written from personal knowledge are Mary B. Claflin, *Personal Recollections of JGW* (C, 1893)–see, also, her *Under the Old Elms* (C, 1895); Mrs. James T. Fields, *W: Notes of his Life and Friendships* (H, 1893), which was reprinted in her *Authors and Friends* (HM, 1896); Thomas Wentworth Higginson, *JGW*, "English Men of Letters" series (M, 1902); J. Warren Thyng, *Reminiscences of the Poet W* (Granite State Publishing Co., 1908); Abby J. Woodman, *Reminiscences of JGW's Life at Oak Knoll, Danvers, Mass.* (Essex Institute, 1908), and somewhat later, Frances Campbell Sparhawk, *W at Close Range* (Boston, The Riverdale Press, 1925) and Emily Binney Smith, *W* (Amesbury, Mass., The Whittier Press, 1935).

Other early books are Richard Burton, *JGW* (Small, Maynard, 1901); Henry Hudson, *W and his Poetry* (Harrap, 1917); B. O. Flower, *W: Prophet, Seer and Man* (Arena Publishing Co., 1896); W. J. Linton, *Life of JGW* (Walter Scott, 1893); C. B. Robertson, *A Talk about W* (Cincinnati, Robert Clarke & Co., 1892). But for grace and skill and literary charm much the most distinguished among the early books is George Rice Carpenter, *JGW*, "American Men of Letters" series (HM, 1903).

See, further, *Proceedings at the Presentation of a Portrait of JGW to Friends' School, Providence, R.I., Tenth Month, 24th, 1894* (Privately printed at The Riverside Press, 1885); *Memorial to JGW by the Citizens of Amesbury, December 17, 1892* (Amesbury, Fred A. Brown, 1893); *A Memorial to JGW from His Native City, Haverhill, Massachusetts* (The City Council, 1893).

The first important "modern" book about W was Albert Mordell, *Quaker Militant: JGW* (HM, 1933). Mordell's use of Freudian methods did not always reveal good judgment, and he convinced few readers that W was a "male coquette," but he dug out new materials, stressed W's heroic aspect, and broke through the common assumption of the time that W was a pale, mild saint of a bygone day who had nothing to say to modern Americans. Whitman Bennett disliked Mordell's book so intensely that he wrote his *W, Bard of Freedom* (University of North Carolina Press, 1941), a much better balanced study, in reply. This was followed in 1949 by what is now (1967) the best biography of W: John A. Pollard, *JGW, Friend of Man* (HM). In 1961 came two excellent biographical and critical handbooks: Lewis Leary, *JGW*, in "Twayne's United States Authors Series" and John B. Pickard, *JGW: An Introduction and Interpretation*, in the "American Authors and Critics Series" (Barnes and Noble). Edward D. Snyder, "Seventy Years of W Biographies, 1882-1952," *BFHA*, XLIII (1954), 1-13, is a curiously disappointing study, and very unfair to Pollard.

The following are unpublished Ph.D. dissertations: Joseph E. Ernest, Jr., "W and the American Writers," University of Tennessee, 1852; Theodore Roosevelt Garrison, "JGW, Pioneer Regionalist and Folklorist," University of Wisconsin, 1960; James Welford Holmes, "W's Prose on Reforms other than Abolition," University of Pittsburgh, 1945; Clara Perry Marcy, "The Literary Criticism of JGW," Boston University, 1945; John B. Pickard, "The Artistry of JGW," University of Wisconsin, 1954; John A. Pollard, "W's Early Years, 1807-1836," Yale University, 1937; Charles Doren Tharp, "The Frontier in the Poetry of JGW," University of Pittsburgh, 1940; Cecil B. Williams, "The Historicity of *Leaves from Margaret Smith's Journal*," University of Chicago, 1933. The University of Chicago Libraries printed Chapter IV of Williams in 1936, and Garrison is available from University Microfilms. George C. Carey's "Folklore in the Writings of JGW," Indiana University, 1966, was completed too late for me to be able to use it.

Authoritative discussions of W's religion from the Quaker point of view may be found in three essays in Howard H. Brinton, ed., *Byways in Quaker History* (Pendle Hill, 1944)—"W's Fundamental Religious Faith," by Rufus M. Jones; "W as Historian of Quakerism," by Henry J. Cadbury; and "JGW, The Quaker Politician," by C. Marshall Taylor. The Jones paper has been reprinted in pamphlet form, together with a paper by Benjamin F. Trueblood, under the title *The Faith of JGW*, by The New England Yearly Meeting of Friends (1957) and is sold at the Whittier Cottage, Amesbury. See further discussion by Jones in "W, the Mystic," *AF*, XIV (1907), 803-4, and in his *The Later Periods of Quakerism* (London, Macmillan, 1921), and by Cadbury in "W's Religion," *Christian Century*, LXXV (1958), 166-7. Other Quaker studies of W include Georgina King Lewis, *JGW, His Life and Work* (Headley Brothers, n.d.); Arthur Rowntree, *W, Crusader and Prophet* (same); C. Marshall Taylor, *JGW, The Quaker* (Friends' Historical Society, 1954); Ernest E. Taylor, *JGW, Poet, Reformer, Mystic*, "Friends Ancient and Modern," No. 17 (New York, Friends' Book & Tract Commission, 1913); Wilfred Whitten, *JGW* (London, Edward Hicks, Jr., 1892). See, also, E. D. Snyder, "W's Relgious Poetry," *FQE*, LXVIII (1934), 146-54, which contains a good commentary on Mordell's glib and snippy judgments, and *A Selection from the Religious Poems of JGW*, with an Interpretative Essay by Augustus T. Murray (Philadelphia, Friends' Book Store, 1934).

See, further, on W's religion: Julius W. Atwood, *The Spiritual Influence of JGW* (Providence, Snow and Farnham, 1894); Elmer James Bailey, *Religious Thought in the Greater American Poets* (Pilgrim Press, 1922); John W. Chadwick, "W's Spiritual Career," *New World*, II (1893), 88-103; Lewis H. Chrisman, *John Ruskin, Preacher and Other Essays* (Abingdon Press, 1921); Ellen E. Dickinson, "A Morning with the Poet W," *Churchman*, XLV (1882), 609; Chauncey J. Hawkins, *The Mind of W: A Study of W's Fundamental Religious Ideas* (Thomas Whittaker, 1904); Howard W. Hintz, *The Quaker Influence in American Literature* (Revell, 1940); Philip C. Moon, "Observations on the Religious Philosophy and Method of W in *Voices of Freedom*," *EIHC*, XCIII (1957), 247-53; W. H. Savage, "W's Religion," *Arena*, X (1894), 153-68; Augustus Hopkins Strong, *American Poets and Their Theology* (Philadelphia, The Griffith and Rowland Press, 1916). Strong's is a very effective presentation from the point of view of "orthodox," Calvinist-oriented Protestant theology, and Hawkins is equally effective from that of modern Protestant liberalism.

Personal reminiscences of W will be found in Charlotte F. Bates, "W Desultoria," *Cosmopolitan*, XIV (1894), 303-6; Charles H. Battey, "W at Home," *FIJ*, XLVIII (1891), 718-20; Joel Bean, "My Recollections of W and His Friends," *FQE*, XLVIII (1914), 449-67; John Wright Buckham, "W Face to Face," *Congregational Quarterly*, XIII (1935), 23-6; Helen Burt, "Reminiscences of the Poet W," *Bookman*, I (1895), 230-34, 309-12; H. J. Cadbury, ed., "A Visit to W in 1881," *BFHA*, XLVI (1957), 108-10; Samuel J. Cappen, "A Visit to JGW," *Leisure Hour*, XXXVIII (1888), 611-15; Mary B. Claflin, "JGW As I Knew Him," *Arena*, XV (1896), 26-8; Robert Collyer, *Clear Grit*... ed. John Haynes Holmes (American Unitarian Association, 1913); John T. Dorland, "A Morning with W," *FQE*, XXVI (1892), 587-95; Wyatt Eaton, "Recollections of American Poets," *Century*, LXIV (1902), 842-50; F. W. Farrar, *Men I Have Known* (C, 1897); Edmund Gosse, *Portraits and Sketches* (S, 1912); Charlotte Forten Grimké, "Personal Recollections of W," *NEM*, N.S. VIII (1893), 468-76; Elizabeth Hume, "Summers with a Poet: Recollections of JGW," *EIHC*, LXXV (1939), 321-5; Christopher C. Hussey, "Some Personal Recollections of W," *Arena*, XV (1896), 376-84; Augustine Jones, "Reminiscences of JGW," *AF*, XIV (1907), 796-800; William Stetson Merrill, "We Talked with W," *EIHC*, XCIV (1958), 156-7; Sarah Ellen Palmer, "A Memory of W," *Century*, XLVII (1893), 152; Robert S. Rantoul, "Some Personal Reminiscences of the Poet W," *EIHC*, XXXVII (1901), 129-44; F. B. Sanborn, "W as Man, Poet, and Reformer," *Bibliotheca Sacra*, LXV (1908), 193-213; Caroline Ticknor, *Glimpses of Authors* (HM, 1922); Isaac Wilson, "Isaac Wilson's Visit to JGW," *FIJ*, XXII (1894), 385; "W as a Man," Boston *Daily Advertiser*, Dec. 17, 1887, p. 8. See also Annie Russell Marble, "Elizabeth Whittier and the Amesbury Home," *Outlook*, LXXXVII (1907), 29-35, with charming quotations from Elizabeth's letters and journal, and Sarah G. Pomeroy's paper about her in *Little Known Sisters of Great Men* (Dana Estes, 1912).

A great many books devoted in the main to other subjects contain references to W. Some of these have been referred to in footnotes. See also: Elizabeth Stuart Phelps, *Chapters from a Life* (HM, 1897); Mrs. John T. Sargent, ed., *Sketches and Reminiscences of the Radical Club of Chestnut Street, Boston* (HM, 1880); Frank P. Stearns, *Sketches from Concord and Appledore* (Putnam, 1895); Laura Stedman and George M. Gould, *Life and Letters of Edmund Clarence*

Stedman (Moffat, Yard, 1910); *Letters of Celia Thaxter* (HM, 1895).

The following are mainly of biographical interest: Betty C. Congleton, "Prentice's Biography of Henry Clay and JGW," *Filson Club Historical Quarterly*, XXXVII (1963), 325-30; Francis P. Dedmond, "A Note on W and Italian Freedom," *BFHA*, XL (1951), 104-5; Cora Dolbee, "Kansas and 'The Prairied West' of JGW," *EIHC*, LXXXI (1945), 307-47, LXXXII (1946), 153-73; E. E. Ericson, "'John Hort' and 'Skipper Ireson,'" *NEQ*, X (1937), 531-2; P. K. Foley, "W and the 'Narrative of James Williams,'" *Nation*, XLIV (1897), 321, with letter by S. T. Pickard, p. 338; Lloyd W. Griffin, "Matthew Franklin W, 'Ethan Spike,'" *NEQ*, XIV (1941), 646-63; C. A. Hawley, "The Growth of W's Reputation in Iowa," *BFHA*, XXVIII (1939), 67-102, "W and Iowa," *IJHP*, XXXIV (1936), 115-43, and "W and Nebraska," *BFHA*, XXX (1941), 17-46; Elizabeth F. Hoxie, "Harriet Livermore: 'Vixen and Devotee,'" *NEQ*, XVIII (1945), 39-50; John J. McAleer, "W's Quest for Humility," *BFHA*, L (1961), 31-45; J. A. Pollard, "W's Esteem in Great Britain," *BFHA*, XXXVIII (1949), 33-6; Arthur H. Reede, "W's Pennsylvania Years," *Penn History*, XXV (1958), 384-409; E. D. Snyder, "W Returns to Philadelphia, after a Hundred Years," *Pennsylvania Magazine of History and Biography*, XLVII (1938), 140-57; Bertha-Monica Stearns, "JGW, Editor," *NEQ*, XIII (1940), 280-304; C. Marshall Taylor, "W vs. Garrison," *EIHC*, LXXXII (1946), 249-78; Thomas F. Waters, "W, the Poet, as Historian," *Massachusetts Magazine*, I (1908), 3-10; Carl J. Weber, "W and Sarah Orne Jewett," *NEQ*, XVIII (1945), 401-7; Roland H. Woodwell, "W's Place of Residence from 1876 to 1892," *EIHC*, LXVIII (1932), 353-8; R. H. Woodwell and Martha H. Dureen, "The Hussey Ancestry of the Poet W," *EIHC*, LXX (1934), 59-68; Jules Zanger, "A Note on 'Skipper Ireson's Ride,'" *EIHC*, XXIX (1956), 236-8.

The following list contains, I think, all the best critical writing on W (as well as some that is less distinguished), with the exception of items cited in the notes: George Arms, *The Fields Were Green* (Stanford University Press, 1953); C. Waller Barrett, "JGW," *Proceedings of the American Antiquarian Society*, LXVII (1957), 125-36; H. W. Boynton, "JGW: An Appreciation," *Putnam's Monthly*, N.S. III (1907), 273-80; J. W. Buckham, "The Unforgotten W," *NEM*, N.S. XXIX (1903), 44-51; Francis B. Gummere, "The Poetry of W," *AF*, XIV (1907), 800-802; John Vance Cheney, *That Dome in Air* (Mc-

Clurg, 1895); Donald Hall, "W," *Texas Quarterly*, Vol. III, No. 3, Autumn 1960, pp. 165-74; W. Harvey-Jellie, "A Forgotten Poet," *Dalhousie Review*, XIX (1939), 91-100; Will D. Howe, "W," in John Macy, ed., *American Writers on American Literature* (Horace Liveright, 1931); Harry Elmore Hurd, "Paradoxes in the Life and Poetry of JGW," *Poetry Review*, XVII (1926), 261-7; Howard Mumford Jones, "W Reconsidered," *EIHC*, XCIII (1957), 231-46; Ernest D. Lee, "JGW," *Westminster Review*, CLXIX (1908), 78-92; John Macy, *The Spirit of American Literature* (D, 1913); Paul Elmer More, *Shelburne Essays*, Third Series (HM, 1906); Harry Oster, "W's Use of the Sage in his Ballads," in Waldo McNeir and Leo B. Levy, eds., *Studies in American Literature*, "Louisiana State University Studies," Humanistic Series, No. 8 (1960); Bliss Perry, *JGW: A Sketch of His Life with Selected Poems* (HM, 1907) and *Park-Street Papers* (HM, 1908); William Lyon Phelps, *Essays on Books* (M, 1914); Elizabeth Stuart Phelps, "W," *Century*, N.S. XXIII (1893), 363-8; John B. Pickard, "W's Ballads: The Making of an Artist," *EIHC*, XCVI (1960), 56-72; Desmond Powell, "W," *AL*, IX (1937), 335-42; Winfield Townley Scott, "Poetry in American: A New Consideration of W's Verse," *NEQ*, VII (1934), 258-75, and "Something about *Snow-Bound*," in *Exiles and Fabrications* (D, 1961); Harriet Prescott Spofford, "The Quaker Poet," *Harper's Magazine*, LXVIII (1884), 171-88; E. C. Stedman, *Poets of America* (HM, 1885); John A. Steuart, *Letters to Living Authors* (Sampson, Low, 1890); George Stewart, *Essays from Reviews* (Quebec, Dawson & Co., 1892); Leon H. Vincent, *American Literary Masters* (HM, 1906); David A. Wasson, "W," *Atlantic Monthly*, XIII (1864), 331-8; E. P. Whipple, *Essays and Reviews*, Vol. I (Appleton, 1848); George Edward Woodberry, *Makers of Literature* (M, 1900); Lewis E. Weeks, Jr., "W Criticism Over the Years," *EIHC*, C (1964), 159-82.

INDEX